RECKLESS
Disregard

RECKLESS Disregard

St. Amant v. Thompson and the Transformation of Libel Law

ERIC P. ROBINSON

LOUISIANA STATE UNIVERSITY PRESS | BATON ROUGE

Published by Louisiana State University Press

Manufactured in the United States of America
First printing

DESIGNER: *Mandy McDonald Scallan*
TYPEFACE: *Whitman*
PRINTER AND BINDER: *Sheridan Books. Inc.*

LIBRARY OF CONGRESS CATALOGING-IN-PUBLICATION DATA
Names: Robinson, Eric P., 1968– author.
Title: Reckless disregard : St. Amant v. Thompson and the transformation of libel law / Eric P. Robinson.
Description: Baton Rouge : Louisiana State University Press, 2019. | Includes bibliographical references and index.
Identifiers: LCCN 2018016034| ISBN 978-0-8071-6940-7 (cloth : alk. paper) |
ISBN 978-0-8071-7017-5 (pdf) | ISBN 978-0-8071-7018-2 (epub)
Subjects: LCSH: St. Amant, Phil A.—Trials, litigation, etc. | Thompson, Herman A.—Trials, litigation, etc. | Trials (Libel)—Louisiana. | Libel and slander—United States.
Classification: LCC KF228.S233 R63 2019 | DDC 346.76303/4—dc23
LC record available at https://lccn.loc.gov/2018016034

The paper in this book meets the guidelines for permanence and durability of the Committee on Production Guidelines for Book Longevity of the Council on Library Resources. ♾

CONTENTS

PREFACE

The *St. Amant* case has faded in prominence to become just one of the parade of Supreme Court decisions that defined and refined the parameters and meanings of the "actual malice" test announced in *New York Times v. Sullivan*. As a result, there has been no comprehensive examination of the *St. Amant* case and its legacy. While there are more than 435 law review and legal periodical articles that mention the *St. Amant* case, none of them focus specifically on the case, and most discuss it only in passing as one of several cases that followed and explained the new defamation law standards announced in the *Sullivan* case.[1]

Detailed discussions of the case are also missing from several books focusing on the Supreme Court and the First Amendment. The case is not mentioned at all in most of the books revealing the inside operations of the Supreme Court in the 1960s and '70s. In addition, only two biographies of the justices sitting on the Supreme Court at the time of the *St. Amant* decision include references to the decision.[2] Lee Levine and Stephen Wermiel, in their groundbreaking book using the justices' notes to portray Justice William J. Brennan Jr.'s efforts to preserve and refine his ruling in *New York Times v. Sullivan*, discuss *St. Amant* in a mere six and half pages.[3]

While the resources for a deep analysis of the *St. Amant* case have not been tapped for a serious scholarly examination, they are readily available. Research materials used for this study include the trial record available at the clerk's office of the East Baton Rouge Parish courthouse in Baton Rouge and the appellate court records available at the Louisiana Supreme Court in New Orleans. The certiorari petitions and other case documents from the proceedings in the U.S. Supreme Court were accessed at the Library of Congress. In addition, the papers of all nine of the U.S. Supreme Court justices who participated in the case were accessed at the Library of Congress (Chief Justice Earl Warren and Justices Hugo Black, Brennan, William O. Douglas, Thurgood Marshall, and Byron White), Yale University (Justices Abe Fortas and Potter Stewart), and Princeton University (Justice John Marshall Harlan II).[4]

The papers of U.S. senator Russell Long at Louisiana State University were also examined for material about the 1962 primary against St. Amant, as was political ephemera held by Tulane University. Also, digital archives of newspapers—primarily the *Baton Rouge Morning Advocate* and *State-Times* and the *New Orleans Times-Picayune*—were accessed through the East Baton Rouge Public Library.

I would like to thank the librarians and archivists at these repositories for their help in locating and accessing the justices' papers and other materials related to the story of *St. Amant v. Thompson*. Thanks also go to Amy Reynolds and Louis Day at Louisiana State University, as well as Lillian Bridwell-Bowles, Erin Coyle, Robert Mann, and James R. Stoner Jr. Thanks also to Jerry Ceppos and to Amy for convincing me to come to LSU in the first place. I also owe a debt of thanks to MaryKatherine Callaway, Rand Dotson, and Catherine Kadair of LSU Press and my copyeditor, George Roupe. I would also like to thank John Maxwell Hamilton and my colleagues Shirley Staples Carter, Myounggi Chon, Elisabeth Fondren, Keith Kenney, Minjie Li, Paromita Saha Killelea, and Lindsay M. McCluskey for their advice. Also, thanks to Lori, Bryan, Cordelia, Dave, Kim, and Ross for their support.

Fifty years after this defining case was settled, I am glad to add a comprehensive examination of *St. Amant* to the literature examining *New York Times v. Sullivan* and the progeny cases that redefined defamation law.

TIMELINE

St. Amant v. Thompson and Related Events

March 29, 1960	"Heed Their Rising Voices" ad published in the *New York Times*, leading to *Sullivan v. New York Times* case
November 4, 1960	Trial verdict in *Sullivan v. New York Times*
November 8, 1960	John F. Kennedy defeats Richard M. Nixon in presidential election
March 28, 1962	**Phil A. St. Amant launches his U.S. Senate campaign**
June 27, 1962	**St. Amant press conference and broadcast**
July 3, 1962	**Thompson files suit against St. Amant**
July 10, 1962	**St. Amant files answer**
July 28, 1962	**Long defeats St. Amant in Democratic primary**
August 30, 1962	Alabama Supreme Court affirms trial verdict in *Sullivan v. New York Times*
August 28, 1963	March on Washington for Jobs and Freedom held Martin Luther King Jr. delivers "I Have a Dream" speech
November 22, 1963	President John F. Kennedy assassinated; Lyndon B. Johnson becomes president
January 6, 1964	U.S. Supreme Court hears argument in *New York Times v. Sullivan*
March 9, 1964	U.S. Supreme Court releases decision in *New York Times v. Sullivan*, 376 U.S. 254

April 22, 1964	First U.S. Supreme Court argument in *Garrison v. Louisiana*
May 4, 1964	Louisiana Supreme Court releases decision in *Matassa v. Bel* (applying *Sullivan* actual malice)
May 5, 1964	**Trial and verdict in *Thompson v. St. Amant***
May 18, 1964	**St. Amant's motion for new trial in *Thompson v. St. Amant* filed**
June 8, 1964	Louisiana Supreme Court denies rehearing in *Matassa v. Bel*
July 2, 1964	Federal Civil Rights Act adopted
October 14, 1964	Martin Luther King Jr. awarded Nobel Peace Prize
October 19, 1964	Second U.S. Supreme Court argument in *Garrison v. Louisiana*
November 3, 1964	President Johnson defeats Barry Goldwater in presidential election
November 23, 1964	U.S. Supreme Court releases decision in *Garrison v. Louisiana*, 379 U.S. 64
January 22, 1965	**Reasons for Judgment [on Motion for Retrial] released in *Thompson v. St. Amant***
January 27, 1965	**Judgment [Denial of Motion for New Trial] issued in *Thompson v. St. Amant***
February 1, 1965	**St. Amant files notice of appeal in *Thompson v. St. Amant***
February 2, 1965	**[Defendant-Appellant's] Original Brief on Appeal filed in *Thompson v. St. Amant***
February 21, 1965	Malcolm X assassinated
August 6, 1965	Federal Voting Rights Act adopted

October 25, 1965	**[Plaintiff-Appellee's] Answer to Appeal filed in *Thompson v. St. Amant***
February 21, 1966	U.S. Supreme Court releases decision in *Rosenblatt v. Baer,* 383 U.S. 75
February 28, 1966	**Louisiana Court of Appeal issues decision in *Thompson v. St. Amant*, 184 So. 2d 314**
April 27, 1966	U.S. Supreme Court hears argument in *Time, Inc. v. Hill*
May 3, 1966	**Thompson files application for review of *Thompson v. St. Amant* with Louisiana Supreme Court**
June 6, 1966	U.S. Supreme Court releases decision in *Sheppard v. Maxwell,* 384 U.S. 333
June 9, 1966	**Louisiana Supreme Court grants review in *Thompson v. St. Amant*, 186 So. 2d 627**
October 10, 1966	**St. Amant changes counsel**
October 18–19, 1966	U.S. Supreme Court hears reargument in *Time, Inc. v. Hill*
October 24, 1966	**Relator's [Thompson's] Brief filed with Louisiana Supreme Court in *Thompson v. St. Amant***
November 4, 1966	**Original Brief on Behalf of Defendant-Respondent [St. Amant] filed with Louisiana Supreme Court in *Thompson v. St. Amant***
January 9, 1967	U.S. Supreme Court releases decision in *Time, Inc. v. Hill,* 385 U.S. 374
February 3, 1967	Louisiana Supreme Court grants review of *Times-Picayune*'s appeal in *Walker v. Associated Press* but denies review of appeal by the Associated Press

February 20, 1967	**Louisiana Supreme Court releases decision in *Thompson v. St. Amant*, 196 So. 2d 255**
February 23, 1967	U.S. Supreme Court argument in *Curtis Publishing Co. v. Butts*
March 27, 1967	**Louisiana Supreme Court denies rehearing in *Thompson v. St. Amant***
June 12, 1967	U.S. Supreme Court releases decision in *Curtis Publishing Co. v. Butts*, 388 U.S. 130
June 26, 1967	**U.S. Supreme Court grants extension for filing of St. Amant's petition for certiorari in *St. Amant v. Thompson***
August 19, 1967	**St. Amant files petition for certiorari with U.S. Supreme Court in *St. Amant v. Thompson***
October 2, 1967	October 1967 U.S. Supreme Court term begins; Justice Thurgood Marshall takes his seat
October 16, 1967	U.S. Supreme Court reverses and remands *Associated Press v. Walker* for reconsideration in light of *Curtis Publishing Co. v. Butts*
November 3, 1967	**U.S. Supreme Court first considers certiorari petition in *St. Amant v. Thompson* at weekly conference meeting**
January 15, 1968	**U.S. Supreme Court grants certiorari in *St. Amant v. Thompson*, 389 U.S. 1033**
February 29, 1968	**Original Brief of Defendant-Relator [St. Amant] filed with U.S. Supreme Court in *St. Amant v. Thompson***
March 31, 1968	President Lyndon Johnson announces that he will not seek reelection

April 4, 1968	**U.S. Supreme Court hears argument in *St. Amant v. Thompson*** Martin Luther King Jr. assassinated (6:00 p.m. Central Time)
April 5, 1968	**U.S. Supreme Court discusses *St. Amant v. Thompson* at weekly conference meeting, votes on result**
April 8, 1968	**Chief Justice Warren assigns majority opinion in *St. Amant v. Thompson* to Justice White**
April 19, 1968	**Justice White circulates draft of majority opinion in *St. Amant v. Thompson***
April 24, 1968	**Justice White circulates revised draft of majority opinion in *St. Amant v. Thompson;* Justice Fortas circulates draft of dissent in the case**
April 29, 1968	**U.S. Supreme Court releases decision in *St. Amant v. Thompson*, 390 U.S. 727**
May 27, 1968	U.S. Supreme Court releases decisions in *Pickering v. Board of Educ.*, 391 U.S. 563, 573 (first citation to *St. Amant v. Thompson*)
May 28, 1968	**Louisiana Supreme Court receives mandate from U.S. Supreme Court (informing of the U.S. Supreme Court's ruling in *St. Amant v. Thompson)***

RECKLESS
Disregard

Introduction

June 27, 1962, Phil A. St. Amant believed, was going to be a banner day in his crusade against anti-Americanism and against the Long family dynasty in Louisiana politics. In a press conference that day—and in a paid television address that evening that he advertised as a "political exposé"—St. Amant would be presenting damning evidence that Senator Russell Long, his opponent in the 1962 Democratic primary for Louisiana's U.S. Senate seat, was "the enemy of the working man." St. Amant would show that Senator Long was involved with corrupt members of the Teamsters Union at both the local and national levels, including Teamsters Union chief James ("Jimmy") Riddle Hoffa. He would demand that Long explain why he had given a character reference for a corrupt local union official to Hoffa and detail "any other deals and influence he may have had with Jimmy Hoffa." St. Amant was also going to explain how Senator Long's corrupt union associates were involved in various crimes and had also consorted with Cuban Communist leader Fidel Castro. Finally, he was going to conclude with the admonition that "the people should ask him these questions. You have a right to know."[1]

St. Amant's most incriminating allegation against Long was that the senator had met with Hoffa to personally vouch for Edward G. Partin, the business agent for Baton Rouge Teamsters Local 5, and that Long had given the endorsement despite Partin's unsavory background. Partin clearly ruled his union local through threats and intimidation, with opponents beaten and often ending up dead. Partin also had his own criminal history, including a conviction for burglary, a rape trial that ended in a hung jury, and unresolved charges in a hit-and-run accident that killed an airman.

Partin also had connections to the New Orleans Mafia operation headed by Carlos Marcello, who was later implicated in the assassination of President John F. Kennedy. Senator Long had his own connections to Marcello, which had been forged by the senator's father, legendary Louisiana governor and U.S. senator Huey Long, and his uncle, Governor Earl Long.

In his speech, St. Amant was going to explain that while Senator Long first denied any connections to Partin, he later admitted that he had indeed given the recommendation, saying that he would do the same "for any other employee for their employer."[2]

But while St. Amant's revelations had little effect on the election, a little-noticed statement during his televised address had a more important legacy, leading to a defamation lawsuit that ended up before the U.S. Supreme Court and resulted in a decision that played a major role in the evolution of American defamation law in the 1960s and 1970s. The decision was once called "the most important of the recent Supreme Court libel decisions," but the libel case against Phil A. St. Amant has now largely been forgotten, subsumed under the rubric of the "progeny" of the *New York Times v. Sullivan* decision that altered understanding of the free speech provision of the First Amendment to the U.S. Constitution.[3]

The story of the case against St. Amant is more than the story of a lawsuit. It is also a story of a unique time in Louisiana politics and of unique personalities that controlled the levers of power in the state—sometimes in the public interest but oftentimes in their own. It is a story not just of law, judges, and precedents but also of history, politics, and corruption. It is also a tale of the elusiveness of "truth" and of the very definition of that word.

(1)

The Gumbo of 1960s Louisiana

Louisiana has long held a unique place in the American imagination, from its conception as a wild frontier territory that doubled the size of the nascent United States in the early nineteenth century to the modern bayou and Cajun adventureland depicted on television programs that showcase the Pelican State's culture and, perhaps, its eccentricities.

Louisiana has been shaped by its geography and history but more importantly by its people. The area has been a crossroads at which various nationalities, ethnicities, and cultures have met and collided. Promoted by New Orleans's role as a trading center for cotton, sugar, and slaves, the state has developed a unique mixture of personalities and perspectives.

At the start of twentieth century, Louisiana was a literal backwater: a state that—beyond the mixture of cultures that constituted the gumbo of New Orleans—was mostly a collection poor, rural towns strung out along dirt roads. But by the dawn of the twenty-first century, Louisiana had transformed itself into a modern, industrialized state that still retains its unique mix of heritage and culture. This progress began with the populism of Huey Long, whose governorship focused on the development of roads, schools, and other necessities of the modern connected world. But toward the middle of the twentieth century the state, like the nation, was forced to face its legacy of slavery and segregation, a process of self-examination and discovery that is still ongoing.

The challenge that Louisiana faced in the 1960s was how it would surmount the cultural, social, and political obstacles to modernity as it overcame its economic and development dilemmas to incorporate itself into the America of the twentieth century and beyond.

THE LEGACY OF HUEY LONG

For the first half of the twentieth century, Louisiana politics was polarized into two camps. The factions were not Democrats and Republicans: since the end of Reconstruction, the state had been a bastion of prosegregationist "Dixiecrats."

Instead, the split was between those who supported the populism of governor and later U.S. senator Huey Long and those who opposed him—a bitter division that cleaved the state into pro-Long and anti-Long factions. This division persisted even after the assassination of "Kingfish" Huey Long, as other members of the Long family continued his legacy in Louisiana politics.[1]

The Longs and their supporters, as well as the family's opponents, shaped much of the history of Louisiana in the twentieth century. A complete retelling of the story of the Longs is beyond the scope of this work and has ably been accomplished by others; a brief summary of the family's history in Louisiana politics is included here as background for Phil A. St. Amant's campaign against family scion Russell Long and the libel litigation that followed.

Huey Long

While the Long family name is legendary in Louisiana politics, the founder of this dynasty was originally a low-profile salesman from rural Winn Parish. The area was characterized by subsistence farms, dirt roads, and barely functioning schools, which Huey Long used to depict his origins as poor. But young Huey's family was actually relatively well off, due to shrewd parceling of the family farm after the arrival of the Arkansas Southern Railroad in 1901. In high school Huey was an enthusiastic member of the debate club and represented his school at debate "rallies" in Baton Rouge in 1909 and 1910. In the second of these events he finished in third place, winning a partial scholarship to Louisiana State University, which he declined. Long later claimed that he did not accept the scholarship because, while it covered tuition, it did not include housing or books, which he could not afford. But the truth was that he could not accept because he had not graduated from high school: he was expelled after opposing the school's principal and faculty on various issues, including expansion of the school to twelfth grade just as Long was prepared to graduate after completing the eleventh. This was not the only time that Huey Long stretched the truth—or outright lied—in order to burnish his supposed humble roots and his unity with "the common man."[2]

After leaving school, Huey Long began his career as a salesman, careening from times of relative prosperity to stretches of abject poverty. Yet he was constantly promoting his products—and himself—through innovative and sometimes audacious schemes. As a salesman for the lard substitute Cottolene, Long arranged for a young woman, Rose McConnell, and her mother to win a baking contest promoting the product. He also convinced the winner to become his wife.

Long attended seminary classes at Oklahoma Baptist University and law classes at the University of Oklahoma Law School. Returning to Louisiana, he took one year of classes at Tulane University Law School and then arranged to take the state bar exam. Taking the exam after only a year or so of law study was how the majority of Louisiana lawyers took the exam at the time. But Long, impatient for the next scheduled test, approached Louisiana Supreme Court Justice Frank A. Monroe, who persuaded his colleagues to give Long a personalized oral exam only a few days after he requested it. Perhaps not surprisingly, he passed.

As a newly minted attorney, Huey first joined his eldest brother Julius in practice in their hometown of Winnfield. But soon afterward, Huey set up his own law office in a space above the bank run by his uncle George. Despite this familial relationship, three of Huey's most prominent cases—the prominence often the result of Long's promotion of his clients' causes—were against his uncle's bank.

In 1918, Huey was elected to the Louisiana Railroad Commission (renamed the Public Service Commission in 1921 to reflect its broad powers over utilities besides railroads) in a campaign that blasted the commission's coziness with business interests. Once elected, Long forged a path as a populist, advocating against utilities and their friends in state government. A particular target of his ire was the powerful Standard Oil Company. After surviving an attempt by his opponents to remove him from office, Long became chairman of the commission in 1922.

In 1924, at the age of thirty, Huey Long ran for governor in a campaign that emphasized the small towns of the state over the major cities. He came in third. Four years later, however, he was elected governor with the slogan "Every Man a King." As governor he pushed for major public works, decent roads, free textbooks for schoolchildren, and literacy classes for adults. As the Great Depression gripped the nation, Long's infrastructure and other projects promoted employment, education, dignity, and a better quality of life for Louisiana's predominantly poor and rural population. But as Louisiana labor historians Bernard A. Cook and James R. Watson point out, Long's support of the downtrodden did not translate into support for laborers and their unions.[3]

Long also used his position—and the state jobs he controlled—to reward supporters and punish opponents. In 1929, his opponents successfully engineered an impeachment vote in the Louisiana House, but the state Senate dropped the matter after it became clear that Long had the support to avoid conviction.

Long ran for the U.S. Senate in 1930 with his "Share the Wealth" platform and easily defeated incumbent Joseph E. Ransdell. But Long did not take his seat in Washington for nine months, until he could install a loyalist who would preserve his state programs as governor. Long finally went to Washington after his hand-picked candidate, Oscar K. Allen, became governor. But Long continued to hold enormous sway over state government and frequently returned to his command center at the Roosevelt Hotel in New Orleans to oversee his empire, promote his programs, and otherwise remain involved in state affairs. One example of Long's continued involvement in state affairs was his apparent involvement in convincing Governor Allen to pardon and subsequently influence federal authorities to be lenient on Carlos Marcello, who went on to become the boss of the Louisiana mob.

In Washington, meanwhile, despite Long's personal enmity for Franklin Roosevelt, whom he deemed too conservative, Long needled the president to expand New Deal programs to focus more on low-income and rural areas like Louisiana. Long also built his own national profile with a network of Share Our Wealth clubs, which had a membership topping eight million—support that he threatened to leverage against Roosevelt in a Democratic presidential primary in 1936.

Long could be ruthless in his dealings with his political opponents. One example was his arranging the imposition of martial law on New Orleans in 1934 by Governor Allen to crush that city's anti-Long political machine. This action led to condemnation not only from New Orleans officials but also from the press both in Louisiana and across the nation and posed a threat to Long's 1936 presidential ambitions. But in the end, this gambit and several others led to Huey Long's complete dominance of New Orleans and Louisiana politics.[4]

Huey Long was shot in the lobby of the Louisiana state capitol building on September 5, 1935, and died two days later. His widow, Rose, was appointed to fill his Senate seat and was elected in April 1936 to serve the remainder of her husband's term. But she declined to run for election to her own term later that year, leading to a Democratic primary for the open seat. Although Long's protégé Governor Allen won the primary, Allen's death after the vote led to the election of Democrat Allen Joseph Ellender to the Senate seat.

Earl Long

Despite Huey's death and the withdrawal of Rose Long from the Senate, the Long legacy remained strong in Louisiana, and the family name continued to hold its populist appeal. Earl Long, Huey's brother, became Louisiana's lieutenant governor in 1936 and then became governor upon the resignation of Governor Richard W. Leche in the face of corruption charges in 1939. Earl Long, known throughout the state as "Uncle Earl," was defeated in his run for election as governor in his own right in 1940 and lost again in a run for lieutenant governor in 1944.

But Earl came back, winning the governor's seat in 1948 on a populist platform that echoed the campaigns of his murdered brother. He solidified his connection with the Kingfish by appointing Huey's son Russell Long—then just out of LSU's law school—as his "executive counsel." This was the start of Russell's meteoric rise, including his election to the U.S. Senate later that year.

Term limits forced Earl Long to give up the governorship in 1952, and he endorsed District Judge Carlos Spaht for the position. But Russell—now firmly established in the Senate—endorsed Congressman Hale Boggs. The two Long-endorsed candidates split the vote of those who had supported Huey Long and his successors Earl and Russell, leading to a victory for the "anti-Long" candidate, Robert F. Kennon.[5]

But the "Long machine" continued with the election of George, another of Huey's sons, to Congress in 1952. And the Longs reunited their loyal voters by presenting a united front in the next gubernatorial election, leading Earl to return as governor in 1956. But as he returned to the political cauldron in Baton Rouge—resisting segregationists in the legislature who bristled under *Brown v. Board of Education* and other rulings by the U.S. Supreme Court—his obsession with politics was clearly taking a toll on Uncle Earl. A drunken evening at a Bourbon Street strip club became public. And he began speaking of ways he could circumvent Louisiana's prohibition on a governor serving two consecutive terms.

On Monday, May 25, 1959, Governor Long hosted a raucous party at the governor's mansion and then held a drunken midnight press conference where he blasted his opponents. The next day, apparently hungover, he delivered an incoherent speech to a joint session of the state legislature. He returned to the legislature two days later, and what began as an apology degenerated into a diatribe against individual legislators who opposed his policies.

The Long family gathered at the governor's mansion and decided to have Uncle Earl committed to a mental hospital. The Longs were united in their intention to commit Uncle Earl and found a facility in Galveston—outside the state—that would accept the governor as long as he came voluntarily. Ultimately, however, Earl Long was sedated and lashed to a stretcher as he was flown to Texas.

Back in Baton Rouge, Russell was given the unenviable task of explaining the situation regarding his uncle to the legislature. Then, a few weeks later, Russell said that he was "very seriously thinking about running for governor," especially "if it were the only way of keeping the Long faction together."[6]

After a Texas judge signed commitment papers at the request of the Long family, Earl demanded a habeas corpus hearing to request his release. As the result was pending, he persuaded his wife to agree that he continue his treatment at a facility in New Orleans. But after a few days there, Earl announced that he was leaving. And as a voluntary patient, no one could stop him.

Once Earl's plans became clear, his wife and several aides worked to involuntarily commit Governor Long to the state hospital in Mandeville. As the governor headed back to Baton Rouge, East Baton Rouge sheriff Bryan Clemmons posted two deputies at the parish line. One of the officers was East Baton Rouge deputy sheriff Herman A. Thompson, who would later rise to prominence when he sued Phil A. St. Amant for libel.

With no commitment papers finalized, the officers were instructed to follow the governor's car once it crossed into the parish. After they did so for eight miles, a radio message told them that the papers had been signed and that they should stop the vehicle. When they did, Thompson told the governor that they would drive him into Baton Rouge, as he took the place of the state trooper who had been driving the governor's car.

As Thompson drove to the county courthouse, the governor figured out what was going on. "Goddamn you," he yelled at Thompson as they exited the car. "I'll get you for this. I'll get all of you." To the other deputy, whose father held a state job, the governor screamed, "Your old man just lost his job." Then two doctors interviewed the governor and decided that his family was right: he needed to be committed. Based on these diagnoses, a Louisiana judge signed the papers. Thompson then took the wheel and drove the governor away, not back to the New Orleans hospital, as the governor expected, but to the state asylum in Mandeville.[7]

But since it was a state asylum, it was under the governor's control. So after eight days, Long got himself out by asserting his authority as governor to fire the acting superintendent of the asylum and the state's hospital director, who both opposed his release. His attorney also waged a legal and public relations campaign blaming Earl's wife and nephew for plotting against the governor.

After his release, Governor Long returned to Baton Rouge to get some revenge, firing forty state employees who had been involved in his commitment. He then returned to his frenzied travels around the state before embarking on a three-week trip around the southwestern United States, which received massive press coverage at every stop. Most of the nation saw the governor's travels—and travails—as a sideshow. But to Louisiana residents, their governor's antics were a serious crisis. They were also a crisis for the Long family.

Earl Long finally returned to Baton Rouge in July 1959 and set upon a plan to run again for governor despite the term limit. When his plan was stymied by the legislature and the state Democratic Central Committee, Long convinced Jimmie Noe to run for governor, with Earl running on the ticket for lieutenant governor. It was clearly an attempt by Earl to hang on to some power, and there was speculation that he had reached an agreement in which Noe would resign after the election, leaving Earl again as governor. Noe himself characterized the race in stark terms, as "Long versus anti-Long."[8]

But Noe and Long lost, with Uncle Earl coming in third in the lieutenant governor race out of six candidates. As the *Baton Rouge Morning Advocate* observed, "the political career of Gov. Long . . . may be near an end."[9]

But Earl Long's efforts to hang on to political office were not over yet. The year after his defeat in the lieutenant governor's race, he won the Democratic primary runoff—tantamount to election in overwhelmingly Democratic Louisiana—for the congressional district representing the Alexandria area. This was the same seat that Earl's brother George had held from 1953 until his death in 1958. But Earl Long never got to take the office: he suffered a heart attack the evening of the runoff and died nine days later.

Russell Long

However, there was one remaining elected official carrying the Long name in Louisiana: Huey's son, U.S. senator Russell B. Long. Russell had enrolled at Louisiana State University after his father's murder and was eventually elected student body president. He interrupted law school to become a midshipman in the navy during World War II, ending up in support roles. After the war he finished law school, then settled in Baton Rouge to establish a law practice.

Russell Long endeavored to develop a reputation separate from his father's. Yet Russell eventually was pulled into the family business. He was an active surrogate in his uncle Earl's 1948 gubernatorial campaign, and when Earl Long was elected, Russell became the governor's counsel.

Three days after Earl Long's inauguration, he had the opportunity to further advance his nephew's career when U.S. senator John H. Overton died. While Russell expressed immediate interest in the seat, Earl was counseled not to appoint him since Russell was less than thirty years old, the constitutionally required age for senators. So instead Earl appointed William C. Feazel to hold the seat for seven and a half months until a new senator could be elected to fill the two years remaining of Overton's term, with Russell the presumed favorite in the election for his seat.

Whatever Russell Long and his uncle Earl Long desired, Russell's election to the Senate seat was not a foregone conclusion. His opponent in the 1948 primary was Judge Robert F. Kennon, who criticized his opponent's youth and his positions on segregation. Long barely won a close primary against Kennon by a vote of 51 percent to 49 percent, with a margin of 10,475 votes. Russell then decisively won the general election against Clem S. Clarke, 75 percent to 25 percent. He was elected to the Senate just one day before his thirtieth birthday.

Despite the close results in his first election, Russell Long was reelected to a full term in 1950 by a wide margin. He continued to win by large margins in 1956, 1962 (after defeating St. Amant in the Democratic primary), and 1968. Senator Long joined the Senate Finance Committee in 1953 and became known as an expert in the arcana of federal tax law. Thirteen years later, in 1966, he became chair of that committee. Long also became Senate majority whip in 1965, a promotion that Louisiana mob boss Carlos Marcello claimed was the result of "a suitcase of cash" that he helped arrange to be distributed among seven undecided senators.[10]

Russell Long remained majority whip until 1969 and chair of the Senate Finance Committee until 1981. He stayed in the Senate until his retirement in 1987.

THE LOUISIANA MOB

Carlos Marcello, well known as the mob boss for New Orleans and surrounding areas, stretching as far west as Dallas, was one of the major contributors to Russell Long's campaigns. Various authors have explained Marcello's exploits in detail, and the story of the mobster and his associates underlay some of the major allegations that Phil A. St. Amant made against Russell Long in his address during the 1962 Senate primary, which was the basis of the libel suit against St. Amant.

The Mafia's "Big Easy" Birth

While New Orleans had been home to Italian immigrants since its founding, it became a primary destination for Sicilians in the late 1800s. Not only were they attracted by weather similar to that in their native land, but the Sicilians were also following the trade route by which much of their homeland's produce came to the United States, through the port of New Orleans.

By the end of the nineteenth century, the New Orleans area was home to the largest Sicilian community in North America, focused primarily in an area of the lower French Quarter that became known as "Little Palermo." Some immigrants brought with them the criminal organizations that had existed in western Sicily since the early part of the century and had become a virtual shadow government after the unification of Italy in 1860. In Louisiana, these groups took the form of criminal enterprises such as the Matranga and Provenzano crime gangs, who competed for control and a share of the profits from trade in the city's French Market and on its lucrative docks. This was among the earliest appearances of the Mafia in the United States.

The Sicilians found themselves in competition with more established immigrant groups, particularly Irish immigrants who had arrived in New Orleans prior to the Civil War. These tensions reached a boiling point when in 1890 New Orleans mayor Joseph A. Shakespeare appointed David C. Hennessy as police chief, with the explicit charge of solving more than one hundred unsolved murders attributed to the feud among the Sicilians in Little Palermo.

While Hennessy had a reputation for successfully prosecuting members of the emerging criminal enterprises in the Italian immigrant community, he eventually allied with the Provenzano gang against the Matrangas.

The Matrangas struck back late on the night of October 15, 1890, by shooting Hennessy, resulting in his death the next day. Hundreds of men of Italian ethnicity were arrested on suspicion of the crime, most of them only because of their heritage. Eventually nineteen members of the Matranga gang were indicted and tried for Hennessy's murder. But despite the out-of-court confession of one defendant, the trial ended with six of the defendants found innocent and a mistrial declared for the remaining defendants.

While there were celebrations of the verdict in Little Palermo, most New Orleans residents were infuriated by the result, and there was widespread suspicion that the jury had been bribed or intimidated. Fueled by these suspicions, a vigilance committee formed and placed newspaper advertisements calling a meeting at which participants were told to "come prepared for action." More than one thousand people attended the gathering at the statue of Henry Clay in the "no man's land" (median) of Canal Street at the corner of St. Charles Street, where organizer William S. Parkerson told the crowd, "When the law is powerless, rights delegated by the people are relegated back to the people, and they are justified in doing that which the courts have failed to do."[11]

The suspects were still being held at the parish prison as their releases were being processed. The group formulated a plan to remove the suspects from the prison and inflict their own form of justice on at least some of them. The group marched to the prison gate but was refused admission. Some of the crowd then used a battering ram to enter through the back. The jailers released the prisoners from their cells so that they could escape the mob, but the horde found nine of them in the jail, where they beat and then shot them dead. The mob took two other prisoners outside, where they were hung from a lamppost and a tree and then used as shooting targets.[12]

Although the leaders of the lynch mob were well known, a grand jury refused to issue indictments in the case on the grounds that it was impossible to charge all of the six to eight thousand people who participated.

This lynching has been called the largest in Louisiana history, garnering newspaper headlines worldwide. It also caused a diplomatic row between the United States and Italy that ended with President William Henry Harrison authorizing $25,000 in reparations to the Italian government.

Although the Mafia had been operating in Louisiana for thirty years by this point, the events in New Orleans were the first exposure that many Americans had to the workings and influence of the Italian crime organizations in the city. Eventually, the Mafia and the government in the Pelican State reached an accommodation in which they coexisted, with officials such as governors, congressmen, mayors, and district attorneys tolerating the criminal activities and in some cases benefiting from them.[13]

By the 1930s, Huey Long was actually courting the mob. Long met mob boss Frank Costello in Long Island, New York, in 1933, and they became fast friends. At the time, Costello was facing pressure from New York City mayor Fiorello LaGuardia's crusade against gambling and vice. Long—by then in the U.S. Senate, but still in control back home through his proxy, Governor Allen—"invited Costello to move his illegal activities to southern Louisiana," as long as Long and his allies received a percentage.[14]

This invitation came in spite of the fact that gambling was technically illegal in Louisiana. But the prohibition was openly flouted: pinball and slot machines were ubiquitous, and illicit casinos openly operated deep in the Louisiana swamps. The offer was also extended despite—and, ironically, perhaps as the result of—Long's use of widespread illegal gambling and other vices in New Orleans as a rationale for declaring martial law in the city in 1934 in an effort to undermine his political enemies in New Orleans city government.[15]

The "Little Man": Carlos Marcello

To establish this venture, Costello needed the help of the Matrangas' successor, the Louisiana crime organization run by "Silver Dollar Sam" Carolla. And to run the gambling operations, Carolla turned to his deputy, Carlos Marcello.

Marcello's birthplace is unclear, but he immigrated as an infant with his mother to New Orleans in 1911, one year after his father came to the city. While his parents eventually became American citizens and his siblings were American by virtue of being born in the United States, Carlos Marcello was never naturalized. While Marcello's lack of American citizenship did little to impede his day-to-day life, it became an Achilles heel that would haunt him and lead to dramatic battles with the U.S. government in his later years.[16]

Marcello dropped out of school at age fourteen and was first arrested five years later, in 1929, for his involvement in a $7,000 bank robbery. Although the police quickly found the money, along with Marcello and his partners, the bank dropped the charges. The next year, Marcello was convicted of assault in a grocery store robbery for which he recruited and convinced two younger boys to actually commit the crime, leading to the press portraying him as a "Fagin," referring to the *Oliver Twist* character who recruits juveniles to carry out his offenses. Marcello was sentenced to nine to twelve years in Louisiana's notorious Angola prison but was released after less than five when he was pardoned by Louisiana governor Oscar K. Allen, Huey Long's hand-picked successor. The pardon was reportedly arranged by Carlos's father and pushed by Long.[17]

Upon his release, Marcello became involved in more criminal enterprises, including illicit gambling and narcotics. In 1938 he was convicted on federal charges of selling more than ten kilograms (twenty-three pounds) of marijuana. Although he was sentenced to one year and one day and a $76,830 fine, Marcello was released after less than ten months and settled his fine for $400.[18]

It was around the time of Marcello's release that Mayor LaGuardia was cracking down on illegal slot machines in New York. When Frank Costello accepted Long's invitation to move the gambling and other operations to Louisiana, Carlos Marcello was put in charge of the enterprise.

Within ten years Marcello controlled not only the pinball and slot machines in Louisiana but also several illicit casinos, betting operations, and brothels throughout southern Louisiana. When Carolla was deported in 1947—the result of a drug conviction in 1938—Marcello became head of the New Orleans Mafia, and by 1950 he was referred to as "the crime czar of New Orleans." He was also known, because of his short stature, as "Little Man."[19]

Under Marcello, Louisiana's mob became a hub for Mafia communications and money laundering nationwide. The illicit operations were linked with various legitimate businesses, including restaurants, motels, banks, beer and liquor distributorships, a fleet of shrimp boats, and the tomato canning company that had been established by Marcello's parents. By the early 1960s, these operations had estimated annual revenues of $1.6 billion, constituting the largest business organization in the state, with offshoots in Texas and Mississippi. Yet Marcello always claimed that his primary occupation was farming and selling tomatoes.[20]

For the most part, state and local officials did not object or interfere. In fact, Governor Earl Long was known to frequent certain mob-controlled New

Orleans gambling establishments. For Marcello's operation, payoffs to local politicians and law enforcement were just the price of doing business.

Marcello was a focus of the two major investigations of organized crime conducted by the U.S. Senate in the 1950s. The first, by the Senate Special Committee to Investigate Crime in Interstate Commerce, was chaired by Senator Estes Kefauver of Tennessee and held hearings in fourteen cities in 1950 and 1951. Altogether, the committee heard from more than six hundred witnesses. Broadcast live, the Kefauver committee hearings were a radio and television sensation and even inspired several television crime shows of the 1950s. The second investigation, by the Senate Select Committee on Improper Activities in Labor and Management, chaired by Senator John L. McClellan of Arkansas, held 270 days of hearings with 1,526 witnesses from 1957 through 1960.

In his appearance before the Kefauver committee on January 25, 1951, in New Orleans, Marcello invoked the Fifth Amendment 152 times, refusing even to answer questions about his age, birthplace, or whether he was married. He only answered questions as to his name and address, plus two questions as to whether he was refusing to answer because doing so might implicate him in a crime. "Not being an attorney I would not know," Marcello responded.[21]

In its reports of its findings, the Kefauver committee described Marcello as a "recognized kingpin of Louisiana racketeering" and "one of the worst criminals in the country" and detailed how his gambling operations continued with the implicit cooperation of local authorities.

Marcello was prosecuted for failing to answer the committee's questions and was charged with forty-nine counts of contempt of Congress. He was convicted in six of these counts, but an appeals court reversed the guilty verdict.[22]

In addition to exploring his criminal operations, the committee also questioned Marcello's immigration status. According to committee chairman Kefauver, "We wanted to find out among other things what was the trouble with naturalization and immigration laws that a man who is apparently having such a detrimental effect on law enforcement and to decency in the community, how can he continue to stay here."[23]

The attention brought to Marcello's immigration status led to the initiation of deportation proceedings, but the process would go on for more than thirty years without any final resolution. Marcello was arrested and found deportable in 1953, but he appealed. The appeal was denied, and Marcello was arrested again. Although Marcello's effort to file a habeas corpus petition was denied, he was still released on $10,000 bail pending appeal. After his release, both the circuit court and the U.S. Supreme Court rejected his arguments and the Justice Department resumed the deportation process.[24]

At the time, deportation law allowed the deportee to choose his destination. Marcello chose France, but that country refused to accept him. The government then tried Italy, which also refused, going as far as revoking the prior permission that it had given Marcello to travel there. In the meantime, Marcello continued to challenge the deportation in the American courts, filing six different lawsuits challenging various aspects of the proceedings to remove him from the United States. While in the end these challenges were all resolved in the government's favor, they effectively delayed the deportation process for several years.[25]

Thus Marcello was still in the United States when the McClellan committee was formed, and he appeared before that committee in 1959. The questions to Marcello stemmed from the testimony of other witnesses who told the committee that he had enlisted the Jefferson Parish Sheriff's Office in forcing stores to accept jukeboxes and slot machines that he controlled. As he did at the prior Kefauver committee hearing, Marcello would only verify his name and address. As before, his only other answer to the senators' questions was to invoke the Fifth Amendment seventy times. Several senators found this ironic, given that Marcello was not a United States citizen.

In addition to the operations of the mob, the McClellan committee also focused on the connections between the Mafia and organized labor, particularly the Teamsters Union and its national leader, Jimmy Hoffa. These links were a particular interest of the counsel to the committee, Robert F. Kennedy. With the support of his older brother, Senator John F. Kennedy of Massachusetts, the younger Kennedy made it his mission to expose and uproot such corruption.

This crusade escalated with the election and inauguration of John F. Kennedy as president and his appointment of Robert Kennedy as U.S. attorney general. Shortly after his confirmation, the Kennedy Justice Department went after Hoffa and other union and mob bosses, establishing a team to specifically focus on the issue.

This included a renewed interest in Marcello's still-pending deportation. Eventually, Attorney General Kennedy convinced the government of Formosa (modern Taiwan) to accept Marcello. But the department later discovered that Marcello had a birth certificate from Guatemala and got the government there—which came to power as the result of an American-sponsored coup—to agree to accept him. Marcello had apparently obtained the fraudulent birth certificate in 1957 by bribing the law partner of the country's prime minister, as an insurance policy to have a refuge relatively close to Louisiana in case he did get deported.[26]

Even though it was clear that the birth certificate was fake, Marcello was deported—kidnapped, his supporters said—to Guatemala in 1961. But his lawyers filed a new challenge, alleging that the Guatemalan birth certificate was fraudulent and that the country had now rescinded its consent to his deportation there. There was even doubt about the legality of the deportation within the Justice Department, since department officials knew that the birth certificate was fake. But the federal courts rejected these arguments, saying that Marcello was now Guatemala's problem.

From Guatemala, Marcello eventually found his way to Honduras. From there, he flew to Miami, possibly on a Dominican Republic Air Force plane. In all, he had been gone for about seven weeks. The FBI suspected that Senator Russell Long played a role in Marcello's return, possibly including arranging for the Dominican plane. The agency also received information that Senator Long was helping Marcello by "sponsoring a Louisiana official for a key INS position from which assistance to Marcello might be rendered."[27]

A few days after Marcello's return, a federal judge dismissed his challenge to the deportation. Marcello later appealed that decision but was unsuccessful.[28]

Upon his return, Marcello was charged with reentering the country illegally. He turned himself in and was again ordered deported, but he was again released pending appeal. The litigation over Marcello's deportation continued through 1981, making it the longest and costliest deportation case in history. But Marcello never was deported again. The case was among the main impetuses for legislative limitations on appeals of deportation proceedings enacted in the 1980s and 1990s.[29]

During Marcello's absence, Attorney General Robert Kennedy launched a second attack on Marcello's empire, with the Internal Revenue Service—which Kennedy was using as another tool against organized crime—filing a $835,000 tax lien against Marcello and his wife.

The mob boss was also ordered to appear once again before the reconstituted McClellan committee. But this time Marcello did not show up when requested, citing poor health. Marcello's brother Joe Marcello and his business partner Joe Poretto did testify, but both invoked the Fifth Amendment when asked about Marcello's health, his gambling operations and other businesses, and his connections to other mobsters. When Carlos Marcello finally did appear before the committee, it was a repeat of his previous appearances: other than verifying his name and address, he declined to answer any questions on the grounds that he might incriminate himself.

In late 1961, the Justice Department filed new charges over the forged Guatemalan birth certificate. According to FBI wiretaps, Marcello tried to get entertainer Frank Sinatra to intervene with Attorney General Robert Kennedy through the crooner's friendship with his father, Joseph Kennedy, but the overture just made Robert Kennedy more determined to get Marcello once and for all.[30]

The animosity was mutual, with Marcello regularly railing against the attorney general and his brother the president. According to Marcello's biographer John Davis, this eventually led to a plan to cut off the harassment by killing President Kennedy. "You know what they say in Sicily," Marcello was captured saying on an FBI wiretap. "If you want to kill a dog, you don't cut off the tail, you cut off the head."[31]

According to Davis, a plan was hatched to kill the president during his visit to Dallas, which was within Marcello's extended territory. And Kennedy was indeed assassinated on November 22, 1963. This was also the last day of the trial over the latest charges against Marcello. The news that the president had been shot and was feared dead reached the court just as the judge finished instructing the jury prior to deliberations. The court recessed for an hour in reaction to the news, after which the jury—including one juror who had been paid by a Marcello surrogate—deliberated for fifteen minutes and returned a verdict of not guilty.[32]

Lee Harvey Oswald was arrested for the assassination and was himself killed by Jack Ruby. After a three-week investigation, the FBI announced its conclusion that Oswald was the lone assassin of Kennedy and that Ruby had acted alone in killing Oswald. The Warren Commission (officially the President's Commission on the Assassination of President Kennedy) agreed, concluding that "the shots which killed President Kennedy and wounded Governor Connally were fired by Lee Harvey Oswald" acting alone, and that there was "no evidence that either Lee Harvey Oswald or Jack Ruby was part of any conspiracy, domestic or foreign, to assassinate President Kennedy."[33]

The conclusion reached by the Warren Commission has been widely rejected. John Davis, based on his detailed investigation, concludes that Oswald was designated by Marcello's operation to be the fall guy for the assassination and that this scapegoat was conveniently eliminated by Jack Ruby.[34]

Davis also alleges that when New Orleans district attorney Jim Garrison launched his own investigation into the murder of Kennedy, it may have been an attempt to deflect attention from Marcello's possible involvement. "Jim Garrison," Davis explains, "was persuaded to open the case by two Louisiana politicians close to Carlos Marcello: Representative Hale Boggs and Senator Russell Long." Garrison—who may have had connections to Marcello himself—confirmed Senator Long's role in instigating the investigation.[35]

The killing of President Kennedy and the subsequent resignation of his brother as attorney general to run for the U.S. Senate in New York did not bring an end to Marcello's legal troubles. On October 6, 1964, he was indicted for attempting to bribe a juror and threatening a witness in the Guatemala birth certificate trial. Again, a jury found Marcello not guilty.

But Marcello's luck in court finally took a turn. Despite his denials of ever being involved in the mob, on September 22, 1966, he was among several Mafia leaders from around the country arrested at a lunch meeting in a New York City restaurant. After his bail was paid, Marcello returned to New Orleans and was greeted by a crowd of reporters, photographers, and curious onlookers at the airport. Marcello claimed that a man got in his way, and he slugged him. But Marcello actually knew the man he hit: he was FBI agent Patrick Collins.

After this incident, Marcello was arrested for assaulting a federal officer, and his 1968 trial on this charge—moved to Laredo, Texas, after he claimed that he could not get a fair trial in New Orleans because of publicity—ended in a mistrial. But the government persisted, retrying Marcello on the charges in Houston. This time, he was found guilty and sentenced to two years' imprisonment. But the sentence was reduced to six months in a prison hospital in light of his alleged poor health.

According to Marcello biographer Dan Moldea, U.S. Supreme Court justice Hugo Black tried to intervene in the case on Marcello's behalf. John Davis says it is clear that Marcello's connections to then-presidential candidate Richard Nixon—based in large part on Marcello's disdain for the Kennedys—led to the sentence being reduced, noting that "the don never looked better than when he was released. . . . The American taxpayers had put Carlos Marcello back in shape."[36]

As Marcello dealt with these legal problems, there were other prominent assassinations in 1968: the killing of civil rights leader Martin Luther King Jr. on the evening of April 4, 1968, and the murder of Robert Kennedy—by then a U.S. senator and presidential candidate—two months later. Davis lays out (mostly circumstantial) evidence that Marcello was involved in these assassinations as well. Davis even speculates that one reason for the mob to have killed Bobby Kennedy—besides Marcello's personal hatred of the man who pursued him for years, including the deportation to Central America—was to remove the most serious opponent to Richard Nixon winning the White House in 1968.[37]

Marcello testified before Congress two more times: in June 1972 before a committee investigating organized crime in sports and in January 1974—with a grant of immunity—before a committee investigating the assassinations of John Kennedy, Martin Luther King Jr., and Robert Kennedy. Unlike in his prior congressional appearances, he actually answered the questions put to him by these committees but only to claim that he was "not in no Mafia" and that "I don't know nothing" about organized crime. Despite this testimony, the House Assassinations Committee reported that both Oswald and Ruby had relationships with individuals who in turn had relationships—albeit tenuous—with Marcello's crime organization and that Marcello "had the motive, means and opportunity to have President John F. Kennedy assassinated." But the committee was unable to establish direct evidence of Marcello's complicity in the assassination and was thus forced to conclude that while "it may be said that it is unlikely that Marcello [himself] was in fact involved in the assassination of the President," it is possible that members of Marcello's organization were involved in the killing.[38]

In the late 1970s, the FBI launched a sting operation in which agents posed as insurance salespeople offering bribes for state business from Louisiana. The so-called "Brilab" investigation—a portmanteau for the words "bribery" and "labor"—led to Marcello's conviction in two separate cases. In one case he was convicted of violating the federal Racketeer Influenced and Corrupt Organizations (RICO) Act by participating in a conspiracy to deprive citizens of honest government, and received a seven-year prison sentence. And through wiretap evidence Marcello was convicted in the second case of attempting to bribe a federal judge presiding over a trial of alleged mob bosses in California and sentenced to ten years in prison and a $25,000 fine. The convictions were both upheld on appeal.[39]

Finally, after years of being pursued by the government, Marcello went to prison for the first time since his five months in Louisiana's Angola prison as a youth. But he was not totally out of options. He continued his legal fight, and the RICO conviction was vacated in 1989 after the U.S. Supreme Court limited application of the RICO law in a separate case.[40]

Marcello was released in October 1989, after having served six years in prison, and died in his Metairie, Louisiana, home in 1993.

The Mob and Louisiana Government

For Carlos Marcello to operate as he did, government officials had to at least tolerate his activities. Some likely actively participated in or profited from them. "In Chicago, people were generally on one side of the fence or the other: honest or crooked," observed Aaron Kohn, who came from the Windy City to New Orleans in 1953 to head the city's Metropolitan Crime Commission. "But in Louisiana there just isn't any fence."[41]

Marcello had relationships with elected and appointed officials at all levels of government in New Orleans and throughout Louisiana, including the state police and local sheriffs and police departments across the state. At the same time, Marcello was careful to keep his political connections indirect. Marcello used go-betweens who would convey information and money between his organization and its various partners and patrons.[42]

So while there are some indicators of connections between Marcello and the targets of Phil A. St. Amant's June 27, 1962, election speech, the specifics of the relationships are unclear.

Ed Partin, the head of Teamsters Local 5 in Baton Rouge—who later provided the testimony that led to the downfall of Teamsters boss Jimmy Hoffa—testified before the House Assassinations Committee that Hoffa had discussed with him the possibility of killing both John and Robert Kennedy and that Hoffa likely had the conversations with him because Hoffa thought that Partin had connections with the Mafia.[43]

The full extent of Marcello's connections to Senator Russell Long are also unclear. Marcello, of course, had a history with Huey Long, Russell's father, and also with his uncle Earl. Marcello was a large contributor to Russell Long's campaigns and boasted about using payoffs to get the senator chosen as majority whip. When Frank Saia, whom Long sponsored for an appointment as a regional advisor to the federal Small Business Administration, was arrested in the bust of a Marcello-sponsored gambling ring in Houston,[44] a subsequent search of Saia's phone records found calls to numerous officials, including Long. Russell Long, Marcello biographer John Davis concludes, was "Carlos's principal contact in the U.S. Senate," whom Marcello enlisted for help in his fight against deportation.[45]

LOUISIANA LABOR

The modernization of Louisiana that Huey Long championed included efforts to move away from a rural, agricultural economy to a more industrial one. These efforts mainly saw success in the state's major cities, particularly New Orleans and Baton Rouge, and brought with them increasing desire among industrial workers to organize to protect their rights and wages.

The union that became the International Brotherhood of Teamsters—known universally simply as "the Teamsters"—began in 1899 when eighteen local unions of drivers of horse-drawn delivery vehicles in several midwestern states joined to form the Team Drivers International Union, under the auspices of the American Federation of Labor. A rival union—the Teamsters National Union—was established in 1902, but the two merged in 1903 and became the International Brotherhood of Teamsters, with its headquarters in Indianapolis under the leadership of Cornelius P. Shea. The union's next president, Daniel J. Tobin, took office in 1907 and saw the vast expansion of the union, from fewer than forty thousand members to more than one million when he stepped down as president in 1952. The membership of the Teamsters had expanded to include workers in all forms of transportation and warehousing, prominently including interstate truckers, and by the 1960s it had become the largest labor union in the country.

Organized Labor in Louisiana

The Teamsters were a significant force in 1960s Louisiana, particularly in New Orleans and Baton Rouge. The union's power inevitably led to involvement and conflict with the political establishment, on both the state and national levels.

During the colonial period, the southern colonies of what would become the United States—Maryland, Virginia, North and South Carolina, and Georgia—developed a primarily agricultural economy, with limited, subsistence manufacturing to fulfill local needs. While there was some industrial development in the South after the American Revolution, the invention of the cotton gin in 1793 increased both the supply and demand for cotton, leading the South to focus on agricultural development, while industry in the area withered.

Of course, underlying the agricultural development of the South was slavery, itself based on a robust international trade in human cargo.

Louisiana's economy as it achieved statehood in 1812 was like that of other southern states except that its agriculture was dominated by slave-based production of sugar, not cotton. In New Orleans, the economy was based on its port and its trade in various goods, including slaves. The port also made New Orleans a cosmopolitan city of diverse peoples.

The city was also home to many skilled workers, who began to form their own trade organizations. A printers' society existed in New Orleans by 1810, and a mechanics' society was established in 1821. But the first union, in the modern sense of issuing demands on wages and working conditions, was the New Orleans Typographical Society, established in 1835. The society later became Local 17 of the International Typographical Union when that national union was founded in 1853. Carpenters and screwmen (who worked on the docks, using jackscrews to reduce the bulk of cotton bales for shipment) also formed their own unions prior to the Civil War. These organizations called a number of strikes in the 1840s and 1850s over wage and workplace issues, but they did so reluctantly because they were concerned about being replaced by slave labor.

After the war, labor organizations in New Orleans began demanding an eight-hour workday for white workers only. With Reconstruction, slaves were nominally transformed into wage-earning workers, but there was little actual change in their working and living conditions. Some former slaves staged violent protests of these conditions but with little change to show as a result. A Colored National Labor Union was formed in 1869, but it failed less than two years later. The Noble Order of the Knights of Labor, which welcomed both black and white workers, began organizing in the South in 1878 and had a primarily black membership in Louisiana by the 1880s. The Knights then began flexing their muscles, calling a strike of plantation workers for better wages and working conditions in 1887. The strike led to violence in several communities. More strikes the following year resulted in similar defeats, and by 1891 the Knights' influence in Louisiana was limited to New Orleans.

Various other unions formed and disbanded in New Orleans in the years following the Civil War, with only cotton stowers and printers maintaining stable organizations. Some of the fleeting unions had impact, such as strikes by drivers, refinery workers, and cigar makers in 1877; waiters at the St. Charles and St. James hotels in 1880; and mule-car drivers in 1884. By 1881 twenty of the city's unions formed a cross-industry (and cross-racial) labor alliance, the Central Trades and Labor Assembly, which grew to include other unions and turned New Orleans into what was called "the center of the strongest labor movement in the South."[46]

In May 1892, New Orleans streetcar drivers staged a strike that resulted in shorter work hours and a closed shop (required union membership). This success led other city workers to organize under the auspices of the American Federation of Labor (AFL). In November, the workers in the city's various services called a strike that was led by the "Triple Alliance," a coalition of the Scalesmen Union, the Packers Union, and the Teamsters. The Workingman's Amalgamated Council, a group of forty-nine more AFL unions representing twenty thousand workers, joined the action, creating a general strike that paralyzed the city. The strike ended after three days, when Governor Murphy Foster threatened to impose martial law. While the city's major employers, represented by the city's Board of Trade, had lambasted the strike leaders and even brought in strikebreakers, they finally agreed to binding arbitration to end the strike. The arbitration resulted in a ten-hour day and overtime pay for workers, but employers refused demands for closed shops and for recognition of the unions. Racial tension and racial quotas on employment in New Orleans led to another, violent strike on the docks in late 1894 and early 1895, which ended only when the militia was called out to restore calm.

While there were scattered union movements in cities and even rural areas across the state by the late 1800s, most organized labor in Louisiana was limited to New Orleans, with a multitude of independent labor groups organized by trade. The leaders of thirteen unions formed the New Orleans Central Trades and Labor Council in 1899, and the Buildings Trades Council reorganized the following year. But these labor groups were only for whites; blacks, barred from membership in these groups, founded their own Central Labor Union in 1901. That same year, amid a steady stream of strikes in the city by new unions flexing their muscles, black and white longshoremen staged a united strike for a wage increase. But the city's first Labor Day parade, also in 1901, was segregated.

Unions organized other strikes over the next several years, many of which resulted in violence and achieved at best only modest gains for workers. Strikes by the New Orleans dockworkers in 1928 and by streetcar drivers the following year both failed miserably. A strike by city sanitation workers in 1935, meant to be a fatal blow to the New Orleans political machine, backfired when the union leaders revealed that Long and his allies had sought to extend the strike to weaken their political opponents in the city.

The Great Depression had a major impact on labor and unionism in Louisiana. The state AFL, which included affiliate unions primarily outside of New Orleans, lost almost half its worker membership between 1928 and 1931. But by the end of the 1930s, public works projects—spearheaded by Governor Huey Long and paid for by the federal government's New Deal programs—led to a resurgence of employment and unionism. Unions were also strengthened by passage of the federal National Labor Relations (Wagner) Act in 1935, which protected workers' rights to organize and to collective bargaining. But Louisiana was still not a union stronghold: by 1939, just under 10 percent of the state's workforce was unionized.[47]

The national upswing in unionism led to a split in the labor movement, with the AFL continuing its practice of organizing workers by craft and the breakaway Committee for Industrial Organization (CIO) advocating organization of workers with different specialties in unions based on the industry in which they work. The newly emerging CIO and the established AFL competed to organize workers in New Orleans and elsewhere in the state. The competition was sullied by charges that CIO organizers had Communist sympathies, which were used to justify police action against the labor movement in general. The AFL and its affiliated unions used and encouraged this criticism of the upstart CIO to retain the AFL's preeminence as Louisiana's leading union organization. The Teamsters, one of the AFL's component unions, was actively involved in this effort.

From the 1930s to the 1960s, Louisiana underwent a fundamental transformation from a primarily agricultural state into one with a major industrial base of oil and petrochemicals. From a labor perspective this change was not always peaceful, with unions fighting and striking for recognition and against open shops. Some of these strikes turned violent.

By 1964, the Teamsters was one of the largest unions in the South, with more than 104,000 members. But Louisiana had a relatively low share of unionized workers. Union membership in the state rose to 19.7 percent of the workforce in 1953 but dropped to 18.4 percent in 1960 and 18.1 percent in 1964. Nationwide, the union membership rate in 1964 was 24.3 percent.[48]

Ed Partin and Local 5

Among the unions in Louisiana, Teamsters Local 5 in Baton Rouge was recognized as "one of the most ruthless [union locals] in the nation." The head of Local 5 was Edward G. "Ed" Partin, whose own brother said that he "had no morals" and "would do anything for a buck." Partin's brother also describes Ed as a childhood bully who stole from their mother. He was sent to reform school after he stole and sold guns, then was released on the condition he join the marine corps. But his behavior there led to a dishonorable discharge.[49]

Partin had several other run-ins with the law. He was convicted of second-degree burglary of a restaurant in Washington State, for which he was sentenced to fifteen years, and was suspected in another instance of breaking and entering. A trial on rape charges ended with a hung jury. Partin reputedly escaped from prison twice during his fifteen-year sentence and was said to have been dishonorably discharged from the marines because of rape accusations.[50]

Partin was the primary subject of St. Amant's June 27, 1962, speech, in which the candidate hoped to tie Partin's corruption and criminal record to Senator Russell Long.

Partin got involved with the Teamsters while working on the construction of an International Paper mill in Natchez, Mississippi, in the 1940s. His success as an organizer brought him to the attention of Local 5 head Paul Kuhns, who hired him. Within a year he was the local's head, in the position of secretary-treasurer / business manager, after forcing Kuhns to resign by threatening to reveal some union improprieties to federal authorities.[51]

Once in control, Partin expanded the size and power of the local, eventually growing it to include seven thousand members in twenty-one Louisiana parishes and adjacent Mississippi counties. He did this by threatening any construction company that refused to negotiate with the union—and, incidentally, give him a cut of the profits—with a picket line. His personal take added up, to the point where he buried money in property he owned in McComb, Mississippi. He was quick to help Teamsters members when they had financial troubles, but he also required a weekly payment from his members—on top of their union dues—in order to keep their jobs.[52]

Partin remained the leader of Local 5 for years, routinely winning union elections through threats and intimidation. Partin's coercion of his members would be subtle but also carried a clear message, as described by Laird Evans, head of the Teamsters local in Shreveport: "Local 5 in Baton Rouge, Louisiana also had a ploy. They would wait until a business meeting was underway. Then, suddenly, the door to the meeting room would swing open and in would walk some huge fellow who would stop and slowly look around the room full of people. After a moment or two, the Business Manager [Partin] would enter, not having to be intimidating at all, since the job had already been done for him."[53]

Using such tactics, by the early 1960s "Partin had controlled Teamsters Local 5 in Baton Rouge for more than a decade with a free-spending, head-knocking, dictatorial style," not unlike the methods Teamsters national head Jimmy Hoffa used to operate and control the union on a national basis.[54]

Partin had a slew of legal problems in 1962, the year of St. Amant's run against Senator Long. In January, Partin was indicted by a parish grand jury for allegedly forging a dissident union member's name on an "honorable withdrawal card," thus removing him from the union. Then in June he was indicted for embezzlement and falsification of records for using union funds to pay for withdrawal cards of thirteen members who he suspected might challenge him for the local's leadership position. (St. Amant claimed credit for this indictment in the press conference held in conjunction with his June 27 televised statement.)

In the union disputes, Partin sought help from Teamsters president Jimmy Hoffa. This was at the core of St. Amant's allegations against Senator Long: he maintained that Long had vouched for Partin when Partin sought Hoffa's support. Partin had every reason to expect Hoffa's assistance. Partin's Local 5 was one of the most successful Teamsters locals in the nation, and Partin was a devoted union loyalist.

Partin had more troubles later in the year. He was arrested twice in September 1962—for a hit-and-run accident in Alabama in which Partin allegedly killed an air force airman, and on charges of aggravated kidnapping for helping fellow union official Sidney Simpson take Simpson's five-month-old son and two-year-old daughter from his estranged wife, who had legal custody.

Despite any endorsement from Long, the national Teamsters Union revoked its payment of Partin's bond in the kidnapping case, which one observer said was why Partin later turned against Hoffa. Partin, for his part, said that he shifted his loyalties after Hoffa personally asked him to obtain "plastic explosives" that would be used to kill Attorney General Robert Kennedy. The national Teamsters Union, he told federal prosecutors, was becoming a one-man dictatorship.[55]

Of course, the same could be said of Local 5. Several members of the Baton Rouge local accused Partin of embezzling union funds, leading the national union to send a team of auditors. Just before the auditors arrived, the safe containing the union's financial records was reported stolen from the union's headquarters. Among the officers who responded to the report of the stolen safe was Baton Rouge deputy sheriff Herman Thompson. The empty safe was found three months later at the bottom of the nearby Amite River.

In the face of Hoffa's refusal to support him, Partin returned to Baton Rouge and turned himself in on the kidnapping charges. Then he offered his jailers the tantalizing information that Hoffa was plotting to kill Attorney General Robert Kennedy, a tale that Partin repeated to the FBI. Eventually, Partin's dramatic testimony about this plot led to Hoffa's conviction and imprisonment.

Jimmy Hoffa and the Teamsters

The McClellan committee's investigation of organized crime included an examination of the connections between organized crime and organized labor. In large part the investigation was sparked by efforts of Jimmy Hoffa, then a leader of the Teamsters Union in the Midwest, to defeat national union president David Beck by creating "paper locals"—imaginary union locals without any actual members—to boost Hoffa's vote totals in the 1957 union election. The committee's revelations led to passage of the Labor Management Reporting and Disclosure Act, requiring secrecy in union elections and allowing for oversight of union elections by the U.S. Department of Labor.

Hoffa's involvement in unions began when he was working at a warehouse of the Kroger grocery chain in Detroit, where he organized the workers and received a local AFL charter. In 1932, the local founded by Hoffa affiliated with the Teamsters. In 1936, Teamsters president Tobin put Hoffa's local into receivership because of questionable financial and election practices. When the trusteeship ended in 1945, Hoffa was elected the local's president.

It was during this time that Hoffa also had his first interaction with organized crime, serving as "muscle" in some of the battles between Jewish and Italian mob factions in Detroit.[56]

Hoffa's Local 299 was already the largest Teamsters local in Detroit, but Hoffa began to expand by absorbing other locals. In doing this, he relied on his ties with the mob that went back to the 1930s, and in the 1940s he was using Mafia muscle in rivalries with other locals. He also became personally involved in some of the mob's illicit business enterprises, including jukeboxes and gambling.[57]

Over the next several years, Hoffa consolidated his control over locals—first in Detroit, then in Michigan, then throughout the Midwest. By the mid-1950s, Hoffa had used his control of the Central States Drivers Council to expand his influence further, into the southern states. He also realized the potential of the union's $200 million pension fund to be wielded as a tool of influence and power. This all paved the way to his being elected national president of the Teamsters Union in 1957.

As he rose in the union, Hoffa had numerous and escalating legal problems. In 1937 he was fined ten dollars for assault and battery in a union picket line. In 1940 he pleaded nolo contendere to charges of conspiring with the union and companies in the wastepaper trades to monopolize that business and was fined $500. In 1946 he was convicted of a misdemeanor for his involvement in a scheme to extort money from small shop owners and was fined $500 and ordered to return $7,500.

In 1957, Hoffa was charged with offering a bribe to one of the McClellan committee's staff attorneys to provide details on the committee's investigations, although he was eventually acquitted. The same year that he was charged in the bribery case, Hoffa was elected national president of the International Brotherhood of Teamsters with 73 percent of the vote of delegates, an election that the McClellan committee characterized as "rigged."[58]

As president of the Teamsters, Hoffa shifted power over major issues from the locals across the country and consolidated it at the union headquarters in Washington, DC, placing himself firmly in charge of the union's political and bargaining operations. With this control, he promoted uniform contracts across the country, eventually culminating in a national master trucking agreement in 1964.

After Hoffa's election, the AFL-CIO expelled the Teamsters from its coalition of unions, based on the McClellan committee's findings regarding the Teamsters Union's involvement with organized crime. The Teamsters' banishment from the coalition lasted thirty years. But while the expulsion was meant as a rebuke to Hoffa, it also allowed him to organize workers without the constraints of the AFL-CIO's "no raid" agreement, which discouraged any union within the alliance from organizing workers already represented by another union.

While Hoffa consolidated the Teamsters' political and negotiating operations, he decentralized the union's organization, dividing it into four regional conferences. Underneath the conferences in Hoffa's structure were joint councils, made up of several Teamsters locals in a geographical area. The grassroots level of the Teamsters was the local, led by a powerful business manager elected by the local's membership. At Local 5, this powerful local business manager was Ed Partin.

As Hoffa rose in the union, he gathered loyal friends throughout the locals. But his imperious style also motivated some dissenters, many of whom fell victim to assaults and some of whom were killed in various "accidents." Two academics who studied Hoffa's leadership techniques observed that while he "look[ed] upon moderate doses of violence as merely another acceptable means for obtaining his ends," it was unfair to impugn him "with every measure taken by local officials or members." They concluded that "the Jimmy Hoffa of the 1960s is much too clever to depend upon brute force to get his way. His reputation for physical retaliation now serves primarily as an unspoken rather than an overt weapon, causing fearful truck owners, local officials and members to succumb before the reputation is tested."[59]

The academics added, however, that "to maintain his various leverage pressures despite the increasing restraints, Hoffa must continually operate on the very edges of legality and even risk breaking the law, so long as he does not get caught."[60]

This included connections to organized crime. Besides his personal involvement with the mob, investments by the union's pension funds in Las Vegas casinos led the Teamsters to have financial connections to the Mafia.

Eventually the Teamsters Union was used as a legitimate cover by the mob for its gambling, narcotics, and other operations, to the extent that in a bugged conversation in 1979, New Orleans crime boss Carlos Marcello told two undercover FBI agents that a group of Mafia chieftains "own[ed] the Teamsters." The increasing power and influence of the union and Hoffa eventually led to political connections, and political enemies.[61]

Hoffa grew the Teamsters into the largest union in the country, with more than two million members. Despite the fissure with the AFL-CIO, he also forged alliances with other unions, which gave the Teamsters enormous power. For example, a general strike by its members and allied unions could paralyze transportation and many other fundamental functions of the American economy and way of life. Hoffa's antagonist, Robert F. Kennedy, described the Teamsters Union as "the most powerful institution in this country, aside from the United States government itself."[62]

Jimmy Hoffa and the Kennedys

To Robert Kennedy, the Teamsters' power was dangerous. As counsel to the McClellan committee, he became obsessed with the corruption and collusion that the committee discovered between union boss Jimmy Hoffa and Mafia kingpins like Carlos Marcello. Hoffa and Marcello returned the animosity. In 1960, Carlos Marcello reportedly gave $500,000 to the Teamsters, which was combined with contributions from mob operations in New Jersey and Miami to donate $1 million to Richard Nixon's 1960 presidential campaign against Robert Kennedy's brother and patron, U.S. senator John Kennedy. After his loss to Kennedy, Nixon spoke to lame-duck attorney general Bill Rogers but was unable to sway career prosecutors to dismiss a federal criminal fraud case against Hoffa over a Florida land deal. But Nixon's intercession may have kept the government from further pursuing the case after a judge dismissed the indictment on the grounds that the grand jury had been impaneled improperly.

After John Kennedy became president and appointed him attorney general, Robert Kennedy continued his search for a criminal case that would bring down Hoffa. He thought he found it in the "Test Fleet" case, in which Hoffa was accused of setting up a fake shipping company in Nashville, Tennessee, as a funnel for payments from legitimate local shipping companies to Hoffa, to keep peace with their workers.

It was during this trial that Ed Partin, the head of Baton Rouge Local 5 and a trusted union loyalist who was later at the center of Herman Thompson's libel suit against Phil A. St. Amant, summoned federal prosecutors to a Baton Rouge jail cell to tell them that Hoffa was planning to kill the attorney general.[63]

Partin returned to Hoffa's camp during the Test Fleet trial as a government informant. While he was trusted enough to be posted outside the door of Hoffa's hotel room during important meetings, his brother Doug Partin claims that Ed never actually made it into Hoffa's inner circle. Whatever his role, Partin remained in touch with congressional investigator Walter Sheridan throughout the Test Fleet trial and recorded several incriminating phone conversations with various union officials, including Hoffa.[64]

The recordings made it clear that Hoffa was trying to bribe jurors in the trial. In the end, three of the jurors were removed from the case because of information from Partin. Nevertheless, the case ended in a mistrial due to a hung jury.

The government then indicted Hoffa and others for jury tampering in the Test Fleet case. Because both of the federal judges in Nashville had been involved in the prior case, the jury-tampering trial was moved to Chattanooga.

After two weeks of trial in this case, on February 4, 1964, Partin appeared as a surprise witness against Hoffa. When Partin was called as a witness, Hoffa was stunned. "My God," he said, "it's Partin." Hoffa later said, "I should have known better than to listen to him," calling Partin "the killing shot that was to nail me to the cross."[65]

Nineteen years after his surprise appearance at the Test Fleet jury-tampering trial, Partin said that it was remarkable that he had not been killed for betraying Hoffa. "I made it longer than anyone else [who led to the downfall of someone as big as Hoffa] has made it," he said in 1983.[66] He died seven years later of natural causes.

With Partin's testimony, Hoffa was convicted and sentenced to eight years in prison and a $10,000 fine, a conviction upheld by the U.S. Supreme Court in 1966.[67]

Four months after the first conviction, Hoffa was convicted in Chicago in another federal fraud case, this one for skimming union pension fund assets, and sentenced to four concurrent terms of five years, on top of the eight-year sentence in the prior jury-tampering case.

The conviction of Hoffa enraged members of his inner circle. Partin later said that Hoffa's loyalists offered him bribes and union positions in which he would oversee and could skim vast union pension funds if he changed his testimony. According to *Life* magazine, the Teamsters also worked another angle, offering $2 million—with the funds entrusted to Carlos Marcello—to anyone who could counter Partin's testimony. Even Partin's brother says he was beaten up by several of Hoffa's men in possible revenge for the testimony. And John Davis reports that there was an aborted effort by Frank Chavez, the boss of Teamsters Local 901 in Puerto Rico, to kill Partin, as well as Robert Kennedy and Walter Sheridan, in retaliation for Hoffa's conviction.[68]

After Partin appeared at Hoffa's trial, all of the pending federal and state charges against him were dropped, although Partin denied that it was in return for his testimony. He returned to Baton Rouge, where he reported being shot at twice, including one shot that hit him in the abdomen. The implication was that Hoffa was out to get him, but Doug Partin alleges that both these incidents were staged, and the wounds self-inflicted.[69]

It is clear, however, that with Hoffa in prison the pressure on Partin increased. He was asked to name his price to recant his testimony. One of the offers was conveyed to Partin by James "Buddy" Gill, head of the Baton Rouge Industrial Contractors Association, who had previously been Senator Russell Long's administrative assistant. When Partin asked how he would be protected if he changed his testimony, Gill reportedly told Partin that "we've got that fixed. Senator [Russell] Long is the most powerful man in the United States today. Don't you worry about it. You will be protected." Another time, Partin was promised that President Nixon would give him immunity from perjury charges if he recanted his testimony against Hoffa.[70]

When Partin refused the bribes, Marcello's associates turned to other means. According to Dan Moldea, this became evident when New Orleans prosecutor Jim Garrison launched his own investigation of the assassination of President Kennedy and alleged that Partin had driven Lee Harvey Oswald and Jack Ruby around New Orleans when he visited the city prior to the president's murder. Partin said that he was told the allegations would be dropped if he recanted. As noted above, Garrison's investigation may have also been an attempt to deflect attention from Marcello's possible involvement in the Kennedy assassination.[71]

At one point Partin appeared to give in as he agreed to give a statement to retract his testimony against Hoffa. An affidavit was drafted, but in the end

Partin refused to sign it. "I said some words, and they wrote them down," Partin explained. "But they were accusing me of everything, including being involved in the Kennedy assassination. So I just told them what they wanted to hear and refused to sign anything." When Hoffa tried to give the unsigned statement to the parole board in March 1971, the panel refused to accept it.[72]

When Partin returned to Baton Rouge after Hoffa's conviction based on his bombshell testimony, he called a vote of the members of his union, Local 5 in Baton Rouge, and received the members' unanimous support. The members emphasized their loyalty by changing the union hall's moniker from Hoffa Hall, and a photo of the national union leader was removed. But Local 5's support of Partin was not shared by the national Teamsters Union. The president of the Teamsters local in New Orleans, Local 270, announced that Local 5 had been decertified by the national union and sent his aide J. D. Albin to Baton Rouge to persuade members of Local 5 to instead join Local 270. These efforts would cease, Partin was told, if he withdrew his testimony.[73]

In 1967, the Department of Justice convened a grand jury to investigate the efforts to bribe and intimidate Partin. According to Walter Sheridan, "When Senator Long learned of this he was furious," and said that if anyone should be investigated, it was Partin. Partin eventually came to believe that Senator Long was behind the campaign against him.[74]

Despite his valuable testimony that led Hoffa to federal prison, Partin's cordial relationship with federal prosecutors soured in 1969, when Partin was charged with extortion to limit competition in the concrete industry. But the government eventually dropped the charges after a mistrial and two guilty verdicts that were both reversed on appeal. Partin was then charged with obstruction of justice for intimidating witnesses in the extortion trial but was acquitted. He was again charged with obstruction, this time related to the previous obstruction trial. Finally, Partin was found guilty on this charge and was sentenced in 1980 to an eight-year term. While in prison, he pleaded no contest to additional charges related to two Local 5 officials who were embezzling union funds and sending them to Partin in prison. In the end, Partin served six years and was released in 1986 when the conviction was reversed. He died in a Baton Rouge nursing home four years later.

Hoffa served his sentence in federal prison from March 1967 until President Richard Nixon granted him clemency on December 23, 1971, commuting Hoffa's sentence from thirteen years to the six and a half that he had already served. The commutation barred Hoffa from being involved in leadership of any union until March 1980, part of a deal that Nixon made with Hoffa's successor, Frank Fitzsimmons, to avoid a threat to his leadership of the Teamsters. There are also allegations—denied by both Nixon and Fitzsimmons—that the union contributed to Nixon's reelection campaign in return for the pardon.[75]

But Hoffa was apparently not originally aware of the condition. Two months after his release, Hoffa asked the U.S. pardon attorney to rescind the leadership ban, a request that would eventually have to be approved by President Nixon. Hoffa sued when the request was denied but eventually lost in court.[76]

Of course, Hoffa famously disappeared on July 30, 1975, and is presumed killed. His last communication with his family was from a pay phone outside a Michigan restaurant where he had an appointment with two alleged mobsters from Detroit and New Jersey. Although mobster Frank Sheeran confessed to killing Hoffa in a posthumously published memoir, several investigations of Hoffa's disappearance have been inconclusive. He was declared legally dead in 1982.

(2)

The Road to *Sullivan*

Congressional committees held hearings throughout the 1960s to investigate the Mafia's influence on organized labor in Louisiana and elsewhere. Meanwhile, across the street from the Capitol, the U.S. Supreme Court was transforming several areas of American law, particularly civil rights.

One area of dramatic change was in the law of defamation, which had not altered much since the first days of the American republic. In the early nineteenth century, the newly independent American states had made a major change in the defamation law inherited from England by making the truth of a statement a conditional defense. But there were no more significant changes until 150 years later, when—starting in 1964—a series of decisions by the U.S. Supreme Court recognized that the constitutional protection of free speech embodied in the First Amendment required further transformation of defamation law. This conversion, which played out over more than two decades, changed these laws in fundamental ways. In this tumultuous setting, an obscure libel lawsuit in Baton Rouge, Louisiana, that went to trial in 1964 and reached the U.S. Supreme Court in 1968 became a storm-tossed ship adrift in this swirling ocean of dramatic change in the law.

DEFAMATION IN ENGLAND AND COLONIAL AMERICA

While defamation law can trace its earliest roots to the ancient Greeks and Romans, defamation law in the United States stems from the common law inherited from the British. This law originated in the tenth century A.D., and over the next nine hundred years—until the era of American independence—the English developed the concept of freedom of speech as a right of Parliament, not of the people. The use of words to damage someone's reputation—defamation, which encompassed both written (libel) and oral (slander) statements—was initially considered a moral failing to be punished by ecclesiastical courts. But eventually it came to be seen as a criminal offense punishable by the state and later as the basis for a private legal action. This history has led to the esoteric contours of defamation as the concept is understood in the United States today. It also shaped the issues that the Supreme Court had to resolve in deciding the appeal in *St. Amant v. Thompson.*

Contrary to American myth, which portrays many colonists as seeking religious and other freedoms in the colonies of the New World, legal historian Leonard W. Levy observes that "the American people simply did not believe or understand that freedom of thought and expression means freedom for the other person, especially the one with hated ideas." Outside of a few large, diverse cities, "colonial America was an open society dotted with closed enclaves" that often prosecuted dissenters who criticized the governing powers or the dominant religion for sedition. Punishments varied and included fines, imprisonment, banishment, forced servitude, and even death.[1]

Colonial courts heard interpersonal defamation cases in the manner that the Crown courts of England did in that era: parties represented themselves, jurors consisted of fellow townsmen (only men could serve on juries), and damage awards were minimal, with courts often requiring losing defendants to formally apologize.

The law applied in these courts was the English common law of defamation, which was described by William Blackstone in his 1769 landmark treatise summarizing English law, *Commentaries on the Laws of England.* As described by Blackstone, defamation was both a criminal and civil offense: the former because "every libel has a tendency to break the peace, or provoke others to break it," and the latter because of the harm to an individual's reputation that could be caused by a defamatory statement. Because of the potential harm to public peace, truth was not a defense in criminal defamation cases. As Blackstone explained, "It is immaterial with respect to the essence of a libel, whether the matter of it be true or false; since the provocation, and not the falsity, is the thing to be punished criminally: though, doubtless, the falsehood of it may aggravate it's [*sic*] guilt, and enhance it's punishment." But truth was a valid defense in civil defamation cases, since a true statement would not harm the reputation of the target.[2]

In addition to continuing common law practices regarding criminal and civil defamation inherited from England, several of the British colonial governments in America passed their own statutes making defamation a crime. In the years immediately following their initial European settlement, Rhode Island, Pennsylvania, and Connecticut all passed statutes outlawing defamatory statements, each allowing for both civil and criminal remedies. While historians differ on how often courts across the colonies prosecuted defamation and related crimes, Bradley Chapin found that defamation cases represented, on average, 17 percent of all criminal cases. Most involved statements accusing someone of criminality (including being a witch, rogue, or thief); accusing a woman of being a whore; or charging a person with incompetence or dishonesty in their business or trade. Punishments often involved monetary damages as well as social censure, placement in the stocks or a pillary, whipping, or even more severe corporal punishments. As in England, slander and libel against noblemen and magistrates resulted in the harshest penalties in the colonies. But "as the struggling English outposts became more stable and secure, criminal penalties tended to become less harsh."[3]

The commonality of such cases, legal historian Norman Rosenberg concludes, resulted from the attitude, widely held in the small communities that populated the colonies, that an ordered society should exact penalties for intemperate speech. Thus the movement away from such cases that occurred in English courts in the seventeenth century was not immediately followed by their colonial counterparts.[4]

But as the colonies and their courts matured during the late seventeenth and early eighteenth centuries, the judicial system's communitarian role waned. "After the earliest years of settlement," Rosenberg writes, "most legal authorities began to consider adjudication of ordinary defamation cases a waste of valuable legal resources." This resulted in prosecutors focusing on defamation in the public arena—against prominent members of the community, including colonial government officials.[5]

The first American newspapers appeared around this time. Colonial printers, who usually operated with the official imprimatur of the authorities, faced the persistent threat of revocation of the licenses granted to them by colonial governments—another aspect of British law imported to the American colonies—and of defamation prosecutions, and thus often imposed self-restraint in their coverage of local affairs. For the newspapers of the time, "Even a casual remark on some petty detail of the administration's policy meant an official inquiry usually followed by the discontinuance of the paper, while any open opposition to the governor soon led to a trial for libel."[6]

The trial of John Peter Zenger in colonial New York in 1735 has become the touchstone for the emergence of the concept of free speech in the United

States. By acquitting Zenger, the jury disregarded the judge's instructions—and the established law at the time—and accepted the argument that truth should be a defense to defamation when the statements at issue involve a public official. While the jury verdict did not make any changes to the substantive law, it was an indicator of changing public attitudes toward the press and the government. The result was widely heralded, and "the importance of Zenger's case in the development of American political opinion could hardly be overestimated."[7]

Common law defamation prosecutions "petered out after Zenger's case," with only four successful prosecutions in the colonies during all of the eighteenth century and only one indictment—which was not prosecuted—in the years leading up to the American Revolution.[8]

While the *Zenger* verdict and philosophers' musings had little practical impact on the law regarding speech freedoms, colonial printers began to realize that it was in their economic self-interest to promote the concept of the press as a conduit of opposing ideas. Their role, they argued, was to publish whatever was submitted to them, regardless of their personal opinion of the arguments made; the printers themselves were not advocates of a specific cause. Benjamin Franklin explained this in his *Apology for Printers*, which he published in 1731 after an advertisement in his *Pennsylvania Gazette* offended some local clergymen:[9] "Printers are educated in the Belief, that when Men differ in Opinion, both Sides ought equally to have the Advantage of being heard by the Publick; and that when Truth and Error have fair Play, the former is always an overmatch for the latter: Hence they chearfully serve all contending Writers that pay them well, without regarding on which side they are of the Question in Dispute."[10]

Levy points out that this declaration "hardly presented a definition or a philosophy of a free press." Nevertheless, Franklin's view did represent the general consensus on the subject in the colonies in the years before the American Revolution: that the press was a hurly-burly venue for political debate, with little regard for the legal restrictions that theoretically limited their activities.[11]

The ire of the colonists against England was finally raised not by defamation law but by another provision that was portrayed as affecting freedom of the press in the colonies: the Stamp Act. This provision, passed by Parliament in 1765, required that all printed material in the colonies use paper embossed and taxed in London. This incited vehement reaction from the colonists. They objected to imposition of the provision by Parliament, in which the colonists had no representatives and thus no voice. They also objected to the purpose of the tax, which was to fund the maintenance of troops in the colonies after the French and Indian War. Finally, many colonists were already distressed by the imposition of new taxes on sugar the previous year.

The colonists' objections to the Stamp Act were expressed in remonstrances and sometimes violent protests. Newspaper editors also took up the cause, particularly because they were directly affected by the provision.

While the Stamp Act was widely ignored when it was in effect and was repealed the following year, it set the stage for wider protests against the English government and the eventual union of the American colonies against the mother country. But freedom of speech was still a minor issue in the overall patriot cause, as protests persisted over other laws passed by Parliament that were seen as oppressive, including the 1764 Currency Act, the 1765 Quartering Act, the 1766 Declaratory Act, the 1767 Townshend Revenue Act, and the 1774 Coercive Acts, referred to by the colonists as the Intolerable Acts.

The newspapers' successful crusade against the Stamp Act had another effect beyond the repeal of that specific tax. It also exposed colonial governments' reluctance to use the charge of seditious libel to suppress popular dissent. Their fear, Lieutenant Governor Cadwallader Colden of New York confessed, was of "raising the Mob, which it is thought proper by all means to avoid."[12]

Printers continued this role after the declaration of American independence and the ensuing war against Britain, as newspapers and broadsides became a primary way to support the revolutionary cause. Loyalist publications lost favor, and their owners and writers were shamed and harassed, often violently. At the urging of the Second Continental Congress, by 1778 all thirteen of the former colonies passed statutes barring speech against the new federal and state governments, the war effort, and the patriot cause. In addition, in October 1776 Virginia passed a treason statute barring "any word, open deed, or act" defending the Crown or Parliament. New York passed a similar law in 1781.

Moderate criticism of the new American government was tolerated, as long as it came from supporters of the basic patriot cause. As Norman Rosenberg observed, "Political leaders found that they could use controls over expression only with great difficulty and at considerable risk to their political fortunes." At the same time, however, newspaper publishers remained skittish about publishing items on particularly sensitive political topics, such as Massachusetts's dire financial state in the aftermath of the American Revolution.[13]

After overthrowing the yoke of British rule, the former colonies had to create a structure for their new government. Their first attempt, contained in the Articles of Confederation, featured a limited national government, with most power and responsibilities held by the newly independent states. Among the states, all but Connecticut explicitly adopted English common law, including the existing common law of defamation. Nine of the new states' constitutions or charters included provisions for freedom of the press, but only two—Pennsylvania's and Vermont's—explicitly protected freedom of speech. This does not mean that there was not robust political debate, both in the press and elsewhere. But the paucity of defamation cases to test these principles left the parameters of the freedom of the speech and press provisions ill-defined. But it seems that the Blackstonian view prevailed: while no prior restraints were imposed, speakers could be punished after the fact, including by prosecutions for common law criminal and seditious defamation. "But the threshold of public tolerance had significantly widened," Levy observes, and freedom of the press "meant the right to criticize the government, its officers, and it policies as well as to comment on any matters of public concern."[14]

But some of the specifics of the Blackstonian conception of defamation fell into disfavor, with general support for the notion from the *Zenger* case that truth is a defense to defamation and that juries should decide whether a particular statement is defamatory. Pennsylvania's 1790 constitution accepted truth as a defense to defamation prosecutions, but only for cases involving "investigat[ions of] the official conduct of officers, or men in public capacity, or where the matter published is proper for public information."[15] It also provided for jurors to determine both the facts in a case—whether the defendant actually published the statement at issue—and the legal question of whether it was defamatory or not. Defense lawyers in a 1791 libel trial in Massachusetts told the jury that it could find their client not guilty on the basis of truth, and the judges instructed the jury to decide whether the statements were actually libelous.[16] But it took several years for these concepts to become widely accepted in American law.

An important influence on popular opinion about freedom of speech in this era was the pseudonymous writer "Cato"—actually two men, John Trenchard and Thomas Gordon—whose articles in the *London Journal* and then the *British Journal* advocating freedom of the press and freedom of speech were widely circulated and read both in England and the colonies. Cato advocated freedom of thought and speech as foundations of liberty and portrayed government officials who restricted speech as oppressors. He also condemned the use of seditious libel to stifle legitimate criticism of government, while defending the government's ability to stifle false statements. He also argued for truth as a defense to defamation in suits involving public officials.

Cato's collection of essays, which was quoted "in every colonial newspaper from Boston to Savannah," "was the most popular, quotable, esteemed source of political ideas in the colonial period." The essays "expressed the fundamental feeling that was gathering force on the western side of the Atlantic," and are credited with fermenting the ideas that were eventually expressed in the Declaration of Independence. But while Cato's ideas joined those of libertarian political philosophers in forming a conception of free speech, American colonists "gave little independent thought and even less expression to a theory of unfettered political debate." On a practical level, the common law of defamation remained unchanged.[17]

CREATING THE FIRST AMENDMENT

After several years of governance under the Articles of Confederation, limitations of the document became manifest and a meeting was called to undertake revisions. The participants soon concluded that a wholesale revision was necessary, and over the summer of 1787 they drafted an entirely new constitution for the nation.

The Constitutional Convention did not dwell on free speech issues. As the convention completed its work, George Mason of Virginia suggested that including a declaration of rights in the document would "give great quiet" to the people. But while Eldridge Gerry of Massachusetts proposed forming a committee to draft such a section, Roger Sherman of Connecticut argued that citizens' rights were protected by state constitutions, which the federal constitution would not preclude. Gerry's proposal was then defeated by a unanimous vote. Two days later, a motion by Gerry and Charles Pinckney of South Carolina to insert into the draft of the Constitution a statement that "liberty of the Press should be inviolably preserved" was also defeated. James

Madison wrote that the convention's failure to seriously consider the motion was the result of haste and fatigue.[18]

The lack of an enumeration of rights in the proposed Constitution was seen as a fatal flaw by those who opposed ratification, such as the columnist "Brutus" (Robert Yates), who wrote in *Antifederalist* No. 84 "that the exercise of [the federal government's] power . . . should be restrained within proper limits, as in that of the State governments." Proponents dismissed this concern, as expressed by Alexander Hamilton in *Federalist* No. 84: "I go further, and affirm that bills of rights, in the sense and in the extent in which they are contended for, are not only unnecessary in the proposed constitution, but would even be dangerous. . . . Why declare that things shall not be done which there is no power to do? Why for instance, should it be said, that the liberty of the press shall not be restrained, when no power is given by which restrictions may be imposed?"[19]

The issue of a bill of rights arose at several of the individual states' conventions on ratification of the Constitution. Three of the first nine states to ratify the Constitution called for changes, including some protection of individual liberties. Three of the remaining states—Virginia, New York, and North Carolina—called for the addition of a bill of rights, including a provision for freedom of the press.

Although the Constitution was ratified by the required nine of the thirteen states, these debates led to a growing general sentiment that an enumeration of rights was required. Fearing that failure to respond to public opinion would undermine the constitutional experiment, James Madison became convinced of the need and argued in the House of Representatives for a statement of rights to be added to the Constitution, including restrictions on both federal and state infringement on freedom of the press. Despite the support of President George Washington, who addressed the issue in general terms in his inaugural address, the reaction in the Federalist-controlled Congress was unenthusiastic. Eventually Madison's nine proposed amendments—in the form of changes in the text of the Constitution, rather than addendums—were referred to a select committee, which reported back a number of proposals, with minor changes to Madison's language. The House eventually passed seventeen proposed amendments—again, as revisions to the text—for consideration by the Senate, including a provision that "the Freedom of Speech and of the Press, and right of the people to peaceably assemble and consult for their common good, and to apply to the Government for a redress of grievances, shall not be infringed." Because of the lack of language limiting this provision, it arguably would have applied to both the federal and state governments.

The Senate initially considered and rejected a provision that would have enshrined a Blackstonian view of freedom of speech limited to a prohibition on prior restraints. The senators then distilled the seventeen House revisions into twelve amendments to the Constitution, now in the form of addendums. In doing so, the senators combined provisions regarding freedom of speech and religion and removed provisions that would have applied the restrictions on government limitations on the press to the states. As a result, the third of the amendments approved by the Senate provided that "Congress shall make no law establishing articles of faith, or a mode of worship, or prohibiting the free exercise of religion, or abridging the freedom of speech, or of the press, or the right of the people peaceably to assemble, and to petition the government for a redress of grievances."

The scant congressional debate over the free speech and free press provisions of what became the First Amendment frustrate attempts to determine the Founders' meaning. But according to Levy, it appears from their choice of language that "the Framers meant *Congress* to be totally without power to enact legislation respecting the press." The other branches of government, and the states, were free to regulate speech as their constituencies would allow.[20]

A conference committee generally accepted the Senate's version, including slight revisions to the third of the proposed amendments, which included the free speech and press provisions. The twelve proposed amendments were then sent to the states for ratification. The first two amendments—regarding apportionment of congressional representatives and barring Congress from raising its own salary for its current session—were not ratified by enough states, renumbering what had been originally designated as the third amendment as the First Amendment. It, along with the nine remaining amendments, was ratified by two-thirds (eleven) of the then-fourteen states and became part of the Constitution in December 1791.[21]

FREE SPEECH UNDER THE CONSTITUTION

The adoption of the Bill of Rights occurred as the new republic established itself under the new form of government prescribed by the Constitution. When

George Washington assumed the presidency in 1789, some of his supporters advocated prosecuting his numerous opponents for seditious libel. But others, arguing that retaliation against such speech would only foster more dissent, urged restraint, and this is the faction that prevailed. This fostered an American press in the early years of the republic that featured robust debate on political issues and personalities and operated, as Levy describes it, "as if the law of seditious libel did not exist."[22]

The 1798 Sedition Act

But the law of defamation inherited from the British did still exist. And upon Washington's retirement, bitter divisions developed between two opposing political factions, exactly the sort of cleavage that Washington warned against upon his withdrawal from public life:

> All obstructions to the execution of the Laws, all combinations and associations, under whatever plausible character, with the real design to direct, control, counteract, or awe the regular deliberation and action of the constituted authorities, are destructive of this fundamental principle, and of fatal tendency. . . . However combinations or associations of the above description may now and then answer popular ends, they are likely, in the course of time and things, to become potent engines, by which cunning, ambitious, and unprincipled men will be enabled to subvert the power of the people, and to usurp for themselves the reins of government; destroying afterwards the very engines, which have lifted them to unjust dominion.[23]

The factions were exposed by the acrimonious presidential election of 1796 between Federalist John Adams and Republican Thomas Jefferson. Adams won the most Electoral College votes, making him president. But under the presidential election rules as delineated in the Constitution, the recipient of the second-highest number of electoral votes, Adams's rival and opponent Thomas Jefferson, became vice president. This result, along with issues in the 1800 election, led to the adoption in 1804 of the Twelfth Amendment, which provides for presidential and vice presidential candidates to run as a ticket and for the Electoral College to vote for the two offices individually.

In 1798, the Federalist Congress passed and President Adams signed the infamous Sedition Act, which made it a crime to "write, print, utter or publish . . . any false, scandalous, and malicious writing against the government of the United States, or either House of Congress, or the President" with the intent to defame or incite opposition. Betraying the partisan motivations behind the legislation, the statute specifically excluded statements about the vice president. According to Levy, this "suggests that the generation that framed the [First] amendment did not consider the suppression of seditious libel to be an abridgement of freedom of speech or press." But Jeffery Alan Smith has a slightly different interpretation, concluding that that the debate over the Sedition Act "demonstrated the existence of two distinct and conflicting interpretations of the First Amendment within a decade of its ratification."[24]

Free speech principles were not totally abandoned in the Sedition Act. In a major libertarian reform for the time, the statute incorporated the principles of the jury verdict in the *Zenger* case: truth was a defense, without any conditions, and the jury was authorized to determine both the law, whether a statement was "false, scandalous, and malicious," and fact, whether a statement was actually published or uttered.

There were not actually very many prosecutions under the statute: only thirty-two people were prosecuted under the act, and thirteen were convicted. The validity of the law was argued primarily along partisan lines, and all of the justices of the Supreme Court—all Federalists—upheld the constitutional validity of the act in various rulings while sitting as federal circuit judges. But while the courts upheld the law, opposition to the provision grew and was crystallized in resolutions passed by the Virginia and Kentucky legislatures, which argued that the Sedition Act was beyond the scope of proper congressional powers.[25]

By its own terms, the statute expired on March 3, 1801, the day before the winner of the 1800 presidential election would be inaugurated—another clear indicator of the statute's political purpose. After it expired, the winner of that election, Thomas Jefferson, pardoned all those prosecuted under the law, and Congress later refunded their fines. But Jefferson's action was likely more an act of political theater than an expression of legal principle regarding freedom of speech: Jefferson himself expressed support for seditious libel prosecutions when they were in his political interest.

The Sedition Act remains an infamous episode in American history that

Justice William J. Brennan Jr. later wrote "first crystallized a national awareness of the central meaning of the First Amendment." In addition to contemporary criticisms of this law, more than 150 years later Brennan led the U.S. Supreme Court in declaring that "although the Sedition Act was never tested in this Court, the attack upon its validity has carried the day in the court of history."[26]

Defamation Law Transforms

As the United States was adopting the First Amendment, in the late 1780s a number of British writers began advocating for changes in the defamation law of England: specifically, truth as a defense—the principle from the *Zenger* case—and giving juries the power to determine not only whether a statement was actually published (the "facts" of a case) but also whether it was defamatory (the "law" of the case). This led to the passage in 1792 of Fox's Libel Act, which expanded the jury's power to include determining both publication and defamation.[27]

In the United States, Pennsylvania had already established truth as a defense to defamation and the dual role of juries in defamation cases in its 1790 constitution. But the experience with the Sedition Act led to a wider rethinking of traditional defamation concepts in the early years of the nineteenth century.

Alexander Hamilton unsuccessfully argued for the concept of truth "with good motives and justifiable ends" as defense counsel in an 1803 libel case in New York, but this principle was adopted by statute two years later. Other states also adopted truth as a defense, with conditions similar to New York's. By 1815, sixteen of the eighteen states—the exceptions were Louisiana and South Carolina—had accepted at least a limited version of these principles, either by judicial decision or statute, and seven of the nine states that wrote or revised their constitutions between 1815 and 1827 included these principles in the new versions.[28]

The end of the federal Sedition Act did not mark the demise of all restrictions on speech. Civil and criminal defamation remained, as did blasphemy. Contempt was also often used by courts and legislatures to punish speech. And starting in the 1820s and 1830s, the fear of slave revolts led the federal government and the slaveholding states to enact laws to suppress abolitionist ideas.

But the end of the Sedition Act was at the forefront of another trend. As Norman Rosenberg explains, "By the early nineteenth century . . . civil libel cases, ostensibly private cases, came to replace criminal prosecutions as the most prevalent restraint on political expression."[29]

Even the few seditious libel cases of this time were more rooted in personal insult as perceived by a public official than in any challenge to the official's authority. In light of these developments, some courts began to recognize a sort of privilege in civil defamation cases for statements about political issues, or at least to require more than falsity as a basis for liability. At first, only a few courts took this approach. But by 1900, twenty-five of the twenty-eight states with post–Civil War appellate decisions involving defamation in a political context had accepted some type of privilege for speech about public affairs.[30]

By the middle of the nineteenth century, American courts had generally accepted the principle that a successful defamation claim required more than just that the statement at issue was false: the plaintiff also had to show that the statement actually hurt the plaintiff's reputation. Courts largely agreed that an otherwise defamatory statement would not lead to liability if the speaker acted with good motives and for justifiable ends. Courts applied these rules to cases involving public officials and also to cases involving other publicly prominent individuals. But there were still calls from lawyers, journalists, and others interested in public affairs to further liberalize defamation law.

DEFAMATION IN LOUISIANA'S CIVIL LAW SYSTEM

When most American courts made these subtle changes to defamation law in the nineteenth century, their starting point was the English common law inherited during the colonial period. In Louisiana, however, the law is the product of the state's distinct colonial history under the French, Spanish, British, and American flags. Thus the defamation law applicable in Deputy Sheriff Herman Thompson's suit against Phil A. St. Amant had a different provenance than the defamation law of every other state. The U.S. Supreme Court ignored these differences when it considered St. Amant's appeal of the result in the Louisiana courts.

Louisiana's Colonial and Territorial Experience

The Spanish were the initial European explorers of the Louisiana coast and Mississippi River, in the 1500s. Yet it was the French under King Louis XIV who made the first land claims to the Mississippi River and its headwaters, including most of modern Louisiana and parts of twenty-four other states. In 1699 Louis XIV administratively split the southern portion of this vast territory from his Canadian realm, with a boundary in modern southern Illinois, and named it Louisiana after himself. He also sent Pierre LeMoyne, Sieur d'Iberville to establish forts and settlements in the territory to thwart English settlement.

In 1712, Louis XIV granted a patent to Louisiana to Antoine Crozat. This patent established the first legal code for the territory, providing that "edicts and ordinances of France and the Custom of Paris were to be in effect in the territory." After Crozat surrendered the patent two years later, a new patent issued to John Law's Company of the West affirmed the laws of France and Paris as controlling the colony.

Despite this declaration, government in the French colony initially consisted only of the royally appointed governor, Antoine Cadillac. He was appointed in 1710 but did not arrive in the territory until late 1712. Upon his arrival, he established an advisory Superior Council, which implemented Custom of Paris laws—the written laws and legal customs used in Paris—as the first legal code in Louisiana.

Such codes are the fundamental source of law in "civil law" systems such as those in France, Spain, and several other nations of continental Europe. This differs from the "common law" system of Great Britain and its former colonies, in which constitutions and statutes are subject to interpretation by the courts in decisions that then become binding precedent on future courts. In pure civil law systems, courts refer to the codes anew in each case, regardless of past decisions.

The code remained when the Company of the West went bankrupt and abandoned its patent in 1731, making the area once again a French colony. In 1762, France ceded Louisiana territory west of the Mississippi to Spain, while the Treaty of Paris the following year ended the French and Indian War by ceding both Canada and all French territory east of the Mississippi River to England. The transfer of the western territory from France to Spain remained secret, and the Spanish did not immediately assert control over their new territory, which sowed confusion and resentment among the Francophile colonists. While the colonists' pleas for reversal of the decision were ignored, the Spanish initially established shared control with holdover local officials, using a hybrid of French and Spanish laws.

The Spanish-appointed governor, Don Antonio De Ulloa, grew wary of this arrangement, and in January 1767 he sought to eliminate the Superior Council. But in the face of dissension from the populace about this maneuver and Spanish restrictions on the colony's trade, he fled to Cuba. Ulloa's replacement, Alejandro O'Reilly, asserted Spanish control, replacing the Superior Council with a new advisory council, the Cabildo. In 1769 O'Reilly enacted a written code of law for the colony, based on existing Spanish law. But the differences between French and Spanish law were relatively minor, and many residents continued to resolve issues extrajudicially, applying principles of French law.

Upon the declaration of American independence by the thirteen British colonies, the Spanish gave covert and later declared support to the American revolutionaries. Spanish forces from Louisiana embarked on military campaigns against other English holdings east of the Mississippi, eventually capturing West Florida, consisting of the modern-day panhandle area of Florida, southern Alabama and Mississippi, and modern Louisiana north and east of the Mississippi River (the so-called Florida Parishes). With the outbreak of the French Revolution in 1789, the Spanish colonial authorities in Louisiana tamped down any rebellious thoughts in the colony by imposing restrictions on materials describing or depicting symbols or slogans of the revolutionaries, with restrictions increasing after Spain declared war on the new French republic in 1793.

The 1795 Pinckney Treaty between the new United States and Spain opened up the Mississippi River to American commerce and also defined the boundary between the United States and Spanish territory. But the nature of this boundary changed when Spain ceded the entire Louisiana territory to France in 1800. Again, the actual transfer of governance was a slow one, with France finally taking possession on November 30, 1803. By that time Napoleon had already sold the territory to the United States in the Louisiana Purchase, and the French ceded control to the Americans after only twenty days. But in that short period the French eliminated the Cabildo and the other components of Spanish governance, including the courts, without establishing a replacement.

The purchase of the Louisiana territory from France more than doubled the territory of the United States, posing the challenge of how to incorporate the new territory into the young nation.

American control brought a new government structure to Louisiana. But the first action taken by William C. C. Claiborne, the commissioner appointed by President Jefferson to administer the territory, was to formally retain existing Spanish law in the territory. This was meant to be a temporary measure until British- and American-style common law could be adapted, but the plan ran into opposition from the public and lawyers in the territory.

In 1804 the Breckinridge Act separated the massive Louisiana territory into the Territory of Orleans, making up most of the modern state of Louisiana, and the District of Louisiana, constituting all the land in the territory above the 33rd north parallel, approximately the northern boundary of the current state. For the Territory of Orleans, Congress established as presidential appointments a territorial governor, a secretary, an unelected thirteen-member legislative council, and a three-judge superior court. The legislative council met and in 1805 passed a "Practice Act" that adopted Spanish civil law but also borrowed several elements of English common law, including the practice of jury trials in civil cases and common law criminal procedure.

The following year, the territorial legislature voted to adopt Spanish and Roman law as it existed at the time of the Louisiana Purchase as controlling law for the territory. Claiborne—now the territorial governor—vetoed the measure, saying that the decision of whether to adopt the civil law system fell solely within the power of the U.S. Congress. A few weeks later, however, Claiborne approved a second measure to appoint James Brown and Louis Moreau Lislet "to compile and prepare jointly a Civil Code for the use of this territory," based on "the civil law by which this territory is now governed."

The resulting Digest of Civil Laws was adopted in 1808 as nonbinding guidelines for the courts. The digest combined Louisiana's various legal legacies. While partially based on the 1769 code, the digest used as its primary source the Code Napoléon, which had recently been adopted in France. But the 1808 digest also continued the elements of English common law that had been enacted in 1804, as well as some elements of Roman law. The digest also provided that Spanish laws that did not conflict with American law remained in effect.

There was apparently no civil action for defamation under the digest, since it did not contain any provisions regarding liability for injury to another. Only with adoption of such a provision would civil defamation later establish a foothold in Louisiana law.

There was, however, a criminal defamation provision, which was quickly put to use. In 1805 the territorial legislature adopted "An Act for the punishment of crimes and misdemeanors," which was based entirely on English common law and included a criminal defamation provision. A criminal defamation provision was included in a criminal code for Louisiana proposed in 1822, but the code was not adopted. This left "a juridical vacuum which the Anglo-American common law of crimes and criminal procedure found relatively easy to fill."[31]

Statehood and Development of a Law of Civil Defamation

In 1812, the Orleans Territory and the western portion of West Florida were admitted into the United States as Louisiana, the eighteenth state of the Union. The new state's constitution, based largely on Kentucky's 1792 constitution, preserved Louisiana's mixed Spanish and French civil law legacy, while providing for English common law in criminal cases. The new state's constitution also included protection for speech: "Printing presses shall be free to every person who undertakes to examine the proceedings of the Legislature, or any branch of the government, and no law shall ever be made to restrain the right thereof. The free communication of thoughts and opinions is one of the invaluable rights of man, and every citizen may freely speak, write and print on any subject, being responsible for the abuse of that liberty."[32]

The 1812 constitution was just the first of ten constitutions that have been adopted in Louisiana, the most of any state. Each of these constitutions, including the current 1974 version, contained a provision for freedom of speech and of the press substantially similar to the 1812 version.

Despite the free speech provision of the Constitution, the existence—and persistence—of a civil action for defamation based on British common law is shown by the passage of a statute in 1821 providing that truth may be used as a defense in "any civil suits for slander or defamation, or for a libel."[33]

Confusion over which body of law was applicable in Louisiana remained after the adoption of the 1805 digest and the 1812 constitution. The state legislature commissioned the drafting of a civil code, which was adopted in 1825. Like the 1805 digest, the 1825 code was a fusion of French and Spanish law and precedents, as well as some concepts from Roman law. But confusion remained, as epitomized by decisions of the Louisiana Supreme Court holding that Spanish colonial laws and provisions of the 1808 code remained in effect long after adoption of the 1825 code, as long as they did not conflict with more recent provisions. Even after statutes adopted in 1828 repealed almost all of the laws that had been in effect prior to adoption of the 1825 code, the state courts still held that pre-1825 court precedents remained valid. Finally, in 1828 the legislature passed the Great Repealing Act, which abrogated "all the civil laws which were in force before the promulgation of the civil code lately promulgated."[34]

The 1825 code, like the 1808 digest, contained no provisions regarding civil defamation. In its first ruling in a civil libel case in 1828, the Louisiana Supreme Court cited Roman, Spanish, French, and English law in rejecting a slander claim against a lawyer for comments made to the court regarding a witness's veracity in the course of a trial.[35] Two years later, the same court rejected the notion that the Great Repealing Act had rescinded the civil action for slander as it existed under Louisiana's colonial law and added that the action was clearly within the provisions of the 1825 Civil Code. In 1840 the court cited provisions of the 1825 code as grounds for recognizing an action for slander and for upholding a damage award in such a case.

The civil code saw its last major substantive revision in 1870, and it still lacks a clear defamation provision even after piecemeal changes in the 1970s, '80s, and '90s. Thus, as the Louisiana Supreme Court wrote in 1888, "Under our laws slander is a quasi-offense, actionable under the broad provisions of our Code." Yet, despite finding its roots in Louisiana's Civil Code, "the Louisiana courts have developed a law of defamation closely resembling that of common law jurisdictions."[36]

The 1921 Louisiana Constitution, which was the version in effect when the trial in *Thompson v. St. Amant* took place in 1964, provided that "No law shall ever be passed to curtail or restrain the liberty of speech or of the press; any person may speak, write and publish his sentiments on all subjects, being responsible for the abuse of that liberty."[37]

The current version of the Louisiana state constitution was ratified in 1974, with only minor changes in the free speech language.[38]

Louisiana Defamation Law prior to Sullivan

Despite the fact that most of Louisiana's civil actions are rooted in the civil law systems of France and Spain, defamation law in the state is very similar to defamation law as it has developed in the other states of the United States, which trace their law back to the British common law system.

But defamation under Louisiana's Civil Code differs from the common law version in two important ways. One major difference is that Louisiana does not distinguish between libel (written defamation) and slander (oral defamation). Second, unlike common law defamation, in Louisiana courts no proof of "special damages"—economic losses—is required in order to win a monetary award in a defamation case. Instead, Louisiana juries have "no fixed rule in assessing the sum for which they are to give a verdict," and can consider the aggrieved party's respect, integrity, and reputation as well as any economic losses.[39] "In Louisiana, the only proof of injury required [was] the establishment of the words as defamatory to the plaintiff": hurt feelings or reputation was enough, and proof of actual economic damages was not required.[40]

This changed with Louisiana's adoption in 1950 of a version of a model statute drafted by the National Association of Broadcasters to require proof of damages for a plaintiff to recover in a defamation case stemming from a radio or television broadcast. The statute also provides that the broadcaster is not liable for a defamatory statement unless it "failed to exercise due care to prevent the publication or utterance of such statement in such broadcast," and—most importantly for the *St. Amant* case—provides that "in no event, shall any owner, licensee or operator, or the agents or employees of any such owner, licensee or operator of such a station or network of stations be held liable for damages for any defamatory statement uttered over the facilities of such station or network by or on behalf of, or in opposition to, any candidate for public office."[41]

The net result of these developments was explained in a 1967 article in the *Louisiana Law Review*, which summarized the requirements of a defamation claim in the state as follows: "In Louisiana, the elements necessary to make defamatory words actionable are: (1) publication, that is, communication to some person other than the one defamed; (2) falsity; (3) malice, actual or implied; and (4) resulting injury."[42]

In the third element in this formulation, actual malice is not the same "actual malice" as defined by the U.S. Supreme Court in *New York Times v. Sullivan* in 1964. Instead, "actual malice" in this context meant "personal ill will," which "may be found from the circumstances" in which the statement is made, and only came into play once a defendant had successfully asserted a conditional privilege:[43] "When defendant has established the existence of his privilege, the burden falls back to plaintiff to bring in further evidence, if he can, which will show that defendant, although he had the privilege, in the first place, to make the communication, yet has exceeded his right by some improper motive or action."[44]

Under this formulation, implied malice came closer to the definition of "actual malice" that the U.S. Supreme Court articulated in *Sullivan*. Implied malice was "closely associated with willful and wanton conduct" and could be found "in the publication of the defamatory statement itself" if "the words are of a defamatory nature with resulting injury." Such imputed malice, the Louisiana Supreme Court held, "is not personal ill will, but merely legal malice implied from willfully and wantonly doing an unlawful act which results in injury." A showing by the plaintiff of such malice "is, in effect, a showing that defendant made the statement for some purpose other than that which the privilege was designed to protect."[45]

By the time of the trial in *Thompson v. St. Amant*, then, it was clear that "suits for libel and slander partake more or less of the nature of a criminal accusation and the preponderance of proof necessary for plaintiff's case is greater than in ordinary civil actions."[46]

The *Louisiana Law Review* article also outlines the possible defenses to a defamation claim that were recognized in Louisiana in the late 1960s. Louisiana provided for two types of privileges: absolute and conditional. Truth and denial that the statement was made were absolute defenses, while there was also an absolute privilege for statements by legislators, judges, and other high-level government officials acting in their official capacity.

Other privileges were conditional and "may be defeated if the communication was made with knowledge of its falsity or if it was made under circumstances showing that the defendant was prompted by an improper motive."[47] These conditional privileges include remarks made to protect one's own social or economic welfare; statements made when the speaker and the recipient share a common interest protected or furthered by the communication; defamatory remarks made to protect close family members; statements made to protect the recipient's interest; statements in the course of public duties by public officials not covered by the absolute privilege; "fair report" news reports of government proceedings; "fair comment" statements of opinion regarding public affairs; and remarks made to protect the public interest concerning public affairs.[48]

DEFAMATION REFORM IN TWENTIETH-CENTURY AMERICA

Despite its more varied lineage, Louisiana's defamation law was similar to the law in other states. But changes in the media and society in the late nineteenth and early twentieth centuries began to reshape the conception of freedom of the speech and the press.

The middle of the nineteenth century saw the emergence of a new form of media, the penny press, which sold mass quantities of newspapers in major cities. While these newspapers originally generally hewed to journalistic standards of ethics and decorum, toward the end of the 1800s newer, bolder forms of coverage emerged: muckraking, which emphasized investigations of social ills and political corruption, and "yellow journalism," which emphasized sensationalism and titillation.[49]

With these developments dissatisfaction with the media rose, particularly among the elites. In the 1870s and 1880s, editor Edwin L. Godkin, appalled at the activities of some popular press at the time, called for more respect of individuals' privacy and reputations. In 1890, Samuel Warren and future Supreme Court justice Louis Brandeis published their famous *Harvard Law Review* article urging the courts to recognize a new right of privacy to wield against the intrusive and unaccountable press. In 1908, President Theodore Roosevelt unsuccessfully sought to have criminal libel charges brought against newspapers that criticized his policies. The U.S. Supreme Court ruled in several cases that the press was subject to the same defamation law that had been articulated in the early 1800s, with no further adjustments necessary. But as the number of civil and criminal defamation cases rose, major newspaper barons, journalists, some attorneys, judges, and legal scholars began to call for reform of defamation law.

America's entry into World War I led to increased concern within the government over press coverage that might undermine the war effort. This led to the creation of the Committee on Public Information, which sought to influence public perception of the war, including production of propaganda materials and "feeding" positive stories to the press.[50]

Eventually, this effort was enhanced with more direct controls on speech regarding the war—passage of the 1918 Sedition Act, which made speech undermining the war effort a crime. A proposed amendment to apply the "good motives and justifiable ends" defense of defamation law as a limitation on the speech restrictions in the act was rejected the Senate. When prosecutions of antiwar dissidents under the act were challenged in the courts, they were upheld by application of the "clear and present danger" test, first articulated by Justice Oliver Wendell Holmes for the majority in the 1919 *Schenck v. United States* case. In that case, the court upheld convictions under the Sedition Act of Communists who distributed flyers arguing against the military draft that the court said undermined the war effort.

In addition to the federal Sedition Act, states also passed their own statutes barring advocacy of "syndicalism," worker control of industrial facilities. The states prosecuted Communists, socialists, and others under these laws. While the Supreme Court's decisions in these cases varied, with some of the statutes being upheld and others held unconstitutional, in 1925 the court firmly established that states and local governments were subject to the free speech and free press provisions of the First Amendment by virtue of the due process clause language of the Fourteenth Amendment.[51]

Despite the increasing limitations on speech in this era, the U.S. Supreme Court did not rely on the First Amendment to strike down a law of any kind until 1931—that is, 140 years after the First Amendment was adopted—and did not hold any federal law unconstitutional under the First Amendment until 1965.

The looming threat of war in the late 1930s and early 1940s led to more restrictions on antigovernment speech in the form of the Alien Registration Act ("Smith Act") of 1940, which included provisions similar to those of the 1918 Sedition Act.

In 1947 the Hutchins Commission—a study group of academics enlisted to examine the state and future of the news media in America—concluded that press freedom under the First Amendment was threatened by the increasing influence of the mass media, inadequate use of the media to serve society, and outrageous behavior of some media outlets. The commission said this could lead to government controls that would imperil freedom for all media. The solution to forestalling such government intervention, the report concluded, was that the press should commit itself to responsibility toward the democratic society that it serves.

The commission gave libel law as an example of how the media already had some obligation to democratic society, which could serve as a model for other legal obligations:

> Though the presumption is against resort to legal action to curb abuses of the press, there are limits to legal toleration. The already recognized areas of legal correction of misused liberty of expression—libel, misbranding, obscenity, incitement to riot, sedition, in case of clear and present danger have a common principle; namely, that an utterance or publication invades in a serious, overt, and demonstrable manner personal rights or vital social interests. As new categories of abuse come within this definition, the extension of legal sanctions is justified. The burden of proof will rest on those who would extend these categories, but the presumption is not intended to render society supine before possible new developments of misuse of the immense powers of the contemporary press.[52]

The commission also recommended that monetary damages as a remedy for libel be replaced with "legislation by which the injured party might obtain a retraction or a restatement of the facts by the offender or an opportunity to reply." One member of the commission, Zechariah Chafee Jr., advocated this change even though his own survey of prominent newspaper executives and lawyers found that most were basically satisfied with existing defamation law and had developed systems to avoid running into legal trouble.[53]

By the late 1950s and early 1960s, libel suits were again perceived by journalists as a growing threat, both with increasing numbers of suits and rising damage awards. In 1956, Fred S. Siebert, Theodore Peterson, and Wilbur Schramm refined the Hutchins Commission prescription under their "social responsibility" theory of the press, which endorsed the Hutchins Commission's conception of the law of defamation as a means of balancing First Amendment freedoms with "private rights or vital societal interests" and ensuring that the media acted responsibly.

NEW YORK TIMES V. SULLIVAN

The trial and verdict in Thompson's case against St. Amant occurred just as the American law of defamation was poised to undergo an extensive metamorphosis, which took it far from its roots in British law. Under the English common law system, the only issue a jury in a defamation case had to decide was whether the alleged defamatory statement had been made. Once that was proven, the falsity of the statement was presumed but could be refuted by the defendant proving that the statement was true. The law also presumed that the statement harmed the subject's reputation, which could also be refuted. But as the American conception of freedom of speech gradually developed, it rejected traditional notions of defamation law, including these presumptions, and eventually severely limited sedition laws and other government limitations on speech.

This trend reached full flower in the 1960s. By that time there had already been several changes in American defamation law from its British antecedents. In order to win their cases, defamation plaintiffs in the United States had to prove that the statement at issue was published, that it was about them, that it harmed their reputation, and that the statement was untrue. But since these changes in the late eighteenth and early nineteenth centuries, the law of defamation remained the same.

While seditious libel was largely rejected in the United States in the early nineteenth century, its spirit lived on through the pursuit of civil and criminal libel charges by government officials and other prominent persons who sued or filed criminal charges against the press and other speakers who they felt sullied their reputations.

New York Times v. Sullivan was just such a case. The case stemmed from an advertisement, placed by civil rights activists and not fact-checked by the newspaper, which alleged several improper actions by authorities and others in Alabama against civil rights leader Martin Luther King Jr. and other civil rights activists, particularly student protesters at Alabama State College in Montgomery. The ad, titled "Heed Their Rising Voices," raised hackles among (white) community leaders in Alabama when it was published on March 29, 1960. Soon several lawsuits seeking a total of $6.15 million in damages were filed against the newspaper and four of the ministers whose signatures appeared as supporters of the advertisement.

The Montgomery city commissioner with responsibility for the city's police force, L. B. Sullivan, was the plaintiff in one of these lawsuits. He sought $500,000 over statements in the advertisement that made various allegations about the police department's treatment of the protesters. Unfortunately for the defendants, several of the details described in the advertisement about the protests and the police response were incorrect. For example, while the ad claimed that the campus dining hall had been "padlocked in an attempt to starve [the students] into submission," in reality the dining hall was never closed, and only a few protestors who had not registered for classes and were thus not enrolled as students were barred from eating there.

The trial in the *Sullivan* case has been well documented by Anthony Lewis and others. It ended with a $500,000 jury verdict for Sullivan against the *Times:* the largest trial award in Alabama history. The newspaper appealed, and the verdict was affirmed by the Alabama Supreme Court.[54]

But the *Times* then appealed to the U.S. Supreme Court, which issued a decision that transformed American defamation law. Invoking the principle that a primary purpose of the First Amendment's protection of free speech and free press was to hold public officials accountable, the court unanimously held that the language of the Fourteenth Amendment—which the court had previously held made the First Amendment applicable to state governments—required that public officials like Sullivan must meet a heightened burden in order to win a defamation case. In addition to the usual required elements of the claim, the court held that public officials must also show that the defendant acted with "actual malice," which the court defined as either actual knowledge that a statement was untrue or "reckless disregard" for the accuracy of the statement. It was unclear whether such "actual malice" was present in Sullivan's case against the *Times.* For while the jury had been instructed that such "actual malice" was required to award punitive damages, the judge had held that the statements at issue were defamation per se—inherently defamatory—so the jury was not told to consider the defendants' state of mind in deciding whether to award compensatory damages. Because of this, the majority ruled, the trial verdict had to be reversed.

This was the first time that the U.S. Supreme Court held that the First Amendment placed limitations on defamation actions, even if such limitations were applicable only to cases involving elected public officials like Sullivan. As Justice Byron White explained in a later case, "In *New York Times* cases, the public official's complaint will be dismissed unless he alleges and makes out a jury case of a knowing or reckless falsehood. Absent such proof, there will be no jury verdict or judgment of any kind in his favor, even if the challenged publication is admittedly false. The lie will stand, and the public continue to be misinformed about public matters. This will recurringly happen because the putative plaintiff's burden is so exceedingly difficult to satisfy and can be discharged only by expensive litigation."[55]

The court decided *Sullivan* only ten years after it had issued its revolutionary decision in *Brown v. Board of Education*, which unanimously held that racially segregated schools deprived minority children of equal educational opportunities. During the decade after the *Brown* ruling, the Supreme Court decided civil rights cases in favor of integration of public and private facilities, including law schools, universities, and eventually primary school education. The court also upheld the privacy of the NAACP's membership lists, upheld federal courts' ability to enforce desegregation, and outlawed racial segregation in public transportation.

Yet despite the court's subsequent instruction that desegregation under *Brown* should proceed "with all deliberate speed," resistance to the Supreme Court's civil rights decisions was fierce, particularly in the South. Most southern state legislatures passed resolutions condemning the *Brown* ruling and passed laws prohibiting implementation of desegregation. Activists on both sides raised the stakes, with civil rights activists conducting sit-ins, boycotts, and protests and their opponents responding with their own protests and violence. In 1957 President Dwight Eisenhower famously nationalized the Arkansas National Guard and sent paratroopers to force the integration of Central High School in Little Rock, Arkansas.

Sullivan and the other cases stemming from the *Times* advertisement, while couched in terms of defamation, were actually part of an effort "to pressure even the largest media corporations to self-censor their coverage from the Deep South." The goal was "to employ state libel laws to cut off outside criticism of 'massive resistance' to racial integration" by limiting coverage that drew the attention of northerners:[56] "Sullivan claimed that he started the law suit because his reputation had been besmirched, but he was cheered on by many southerners who wanted to silence the northern press, which they believed had painted a false picture of southern society. And no media member bore more blame on this count than did the *New York Times*."[57]

Sullivan's lawsuit was just one of several filed by southern officials against the *Times* and other news organizations based in the North. Their goal, simply, was to use the threat of defamation damages as a way to dissuade newspapers and the television networks from covering the civil rights movement. The plaintiffs in these cases admitted as much. An article by Associated Press Alabama correspondent Rex Thomas that ran in the *Montgomery Advertiser* and other newspapers pointed out that with defamation lawsuits "state and city authorities have found a formidable legal bludgeon to swing at out-of-state newspapers whose reporters cover racial incidents in Alabama." The *Alabama Journal*, meanwhile, had boastfully observed that the trial verdict in *Sullivan* "could have the effect of causing reckless publishers of the North . . . to make a resurvey of their habit of permitting anything detrimental to the South and its people to appear in their pages."[58]

As Anthony Lewis observed, "Commissioner Sullivan's real target was the role of the American press as an agent of democratic change. He and the other Southern officials who had sued the *Times* for libel were trying to choke off a process that was educating the country about the nature of racism and was affecting political attitudes on the issue."[59]

Legal scholar Melvin Urofsky reinforces this observation: "L. B. Sullivan and the other commissioners wanted to punish the *Times* and, through a victory in court yielding large damages, to stop the newspaper and other northern media from reporting what they considered a biased and unfair view of the events in the South."[60]

Urofsky even argued that the civil rights context preordained the result in *Sullivan:* "The Court could not have found against the *New York Times* [in *Sullivan*] because in large measure the Court's decisions beginning with *Brown v. Board of Education* in 1954 had led the newspaper into the predicament it found itself in during the early 1960s."[61] He also observed that while the majority opinion in *Sullivan* "paid practically no attention to civil rights activities," the court itself clearly recognized the *Sullivan* case as part of this civil rights context.[62]

In his concurring opinion in *Sullivan*, Justice Hugo Black noted, "The factual background of this case emphasizes the imminence and enormity of that threat. One of the acute and highly emotional issues in this country arises out of efforts of many people, even including some public officials, to continue state-commanded segregation of races in the public schools and other public places, despite our several holdings that such a state practice is forbidden by the Fourteenth Amendment."[63]

Legal historian Harry Kalven Jr. asserted that the ruling in favor of the *New York Times* in the *Sullivan* case was predictable given the historical context: "Even a cursory examination of the case reveals that the decision was responsive to the pressures of the day created by the Negro protest movement and thus raises the question so frequently mooted whether the Supreme Court has adhered to neutral principles in reaching its conclusion."[64]

Aside from its roots in the civil rights movement, the *Sullivan* decision also served to further the civil rights cause. "Through the use of libel suits, a minority of segregationists threatened to disrupt the flow of information through the marketplace of ideas and to delay the march of civil rights programs through the political marketplace. . . . Once freed to operate freely, the process of unblocked discussion would help people of good will discover the best solution to the racial problems besetting the nation."[65]

The *Sullivan* decision also fundamentally transformed defamation law in the United States. The court's decision attributed heightened requirements for defamation plaintiffs who are public officials to the First Amendment's free speech provision. The First Amendment, the court said, was the expression of "a profound national commitment to the principle that debate on public issues should be uninhibited, robust, and wide-open, and that it may well include vehement, caustic, and sometimes unpleasantly sharp attacks on government and public officials."[66]

Such a commitment, the court continued, required a heightened standard for defamation suits by public officials: "The constitutional guarantees require, we think, a federal rule that prohibits a public official from recovering damages for a defamatory falsehood relating to his official conduct unless he proves that the statement was made with 'actual malice'—that is, with knowledge that it was false or with reckless disregard of whether it was false or not."[67]

Since the *Sullivan* decision based the new "actual malice" standard on the First Amendment, under the principles of federalism the ruling and the standard it created apply to defamation claims by public officials nationwide, in both state and federal courts. The ruling thus swept away the existing disparate standards that individual states had developed for use in such cases. Prior to *Sullivan*, these different state standards resulted in uneven free speech protections from one state to another.

The Supreme Court's ruling also fundamentally changed defamation law to give greater deference to media coverage of public affairs and played a major role in the growth of the media and journalism in the decades that followed. By imposing new requirements on civil defamation claims brought by public officials, the *Sullivan* ruling emboldened the media to be more assertive—some would say reckless—in their coverage of government officials and their activities. In the years following the *Sullivan* decision, investigative journalists revived the muckraking tradition that had flourished in the late nineteenth and early twentieth centuries with investigative efforts such as examining the murders of civil rights activists, the (ethically controversial) creation of a tavern by the *Chicago Sun-Times* to capture state and city inspectors demanding bribes, and Bob Woodward and Carl Bernstein's revelations of the Watergate scandal.

But some critics saw the changes wrought in defamation law by the *Sullivan* decision as negative developments. Rosenberg observed that the "actual malice" test "required post-publication scrutiny of the motives, the choice of language, the editorial judgment, and even the intellectual significance of publishers' products." And he added that judges now had the constitutionally sanctioned authority to become "editors of last resort for the American media," using their own editorial judgment to decide questions of liability.[68]

Attorney Francis Murnaghan saw the effort at standardization of defamation standards as a means of reducing the need for judicial intervention. He conceded, however, that the rationale used to decide *Sullivan* "puts the already over-burdened Supreme Court in the time-consuming business of case-by-case independent examination of the record as a whole to determine whether the public interest suffices to give first amendment protection to the utterance and whether the evidence of 'actual malice' is convincing enough to meet constitutional standards."[69]

Some observers foresaw the expansion of the *Sullivan* "actual malice" rule to plaintiffs other than public officials. As the Second Circuit observed just four months after the *Sullivan* ruling, "Although the public official is the strongest case for the constitutional compulsion of such a privilege, it is questionable whether in the principle the [*Sullivan*] decision can be so limited."[70]

One prescient law scholar observed, "The law of defamation will undergo a significant change if the indicated extensions are fully exploited."[71] But most commentators celebrated the *Sullivan* decision as a new apogee in recognition of the importance of the free speech and press principles contained within the First Amendment. To these observers, with the ruling "a sea change began in the law of the First Amendment" that "resoundingly vindicated the promise of the First Amendment."[72]

Just a few months after the ruling, scholar Harry Kalven Jr. wrote that the *Sullivan* decision "may prove to be the best and most important [decision the court] has ever produced in the realm of freedom of speech." Arthur Ochs Sulzberger, publisher of the *New York Times* when the decision was announced, congratulated the newspaper's attorneys for "the significant decision handed down by the Supreme Court today that is of such fundamental importance not only for the *Times* but for all newspapers and other news media." First Amendment attorney Floyd Abrams called it "a majestic opinion." And scholar Alexander Meiklejohn famously called the decision "an occasion for dancing in the streets."[73]

But for Herman Thompson, the *Sullivan* decision and the new legal standard that it imposed in defamation cases brought by public officials was an unforeseen development that doomed his efforts to remove the blemish on his reputation that Senate candidate Phil A. St. Amant imposed during his television address on June 27, 1962. It did not matter that St. Amant's primary target in the address was incumbent U.S. senator Russell Long and that the mention of Thompson was merely an aside. Thompson's defamation case against St. Amant had not even gone to trial when the U.S. Supreme Court announced its ruling in *Sullivan*. But Thompson's case was fundamentally altered by the changes in defamation law that *Sullivan* introduced.

(3)

Philosophies of Communication and Defamation

Academics and legal scholars have crafted a number of theories to explain and analyze the freedom of speech and freedom of the press encapsulated in the First Amendment. There are several conceptions of harm that defamatory speech can cause and what measures, if any, should be taken to curb such harmful speech. Each of these philosophies is based on different ideas of the goals of society, the relationship between the state and the individual, and the role that government should play in shaping public and private discourse. And each of them has had some influence on the development of a uniquely American brand of defamation law in the *Sullivan* decision and its progeny that differs in significant ways from its British antecedents.

THE BLACKSTONIAN THEORY OF DEFAMATION

The earliest conception of defamation comes from the common law. The basis of the common law approach was that "government must necessarily exert some control over the press as it must over all other types of institutions operating in society."[1]

English jurist William Blackstone described the common law of defamation in his *Commentaries on the Law of England*, which explained that while freedom of speech and the press meant that there could be no restrictions prior to publication, the law could punish speech that has deleterious social impact. Such speech included libel and slander:

> Where blasphemous, immoral, treasonable, schismatical, seditious, or scandalous libels are punished by English law . . . the liberty of the press, properly understood, is by no means infringed or violated. The liberty of the press is indeed essential to the nature of a free state; but this consists in laying no previous restraints upon publications, and not in freedom from censure for criminal matter when published. Every freeman has an undoubted right to lay what sentiments he pleases be-

> fore the public; to forbid this, is to destroy the freedom of the press; but if he publishes what is improper, mischievous or illegal, he must take the consequence of his own temerity.[2]

By Blackstone's time the restrictions on speech under the British Crown were actually more relaxed than in prior periods. Before the Blackstonian era, speech could be considered harmful and be punished if it tended to undermine any of the institutions of society, from the Crown to the church. This approach was forged by a special tribunal in the English legal system, the Star Chamber, which handled defamation cases involving nobles and other "best men" of the realm. The Star Chamber, which is now infamous for its unjust procedures, heard seditious libel cases against those who insulted the British monarchy from the late fifteenth century through the chamber's elimination in 1641. In the 1606 *De Libellis Famosis* case, the tribunal expanded the scope of seditious libel to include insults not only to the monarch but of the government as a whole.

Blackstone, writing a century after the elimination of the Star Chamber, articulated the different standards applicable to civil and criminal defamation, including the role of falsity as an element of the offense:

> It is immaterial with respect to the essence of a [criminal] libel, whether the matter of it be true or false; since the provocation, and not the falsity, is the thing to be punished criminally: though, doubtless, the falsehood of it may aggravate its guilt, and enhance its punishment. In a civil action, we may remember, a libel must appear to be false, as well as scandalous; for, if the charge be true, the plaintiff has received no private injury, and has no ground to demand a compensation for himself, whatever offence it may be against the public peace: and therefore, upon a civil action, the truth of the accusation may be pleaded in bar of the suit. But, in a criminal prosecution, the tendency which all libels have to create animosities, and to disturb the public peace, is the sole consideration of the law.[3]

While falsity was a requirement for a civil defamation case, it was presumed; rather than falsity being something that the plaintiff had to prove, as it is in current American law, the defendant in a civil defamation case had the burden of proving that the statement at issue was *not* false. In a criminal case, however, the truth or falsity of the statement was not an issue in determining guilt, since, as an oft-quoted maxim stated, "The greater the truth, the greater the libel."[4]

DEFAMATION AND FIRST AMENDMENT ABSOLUTISM

The development and adoption of the First Amendment rejected the Blackstonian view of freedom of speech and of defamation. The First Amendment clearly states that "Congress shall make no law . . . abridging the freedom of speech, or of the press." While there is much scholarly debate over what exactly the Founders meant by this language, a few scholars and Supreme Court justices have taken this statement to heart and advocated an absolutist position regarding the free speech provisions of the First Amendment: that all speech, regardless of content or societal consequences, should be protected from any sort of government restriction or censure.

The primary advocates of the absolutist position on the court were Justice Hugo Black and, to a lesser extent, Justice William O. Douglas. Black declared that "First Amendment rights are beyond abridgment either by legislation that directly restrains their exercise or by suppression or impairment through harassment, humiliation, or exposure by government," explaining that "the men who drafted our Bill of Rights did all the 'balancing' that was to be done in this field."[5]

But Black drew a line between speech and conduct, holding for the majority in *Cox v. Louisiana* (1965) that "we emphatically reject the notion urged by appellant that the First and Fourteenth Amendments afford the same kind of freedom to those who would communicate ideas by conduct such as patrolling, marching, and picketing on streets and highways, as these amendments afford to those who communicate ideas by pure speech."[6]

Justice Douglas also defined a distinction between speech and action. While speech cannot be constitutionally limited, he argued, harmful action can be restricted by law under the First Amendment. For example, in *Schenck v. United States* (1919), Douglas cited the classic scenario of someone "falsely shouting fire in a theater and causing a panic" as justification for the "clear and present" danger standard for restrictions on speech—as a circumstance in which the "speech is brigaded with action" and the speech and action "are indeed inseparable," so that "a prosecution can be launched for the overt acts actually caused." In the view of Douglas and Black, this was probably the only sort of case in which a person could be prosecuted for speech.[7]

Douglas was somewhat equivocal on free speech absolutism over the course of his long tenure at the court. While in *Dennis v. United States* (1951) he wrote that "the freedom to speak is not absolute," twenty years later in the Pentagon Papers case (*New York Times Co. v. U.S.*, 1973) he declared that the language of the First Amendment "leaves, in my view, no room for governmental restraint on the press."[8]

DEFAMATION IN THE MARKETPLACE OF IDEAS

The conception of public discourse as a "marketplace" in which ideas are introduced and then become either valuable or insignificant based on the "demands" of the public has been traced back to British philosophers such as John Milton and John Stuart Mill and was based on scientific precepts of research and discovery. Milton expressed this in terms of his argument against censorship in his *Areopagitica:* "Let [Truth] and Falsehood grapple; whoever knew Truth put to the worse, in a free and open encounter?" Mill, for his part, argued that "truth," rather than being fixed and objective, often had "many sides" that should receive equal expression, and thus argued vehemently for a free press. But when there is actual truth, he believed, it will always win out in the marketplace of ideas, at least in the long term.[9]

While the marketplace of ideas concept was widely accepted in America from colonial times, it was not formally introduced into American First Amendment jurisprudence until 1919, when Justice Oliver Wendell Holmes wrote in his dissent in *Abrams v. U.S.* (1919) that "the best test of truth is the power of thought to get itself accepted in the competition of the market." A majority of the court later accepted this concept in *Gertz v. Robert Welch, Inc.* (1974), writing that "under the First Amendment there is no such thing as a false idea. . . . However pernicious an opinion may seem, we depend for its correction not on the conscience of judges and juries but on the competition of other ideas."[10] Legal scholar Stanley Ingber expanded on the rationale for such a conception of free speech: "This theory assumes that a process of robust debate, if uninhibited by governmental interference, will lead to the discovery of truth, or at least the best perspectives or solutions for societal problems. A properly functioning marketplace of ideas, in Holmes's perspective, ultimately assures the proper evolution of society, wherever that evolution might lead."[11]

This conception of speech is rooted in the laissez-faire economic theory of Adam Smith, who conceived of an "invisible hand" that balanced supply and demand in an economy, removing the need for government intervention. This understanding of freedom of speech has been called "perhaps the most powerful metaphor in the free speech tradition," and "framed free press theorizing in twentieth century." The concept has come to be seen as the idealized, proper form of American political debate and a means of determining the good of society as a whole. But this theory has also been criticized for its naïve denial of the understanding that markets can be manipulated and controlled by particular interests or warped by charlatans and dupes, but it is also aspirational in its belief that in the end truth and justice will win out.[12]

While a true laissez-faire approach would involve little or no regulation, realists understand that some government regulation is necessary. The purpose of such regulation of the marketplace of ideas is to keep the market functioning and fair and to provide access to the ideological marketplace "to overcome disparities in speakers' capitalization, communicative and marketing skills, perceptivity, popular acceptance, organizational skills, continuing commitment, stature, hard work, charisma, luck, and all other factors which traditionally determine a speaker's effectiveness in communicating with his audience."[13]

In this conception, the government's role is to enforce "rules of the game" and ensure that virtually all ideas, "true" and "false," defamatory or not, have equal chance to be heard and to attract adherents, so that the better ideas—the "truth"—will win out.

Mill saw this as an integral part of government's role in maximizing human enlightenment and the pursuit of truth while also limiting personal harm. This view is similar to sentiments expressed by Adam Smith and Immanuel Kant, as well as in the French *Declaration of the Rights of Man and of the Citizen*. Based on this "harm principle," Mill argued that speech that causes specific harm to an individual, including defamation, may be punished. As an example, he described criticism of corn dealers. In general, Mill said that criticizing corn dealers for selling their product at too high a price, leading to starvation among the poor, is acceptable and cannot be restricted. But if the same statement is made to an agitated mob in front of a corn dealer's home and harm to the corn dealer is imminent, the speech may be restricted. Under this formulation, "harmful speech" such as defamation may be restricted and punished.

One prominent twentieth-century proponent of the marketplace theory of free speech was Zechariah Chafee. But Chafee was not an absolutist: he agreed with Mill that government need not be totally agnostic as to the value of different types of speech. "We all agree from the very start," Chafee wrote, "[that] there must be some point where the government may step in" to impose limits on speech. He advocated full protection for expression that was valuable to civic discourse but argued that speech without civic value—such as obscenity or insult—should not be protected. Such speech was harmful to society, so it could be punished. He also saw dangers in the increasing concentration of media ownership and the growth of advertising and public relations over news and informational content.[14]

The Supreme Court adopted the approach of Mill and Chafee in *Chaplinsky v. New Hampshire* (1942), in which the unanimous court held that the government could restrict expression of "fighting words," which it described as a "certain well-defined and narrowly limited classes of speech, the prevention and punishment of which have never been thought to raise any constitutional problem." These included "the lewd and obscene, the profane, the libelous, and the insulting or 'fighting' words those which by their very utterance inflict injury or tend to incite an immediate breach of the peace." The court took a similar approach twenty-seven years later in *Brandenburg v. Ohio* (1969), in which the majority held that incendiary speech could be punished only if it presented a threat of "imminent lawless action."[15]

This approach to the First Amendment "guided the Court for two decades," until the Supreme Court's decision in *New York Times v. Sullivan* in 1964. Under this approach, defamation was considered to fall outside the marketplace of ideas, and received no First Amendment protection. But as scholars Kermit Hall and Melvin I. Urofsky explained, the holding in *Sullivan* indicated that even "speech characterized as defamatory under the common law . . . can . . . be beneficial to the public debate."[16] Daniel Scardino expanded upon this philosophy: "If the debate itself is what is protected, the plain reality is that we must ensure that both 'truth' and 'falsity' are permitted in the marketplace; otherwise, there is no debate. Some types of falsity must be protected."[17]

DEFAMATION AND DEMOCRATIC SELF-GOVERNANCE

While some language in the *Sullivan* decision supports the marketplace of ideas conception of free speech, the decision's author, Justice William J. Brennan Jr., described the ruling as based on the conception of free speech formulated by Alexander Meiklejohn, who saw the right of free speech as a necessary and integral component of Americans' moral obligation to actively participate in democratic self-governance. Thus the purpose of freedom of speech and the press under the First Amendment was to provide the information necessary for such civic involvement. In the freedom of speech provision of the First Amendment, Meiklejohn wrote, "We are saying that the citizens of the United States will be fit to govern themselves under their own institutions only if they have faced squarely and fearlessly everything that can be said in favor of those institutions, [and] everything that can be said against them."[18]

The Meiklejohnian approach gives more protection to speech that furthers the goal of citizen participation in governance and less protection to other types of speech. In this conception of the First Amendment, only speech on matters of public interest is fully protected from government restrictions, while private speech receives only limited protection. "The guarantee given by the First Amendment is not . . . assured to all speaking," he wrote.[19]

Thus defamatory speech may be protected, depending on the context: "In cases of private defamation, one individual does damage to another by tongue or pen; the person so injured in reputation or property may sue for damages. But, in that case, the First Amendment gives no protection to the person sued. His verbal attack has no relation to the business of governing. If, however, the same verbal attack is made in order to show the unfitness of a candidate for governmental office, the act is properly regarded as a citizen's participation in government. It is, therefore, protected by the First Amendment."[20]

Meiklejohn's ideas were echoed by other influential thinkers. Justice Louis Brandeis wrote what is perhaps the most eloquent statement of this rationale in his concurring opinion in *Whitney v. California* (1927), upholding the conviction of a founder of the Communist Labor Party of America under the state's Criminal Syndicalism Act, which barred subversive speech. While concurring with the majority on Fourteenth Amendment grounds, Justice Brandeis included in his opinion a strident statement advocating broad protection of free speech as an essential element of democratic government:

> Those who won our independence by revolution were not cowards. They did not fear political change. They did not exalt order at the cost of liberty. To courageous, self-reliant men, with confidence in the power of free and fearless reasoning applied through the processes of popular government, no danger flowing from speech can be deemed clear and present, unless the incidence of the evil apprehended is so imminent that it may befall before there is opportunity for full discussion. If there be time to expose through discussion the falsehood and fallacies, to avert the evil by the processes of education, the remedy to be applied is more speech, not enforced silence.[21]

The principle of free speech as a bulwark of democratic self-governance also underlay the work of the Hutchins Commission, a group of scholars organized in 1942 by *Time* magazine publisher Henry Luce to address the question of whether freedom of the press was endangered in the United States. One of the commission's basic assumptions was that "the social justification for freedom of expression is a matter of common knowledge: genuine progress in all areas of human concern is best achieved in a society that ventilates its problems thoroughly."[22]

From this perspective, defamation was a legitimate recognition "that an utterance or publication invades in a serious, overt, and demonstrable manner personal rights or vital social interests," and "as new categories of abuse come within this definition, the extension of legal sanctions is justified." But as an alternative to lengthy and expensive defamation litigation the commission recommended the adoption of legislation allowing a streamlined process for a party injured by the press to "obtain a retraction or a restatement of the facts by the offender or an opportunity to reply."[23]

The Hutchins Commission analysis gave rise to the "social responsibility" theory of the press. Under this theory, "the press, which enjoys a privileged position under our government, is obliged to be responsible to society for carrying out certain essential functions of mass communication in contemporary society." Thus the press has a duty to serve the public benefit by facilitating democratic discussion and policy formulation.[24]

Defamation claims, the scholars who formulated this theory observed, were often used in authoritarian systems as a means of controlling the media. But these scholars explained how libertarian systems, such as that of the

United States in the early nineteenth century, broke away from this use of defamation as a means of repression, reconfiguring it to focus on protecting the reputations of individuals. The courts, meanwhile, took on the role of defining the limits of freedom of speech in the libertarian system, while also determining the limits of government intrusions on this freedom. By defining these boundaries, the courts also instilled them in the American media, engendering notions of professionalism and objectivity.

The social responsibility structure accepted restrictions on speech as a means of balancing freedom of speech "against the private rights of others and against vital social interests." In addition, such legal restrictions could be extended if new abuses arise. "However, the burden of proof that society's interests were harmed [and new restrictions were thus necessary] would rest with whoever would extend the law to cover new areas of abuse."[25]

Scholar Thomas I. Emerson also saw free expression as a bulwark of democracy and attempted to formulate a systemic understanding and doctrine to replace the ad hoc decisions of the Supreme Court, which Emerson said created an "existing legal theory [that] is inadequate to support an effective system of freedom of expression." This doctrine, he said, should recognize the societal interests that free speech serves in a democracy, including ensuring individual self-fulfillment, advancing knowledge and the discovery of truth, fostering participation by all in decision making, and promoting orderly societal and cultural change. Emerson's system encompassed ten major points, including a distinction between actions and speech and limitations on government intervention. Sanctions for defamatory speech were justified by the harm that it does to individuals' private interests, which he analogized to a physical assault.[26]

DEFAMATION AND HUMAN DIGNITY

Another theory regards freedom of speech as fulfilling "not only the needs of the polity but also those of the human spirit—a spirit that demands self-expression." Under this conception, free speech "is founded on respect for the autonomy and dignity of human beings" and "is a right defiantly, robustly, and irreverently to speak one's mind *just because it is one's mind.*"[27]

Steven Heyman championed this approach, explaining that aside from the civic and governmental rationales, the Constitution protects free speech because it is "an inherent right which is rooted in human dignity and autonomy." This approach is based on John Locke's concepts of inherent human rights and finds support in John Stuart Mill's recognition of such rights as an element of human dignity, and ultimately of human pleasure. These ideas "had a profound impact on American political thought" in the late eighteenth century, particularly in essays by the pseudonymous author "Cato," who was very influential in colonial America.[28]

The problems with this approach arise when the fundamental right of free speech comes into conflict with other fundamental human rights. The result is that free speech must sometimes yield. "As a general rule," Heyman wrote, "speakers should be required to respect the fundamental rights of others." But Heyman criticized the Supreme Court's "content neutrality" approach to free speech issues, particularly the court's focus on the "communicative impact" of particular speech, saying that a better approach is to protect free speech on the basis of individual autonomy, restricting it only when it infringes on the autonomy of another. "In regulating speech," he explained, "the government is not invading the province of the speaker or the community but is protecting the rightful freedom of others."[29]

Thus Heyman explains that personal defamation may be punished under this schema as the result of balancing the natural right to free speech with others' right to personal reputation. For Heyman, defamation law is justified as a means to protect individuals' reputations—an inherent natural right—rather than on the basis of harm to individuals' dignity, which he says is a socially constructed artifice. But Heyman had a starkly different opinion about defamation claims by public officials, including the concept of seditious libel, seeing it as an affront to the natural conception of free speech since it limits the basic human right to freely determine the form of self-governance.

Unlike Heyman, other advocates of natural rights see seditious libel as a necessary limitation on speech for preserving government authority. The constitutional founders, as explained previously, generally held the latter view.

PHILOSOPHY AND *NEW YORK TIMES V. SULLIVAN*

These various philosophies of free speech are also reflected in the U.S. Supreme Court's decisions in *New York Times v. Sullivan* and the cases that followed it, including *St. Amant v. Thompson*.

The *Sullivan* ruling was a clear rejection of the Blackstone view of speech and defamation, particularly because the Alabama trial court had held that if the statements at issue in the case represented defamation per se—in accordance with the common law outlined by Blackstone—that damages could be presumed. When the plaintiff in a defamation case is a public official, the court held, such a rule cannot withstand First Amendment scrutiny.[30]

The court in *Sullivan* expressed some absolutist sentiments, saying, "We consider this case against the background of a profound national commitment to the principle that debate on public issues should be uninhibited, robust, and wide-open." In such robust debate, the court added, some erroneous statements are inevitable. But while the court placed limitations on public officials' ability to sue for defamation, it did not hold that the First Amendment immunized all defamatory statements from liability.[31]

Justices Black and Douglas used a concurring opinion in *Sullivan* to endorse an absolutist approach. "The First and Fourteenth Amendments not merely 'delimit' a State's power to award damages to 'public officials against critics of their official conduct,'" they wrote, "but completely prohibit a State from exercising such a power." In a separate opinion concurring in the result, Justice Arthur Goldberg went even further, saying, "In my view, the First and Fourteenth Amendments to the Constitution afford to the citizen and to the press an absolute, unconditional privilege to criticize official conduct despite the harm which may flow from excesses and abuses."[32]

While the court's majority did not embrace absolutism, it did justify its decision on the value of speech critical of public officials in terms relating to the conception of free speech as an essential component of democratic self-governance. Thus the majority quoted one of the court's earlier decisions that said that "the maintenance of the opportunity for free political discussion to the end that government may be responsive to the will of the people and that changes may be obtained by lawful means, an opportunity essential to the security of the Republic, is a fundamental principle of our constitutional system."[33]

(4)

“The Story of Politics in Louisiana Today”

The politics, the mob, and the unions of 1960s Louisiana formed the backdrop of the political campaign that led to the *Thompson v. St. Amant* defamation case. These circumstances combined with other, national factors such as the ongoing civil rights movement and political battles between conservatives and liberals would continue for the next several decades. In this environment, an offhand comment made in a campaign speech blew up into a massive proxy war between political and other factions in Louisiana. The statement also eventually led to an important decision of the U.S. Supreme Court that helped establish defamation standards that persist today.

ST. AMANT FOR SENATE

While the Long family was establishing itself as a boisterous force in Louisiana politics starting in the 1920s, another Baton Rouge family was making a public name for itself in a quieter way, through development and involvement in the community and through military service.

Alfred D. St. Amant, who traced his lineage in Louisiana to French immigrant Jean François D’Aspit de St. Amand, who arrived in New Orleans in 1720, was a university professor turned Baton Rouge insurance salesman. He purchased a portion of the former Richland Plantation outside of Baton Rouge in the 1920s and developed it as Southdowns, which was later annexed into the city.

Alfred St. Amant had long-running disputes with Huey Long, starting—according to his son—when he refused Long’s demands for a kickback from St. Amant’s insurance contracts with the state. They had another run-in in 1934, after Governor Oscar K. Allen, Huey Long’s successor and puppet, ordered the National Guard into New Orleans as part of the Long machine’s attempt to dislodge its opponents in city government. Among the troops was the Baton Rouge 156th Infantry, including Alfred’s son Thomas Harris St. Amant. “This is to notify you,” Alfred St. Amant wrote in a telegraph to Huey Long that he released to the press, “that should any harm or injury come to him as a result of this mad effort of yours, either by accident or otherwise, I will personally kill you as I would any other mad dog."[1]

"He was very opposed to Huey," Alfred's fifth child, Philemon "Phil" A. St. Amant, recalled about his father. "They were bitter enemies."[2]

Phil St. Amant was born on February 3, 1918. After graduating from Louisiana State University in 1939, Phil joined the army and rose to the rank of lieutenant colonel in a twenty-year military career that included commanding a parachute artillery battalion and serving in Europe with the Office of Strategic Services and as an agent of the Counterintelligence Corps. Retiring from the military in 1959, St. Amant returned to Baton Rouge, started a family, and established himself as a tax and business consultant.

Politically, St. Amant was a conservative Democrat who favored low taxes and limited government and urged mobilization of the military to counter the threat of the Soviet Union. "I was very conservative," he said many years later. "Like many of the white people in Louisiana, I was a Democrat then."[3]

In the early 1960s, St. Amant set his sights on the U.S. Senate seat held by Russell Long, who was up for reelection in 1962. "After much thought on the matter I have decided to run for the Senate post now held by Russell Long," St. Amant said in announcing his candidacy in September 1961, adding that his small government and robust foreign policy ideas were "the direct opposite of what we have been getting from the Kennedy Democrats, and specifically from the Share-the-Wealth senator currently representing us."[4]

THE CAMPAIGN AND THE SPEECH

St. Amant's challenge was reportedly not a major worry for Senator Long. But he did campaign extensively before the 1962 primary, possibly in preparation for an expected gubernatorial run in 1963.

On July 11, 1961, St. Amant purchased forty minutes of airtime on Baton Rouge radio station WJBO to deliver a speech titled "The Decline and Resurrection of the American Republic," which he rebroadcast on several other stations and later published as a pamphlet. The speech described several perceived problems in American society and politics, including self-serving politicians, failing schools, flagging patriotism, and lack of support for the military. It also attacked the civil rights movement and agitators for racial integration, alleging that "it is highly unlikely that this new burning zeal to destroy social institutions of long standing in the name of constitutionality and human rights is of domestic origin."[5]

The week after his radio address, the *Baton Rouge State-Times* newspaper published a letter from St. Amant criticizing Attorney General Robert Kennedy for not sending U.S. marshals to Illinois to "protect embattled and innocent Caucasians," in the wake of protests and violence during a civil rights protest at the whites-only Rainbow Beach in Chicago. St. Amant's letter also accused Kennedy of recognizing only "the constitutional rights of agitators."[6]

St. Amant formally announced his candidacy for the U.S. Senate on September 18, 1961. "I'd been watching Russell for a long time," he explained many years later, "and he wasn't my kind of man."[7]

St. Amant was running in the Democratic primary, but his conservative positions garnered support from groups such as the John Birch Society in northern Louisiana, which raised money for St. Amant as a way of "softening up" Russell Long for the general election against Taylor W. O'Hearn, who had switched parties to become a Republican because of his opposition to President Kennedy.

Although he had already announced his campaign against Long, the official launch of St. Amant's campaign was made with a paid television address on March 28, 1962, on WAFB-TV (channel 9) in Baton Rouge. In the address St. Amant criticized Senator Long as "the enemy of the working man," who he claimed was part of the "Kennedy combine" that "legislate[s] outside of Congress."[8]

"I will go to Washington to return the government to the people as stated in the Tenth Amendment," St. Amant said, adding that he would "lead the American people back into the path of constitutional government."[9]

St. Amant paid for the address after another Baton Rouge station, WBRZ-TV (channel 2), refused his demand for time under the Federal Communications Commission's equal time rule, which required broadcast stations that gave broadcast time to one candidate in a federal election to offer the same amount of time, with similar viewership, to other candidates for the same office. St. Amant sought equal time for Senator Long's weekly "public service" broadcasts on WBRZ, but Long made those broadcasts as a senator, not a candidate. Later, after Long officially launched his reelection campaign, St. Amant was able to get television time under the rule.

St. Amant continued to deliver both paid and "equal time" radio and television addresses, including broadcasts in Baton Rouge on April 26, 1962; in New Orleans on June 17; and in Baton Rouge again on June 27.

The June 27 address, which led to Thompson's libel suit, was billed as major event. In that morning's newspaper, St. Amant's campaign advertised the program as a "political exposé." That afternoon, St. Amant held a press conference at the Capitol House hotel in Baton Rouge at which he promoted the address that evening. He also took credit for the federal indictment the day before of Edward G. Partin, the business agent for the Baton Rouge Teamsters Local 5, whose activities were to be a major feature of the speech.

Several dissenting union members had been working against Partin's ruthless methods of running Local 5, but J. D. Albin and Adolph G. Klein Jr. were leading the charge. Albin was a leader of Teamsters Local 270 in New Orleans, while Klein was involved in Partin's Local 5. Both had testified against Partin in a union disciplinary hearing and were beaten by Partin's supporters as they left. (Six union members, including Partin's brother, pleaded guilty to the beatings.) Klein had also testified before a federal grand jury investigating Partin.

Albin and Klein had contacted St. Amant to talk about Partin's corrupt leadership of the union. But Klein was killed at his workplace on June 7, 1962, when a trailer full of sand slipped off the bulldozer holding it up and fell on him while he was placing bolts on the trailer. Six months later, Klein's widow placed a memorial ad in the *Baton Rouge Morning Advocate* hinting that his death was not accidental. "Amid strife and corruption stood a man so great," the ad read. "He worked so devoutly for his fellow members 'til the day he met his fate. Neither hoodlums nor corrupt officers could stop him, he had one goal in sight. A clean and decent organization to protect a workers's [*sic*] right."[10]

Despite Klein's death, Albin appeared with St. Amant at the June 27 press conference, where St. Amant presented a filmed interview that he had conducted with Albin about Partin's activities and his connections to Senator Long. St. Amant also distributed a transcript of the interview, which Albin signed and swore to at the press conference as an affidavit.

One of the charges in Albin's statement alleged that Ed Partin had visited with Fidel and Raúl Castro on behalf of national Teamsters president Jimmy Hoffa during a trip to Cuba in 1960. Although neither Albin nor St. Amant alleged it at the time, according to Ed Partin's brother, Partin's connections to the regime in Cuba were more extensive than a single visit. He had actually gone to Cuba twice and had made a deal to supply Fidel Castro's nascent government with military equipment.

In the years immediately after the 1959 Cuban Communist revolution, Teamsters boss Jimmy Hoffa was serving as a middleman between the Central Intelligence Agency and the mob, which were both trying to undermine the new Communist regime in Cuba. For the CIA, a Communist country off the coast of Florida was a national security threat. For the mob, Castro's revolution meant the loss of its drug and gambling operations on the island. The mob had actually supplied arms—financed from Teamsters Union pension funds—to both sides in the revolution, but superficially at least supported the new regime. In 1962 Partin was charged with conspiring to smuggle arms to Castro's opposition. Later, the CIA used the Mafia as a go-between for help in plans to assassinate Castro or overthrow him by invading the island.

In the affidavit presented at St. Amant's press conference, Albin also alleged that Partin had used union funds for personal expenses and had covered up his misdeeds by arranging for the theft of the union's safe and destruction of the papers stored in it. The affidavit also detailed Partin's criminal past and noted the recent hit-and-run incident that had killed an airman in Alabama, for which Partin was later arrested.

St. Amant later testified that in his filmed interview with Albin and the resulting affidavit, "the replies by the witness were ad-libbed by him. They were not prompted nor did I in all cases know the exact way he was going to present it." But he added, "I had certainly discussed the material and had checked out its veracity before we ever presented it."[11]

St. Amant had planned to present the filmed interview during his paid political advertisement that evening on WAFB. But the television station's attorneys required St. Amant to instead read the transcript of the interview on the show, with St. Amant reading both his questions and Albin's answers. According to St. Amant, the lawyers were concerned that airing the original film, in which Albin was shown making most of the allegations against Long and others, could subject the station to liability for broadcasting defamatory statements.

Federal law still requires broadcasters to offer "reasonable access" to legally qualified candidates for federal political office who are able to pay for the time. Broadcasters are prohibited from editing the broadcasts and are not legally liable for the content of such broadcasts, provided the comments are made by the candidate him- or herself. But the station is not immune from liability for statements made by anyone other than the candidate in the course of the program.

To assuage the station's concerns, after his press conference St. Amant recorded a second film in which he read the entire affidavit that Albin had sworn to at the press conference, including both St. Amant's questions and Albin's responses. This is the film that actually aired on WAFB that evening.

Before reading the affidavit, St. Amant gave a short introduction in which he promised to tell a sordid tale of union corruption and its political enablers: "I have a story to reveal tonight which is so unusual that I have bought this time on the television to inform the public. This story involves a well-documented criminal, an ex-convict who became a labor chieftain. It involves misuse and theft of union funds, dealings with Communist officials of Cuba, a criminal conspiracy to destroy evidence and the destruction of that evidence[,] death resulting from the commission of a felony and a second death by a hit and run by a union car. . . . This . . . is the story of politics in Louisiana today."[12]

He also explained the last-minute change that led to his reading the affidavit rather than showing his filmed interview with Albin:

> Ladies and gentlemen; I would like to tell you that at this time we have had to refilm this part because as filmed originally Mr. J. D. Albin appeared on the screen live and told his story in answer to the questions that I gave him. However, because of legal advice to the station and checking with the F.C.C. of their legal responsibility, at this time it was determined that the original film would not be used on this program. Instead, I will read to you the signed affidavit of Mr. J. D. Albin as the testimony exactly as given.[13]

Of course the address was a campaign commercial and was meant to persuade voters to reject Senator Long. But the only incriminating evidence against Senator Long in St. Amant's address was an allegation that the senator had met with Hoffa to personally vouch for Partin despite his unsavory background. According to Albin, as repeated by St. Amant, Senator Long first denied that he had supported Partin with Hoffa but later admitted that he had, as Albin conveyed it, the same as he would "for any other employee for their employer."[14]

There are other indications of connections between Long and Hoffa beyond the ones noted in St. Amant's address. For example, D'Alton Smith, an associate of New Orleans crime boss Carlos Marcello, reportedly said that he had helped Senator Russell Long get elected whip (in 1965) by "carr[ying] money to Long from [Marcello in] New Orleans and that he and Teamsters consultant Allan Dorfman had bought seven [senators'] votes for Long in the leadership election." Later, in trying to get Partin to assist in efforts to get Hoffa out of prison, Buddy Gill, a former staffer to Senator Long, reportedly told Partin that the senator would make sure that the government ensured Partin's safety. "We've got that fixed," Gill reportedly told Partin. "Senator Long is the most powerful man in the United States today. Don't worry about it, you will be protected." After Partin refused, he was told that Senator Long had taken a special interest in the government's extortion case against Partin and had told Attorney General Ramsey Clark that if the prosecution was dropped, twenty-five senators would raise strong objections. Partin then spoke to Senator Long on the phone, but the conversation ended in an argument.[15]

In passing, Albin's affidavit made another accusation, not involving Long. Albin—and thus St. Amant's address—alleged that East Baton Rouge deputy sheriff Herman A. Thompson was Ed Partin's "connection" to the East Baton Rouge Parish Sheriff's Office. Albin also claimed that Thompson visited Partin at the union hall and that money "had passed hands" between Partin and Thompson during these visits. The affidavit also noted that Thompson was one of the deputies who arrived to investigate the disappearance of the union's safe, insinuating that the investigation of the theft was fruitless because Thompson had received money from Partin.[16]

Albin explained this in the context of the national Teamsters Union's investigation of Local 5's finances:

> . . . We knew something had to be done if we were to ever straighten out the local union, and the onliest [*sic*] way to straighten it out was the removal of E. G. Partin. Now, we knew that this safe was going to be removed that night, but imagine our predicament, knowing of Ed's connection with the sheriff's office through Herman Thompson, who made recent visits to the hall to see Ed. We also knew of money that had passed hands between Ed and Herman Thompson, from Ed to Herman. We also knew of his connections with State Trooper Lieu-

tenant Joe Green. We knew we couldn't get any help from there and we didn't know how far that he was involved in the sheriff's office or the State Police office through that, and it was out of the jurisdiction of the city police.

Q: What did you do then?

A: Well, we rode around awhile trying to decide what to do. Finally, we decided that we would go to the hall ourselves and see if there was any way we could stop them if we saw them coming out with the safe. We arrived a little too late. Somewhere in the neighborhood of 9 o'clock, the safe was gone. The next morning there was an investigation. Brother Herman Thompson came out and investigated it and I understand that Lieutenant Joe Green showed up. They seemed to think it was a job by a professional. I agree with them.[17]

When St. Amant gave his televised address, he did not know Herman Thompson. In fact, St. Amant said they did not meet until the trial began in Thompson's defamation case against St. Amant, although it turned out that St. Amant and Thompson's older brother had been Sunday school classmates. St. Amant later said that Thompson played up this connection, tenuous as it was, in order to portray his family as close friends of the St. Amants, to elicit sympathy in the case at the apparent betrayal of that relationship. "He did it to establish that he was a friend of the St. Amant family and he didn't understand why I had done this to him," he recalled.[18]

The mention of Thompson was only in passing, since the real target was Long and his associations with Partin and Hoffa. So there was no thought that the statements involving Thompson would be an issue. "Certainly it never occurred to anyone that Herman Thompson would have anything to do with [any concerns about the station's liability for the original film,] because he was so collateral," St. Amant testified at the trial. He also denied any personal knowledge of improper behavior by Thompson: "I have no personal knowledge of it nor did I impute it," St. Amant testified. "Nor did I intend to."[19]

But the allegations against Thompson were covered by both of Baton Rouge's daily newspapers, with the *Morning Advocate* reporting that St. Amant had "made serious charges involving state and parish police officers, implying bribery was involved” and the *State-Times* explaining that St. Amant had alleged “corrupt tie-ins between certain labor officials and certain law enforcement officers here.”[20]

The evening after the broadcast, Thompson publicly denied the allegations. He said that he first learned of the contentions when a neighbor told him that “some man had been on the radio or the television and had called me some kind of thief and all kind of names.”[21] He said that St. Amant’s allegations caused him embarrassment and hurt his reputation as a law officer and that he endured taunting that frayed his nerves. “For quite a while [after the broadcast] every time I would go bowling or play golf or go out in the public somebody would have some kind of comments. Of course, I think most of it was joking but it did get to where it was irritable and I have had to control my temper quite a few times.”[22]

St. Amant expressed surprise when Thompson filed his lawsuit, noting that there were others who could have possibly sued for defamation over the program, but did not: “There was a contractor there that could have objected to saying that he had given permission to cut a safe open in his office, but he did not, and I believe the time in which he would normally have made such an objection has expired. There were certain other people that could have required proof of these things in court. I was prepared to go as far as was necessary because I had the statements and testimony of people who knew about these things.”[23]

While St. Amant’s speech and the subsequent legal case have had a lasting legacy, his Senate campaign did not. St. Amant ended up losing badly in the July 28, 1962, primary, with Russell Long garnering 80.2 percent of the vote and going on to win the general election against Taylor W. O’Hearn with 75.6 percent of the vote. Long would go on to easily defeat primary candidates in 1968, 1974, and 1980 and faced no opponents in the general elections in those years. He remained in the Senate until his retirement in 1987, after a total of thirty-eight years in the Senate.

HERMAN A. THOMPSON

Herman A. Thompson, the incidental victim of St. Amant’s address, actually had some similarities to the candidate. He served in the navy during World War II and worked for Shell Oil Company after returning to Baton Rouge. In

1945, Thompson became a deputy with the East Baton Rouge Parish Sheriff's Office. He did well as a deputy sheriff, with just one disputed incident, when a woman filed a civil lawsuit in 1949. The lawsuit accused Thompson of physically attacking her after she called the police to protect her from a drunken man. However, a jury trial ended with a verdict for Thompson, which was affirmed on appeal. By 1956, Thompson had been named chief of detectives and had risen to the rank of captain.

In 1959, Thompson had a brush with notoriety when he was involved in the involuntary commitment of Governor Earl Long to Southeast Louisiana Hospital in Mandeville. Two years later, in 1961, Thompson was one of the responding officers when a safe was stolen from the headquarters of Baton Rouge Teamsters Local 5.

By 1962, he was in charge of the sheriff's office's Uniform Division and was involved in a number of charitable groups. He and his wife were also socially active in the Baton Rouge community.

In his lawsuit against St. Amant, Thompson claimed that the comments in the July 27 speech hurt his reputation as a deputy sheriff and hurt his standing in the community. He also claimed that the allegations in the broadcast upset his wife and his mother, who had a heart condition.

(5)

Thompson Goes to Court

St. Amant's Senate candidacy ended a few weeks after his television address, with his defeat in the primary. But the libel suit that came out of that campaign lasted six years, with rulings that flipped the result of the case at every level of court that considered it. This was due in large part to the timing. Right before the trial in Thompson's lawsuit against St. Amant, the U.S. Supreme Court had upended more than 150 years of American defamation law in its landmark decision in *New York Times v. Sullivan*. Thompson's case against St. Amant was caught in this sea change in the law and ultimately became a means for the Supreme Court to continue to make more changes in the law of defamation.

THOMPSON'S LAWSUIT

The week after St. Amant's broadcast, Baton Rouge attorney Robert L. "Buck" Kleinpeter, a personal friend of Thompson's, filed three lawsuits based on St. Amant's speech on Thompson's behalf in the Nineteenth Judicial District Court in Baton Rouge. The lawsuits sought $150,000 in damages each from St. Amant, Albin, and the corporate owner of radio station WLCS, which Thompson claimed had repeated the affidavit's allegations in its newscasts. Thompson did not sue WAFB-TV, likely because of the federal law providing immunity to broadcasters for political programs.

The suit against St. Amant stemmed from not only the statements about Thompson during the broadcast but also St. Amant's distribution of a transcript of the remarks at the press conference earlier in the day.

The lawsuit against St. Amant claimed that the statements about Thompson in the broadcast and the transcript "were intended to belittle, degrade and ridicule him and clearly reflects [*sic*] a design and intent on the part of the said defendant to defame, slander and libel Thompson's good name, reputation and character before his friends, the Courts, and the Public in general." Thompson sought a total of $150,000 in damages from St. Amant: $50,000 for "humiliation and mental suffering," $50,000 for "injury to his personal and private reputation," and $50,000 for "loss of public confidence and injury to his professional reputation."[1]

Thompson apparently made the same claims, seeking the same amounts of damages, in his separate lawsuits against Albin and WLCS radio.[2]

In his response to Thompson's suit, St. Amant—represented by attorney Richard G. Van Buskirk of Clinton, Louisiana—called for a special session of the court to consider dismissal of the case. He also specifically denied that the statement at the start of his address—the preface promising a "story [of] . . . misuse and theft of union funds, dealings with Communist officials of Cuba, a criminal conspiracy to destroy evidence and the destruction of that evidence: death resulting from the commission of a felony and a second death by a hit and run by a union car"—referred to Thompson. Instead, he argued, that portion of the statement referred to "individuals other than the Plaintiff and [that portion] did not [refer to] Plaintiff in any manner or way."[3]

The answer continued: "At no time and in no manner was any utterance made that could fairly be interpreted to mean or that would suggest or connote that the Plaintiff committed any of the acts stated in the above quoted words."[4]

As for the statements regarding Thompson himself later in the address—about his visiting Ed Partin at the Local 5 union hall and that money "passed hands" between them—St. Amant argued that "any such words were not written or spoken for any vindictive or selfish interest, but were uttered because they were true and their distribution, dissemination or broadcast was for the public good." He also argued that the statements were true and that "truth is an absolute defense to all of the allegations made by the Plaintiff."[5]

As described above, truth as a defense to civil defamation claims dates back to 1805 and was first formally adopted in Louisiana by statute in 1821. St. Amant's defense was thus a viable one under existing Louisiana law. But to use this defense, St. Amant would be forced to prove that his statements regarding Captain Thompson were actually true.

St. Amant appeared undaunted by this challenge, saying in his testimony during the trial, "I never ran away from a fight and I felt that this was my presentation of what's going wrong around here and I thought I had better tell the voters about it. Looks like nobody else has the courage to tell them around here. Everybody is scared somebody is going to sue them. I told them the truth and I can stand on this truth and I can, as we did, back this up with other witnesses. Basically speaking, this is a true story."[6]

In accordance with Louisiana's process for civil cases, the next step was for

Thompson to submit questions ("interrogatories") for St. Amant to answer about the witnesses and evidence that he planned to present in the case. In one of these interrogatories, Thompson asked St. Amant about his statement that money had passed between Partin and Thompson. St. Amant's response listed several individuals who he said could testify about the monetary transfers and said that the transfers were in the form of cash and checks and had occurred "on or about March 20, 1962."[7]

Another query asked whether St. Amant knew of any activity by Thompson that was illegal or "might reflect upon him as a Deputy Sheriff, or the Sheriff's Office as a whole." St. Amant responded, "As to any illegal act on the part of Herman Thompson the answer is no," but "as to actions which would reflect on Herman Thompson and the Sheriff's Office the answer is yes."[8]

By this answer, St. Amant was denying that Albin's statements that Albin and other leaders of the union "[knew] of Ed [Partin]'s connection with the sheriff's office through Herman Thompson" and that they also "knew of money that had passed hands between Ed and Herman Thompson, from Ed to Herman" implied bribery. Instead, St. Amant argued that the statements only implied some impropriety in the relationship between Thompson and Partin. In other words, *any* sort of relationship between a sheriff's deputy and an unsavory person like Partin would reflect badly on both the deputy and the sheriff's office.

THE TRIAL

The bench trial in the case of *Thompson v. St. Amant* was held on Tuesday, May 5, 1964, before Louisiana District Court judge Fred A. Blanche Jr., without a jury. Judge Blanche already had some familiarity with one of the major players in the libel case. In January 1963, he had presided over a criminal battery trial in which Ed Partin was acquitted over a melee on a picket line.

By the time of the trial, the primary and election were long over, and Senator Long had returned to the U.S. Senate seat he would hold for another twelve years.

The trial began with cross-examination of Phil A. St. Amant by Thompson's attorney, Robert L. Kleinpeter, in which St. Amant verified basic information about himself, the 1962 Senate primary, and the television address on July 27, 1962. This included a basic explanation of how he had filmed an interview with J. D. Albin that he intended to be broadcast, but that WAFB instead required him to read a transcript of the original film, including both his questions and Albin's answers. Kleinpeter introduced into evidence a transcript of the broadcast, as well as an audio recording, which he played in court.

After playing the recording, Kleinpeter asked St. Amant about his relationships with the various players in the case and about his allegation that money "had passed hands" between Partin and Thompson. St. Amant claimed that this statement did not impute any nefarious behavior and was only meant to show that there was a relationship between Partin and Thompson: "I don't know what this money was for, Mr. Attorney. I did not suggest what the money was for, nor has—did Mr. Albin suggest what it was for. This could have been for his favorite charity for all I know. But as Mr. Albin explains, he couldn't go to him [Thompson] [about the union troubles] because he was contributing to this man, for whatever purpose. A close personal relationship existed."[9]

Thompson's attorney pointed out that this relationship could have been a professional one, and that "because of some disturbances one way or another, it might be necessary for the law enforcement officers at one time or another to come in contact with and know business agents [of local unions]." St. Amant replied that he was aware of such a possibility.[10]

In his testimony St. Amant explained how he had gotten involved with the union issues: Albin and other union dissidents sought his help after "getting the run around" in their efforts to challenge Partin's control of Local 5, including "two different stories from my opponent [Senator Long]." He also said that he requested the affidavit from Albin and others in order to verify the information about the situation with the union before he broadcast it on television:[11] "I wanted to have some signed statements to know what the situation was. I have other affidavits, by the way, concerning some of the other details from other people, and I had them in my possession and had seen them and interviewed the other witnesses prior to such a broadcast to be sure that my facts were at least well substantiated."[12]

He added that when asking for the affidavits, "I never mentioned the name of Herman Thompson. Herman Thompson wasn't even in my mind." Thompson's name had just come up as part of the larger story of Ed Partin, St. Amant added, and Senator Long's character reference for Partin to Jimmy Hoffa:[13]

> I had no interest at the time in Mr. Thompson. I had interest in Senator Russell Long, and I wanted to establish that here is a man in the public

> eye in a most disreputable fashion, and I am sure Mr. Thompson did not think I was speaking of him.
>
> I was speaking of the business agent who was notoriously in trouble at the time and was being helped out by a United States Senator to the detriment of his men; to the detriment of the working people of this parish.[14]

St. Amant also testified that he did not think that his broadcast had harmed Thompson, particularly because he still had his job and had not been suspended or lost any pay.

The second witness in the trial was East Baton Rouge sheriff J. Bryan Clemmons, Thompson's boss. He confirmed that Thompson's responsibilities had broadened and his salary had increased since St. Amant's televised address.

Clemmons also spoke of his office's numerous charitable involvements. Thompson, he said, had "been in charge of practically all the fund-raising drives" and had the "particular assignment to contact the labor unions and trade unions in the parish" for these charity drives. This included, Clemmons said, raising funds for the annual Baton Rouge Kids' Baseball Clinic, to which he said Partin contributed each year. Thompson later testified that Partin "refused" to contribute in 1963. Thompson was involved with the clinic for many years, and later was elected to its board.[15]

Clemmons said that this was the only money that he was aware of that had "passed" between Partin and Thompson.

Thompson was the next witness. He said that the baseball clinic contribution was the only check he ever accepted from Partin. But when he was asked whether this made St. Amant's statement about funds passing between himself and Partin literally true, Thompson responded, "[St. Amant] didn't state what it [the money] was for. It was an inference of what he said." It was this inference, Thompson testified, that hurt his reputation as a deputy sheriff and in the community.[16]

Thompson added that he had refused Partin's offer of a free suit when Thompson had graduated from the FBI Academy in 1959. Thompson said that he told Partin that if he accepted, it would destroy his career and "would be the most expensive thing I had ever done in my life." Thompson added that he also declined Partin's offer of cash or a check as an alternative, and that he had reported Partin's offer to his boss, Sheriff Clemmons. Thompson said, "I told [Partin], 'No, thank you, I don't want anything. I am just doing my job.'"[17]

But the next witness—Marjorie Anne Smith, a secretary at the Local 5 union office—testified that Thompson had taken one hundred dollars in cash from Partin in March of 1961. She testified that Partin gave her an envelope containing five twenty-dollar bills, which she transferred to another envelope before giving them to Thompson, as she had been instructed by Partin. Smith said that she and the other union secretary opened the original envelope because "we knew Mr. Partin was under investigation and we was [*sic*] just wondering what was in the envelope." She also said that she had told Albin about the payment but that she did not recall whether she spoke about the one hundred dollars when she testified before the federal grand jury investigating Partin and the union. Later, when St. Amant asked her about it after he had given his televised address, she assumed that Albin had told him about the incident.[18]

After Smith's testimony, St. Amant retook the stand, this time for direct examination by his own attorney. St. Amant explained the circumstances of the broadcast, including the last-minute substitution of the film of him interviewing Albin with the film of him reading the entire affidavit, including his questions and Albin's answers. St. Amant's attorney then ran the film that St. Amant had originally intended to broadcast, which showed St. Amant asking questions to Albin and Albin responding.

Albin did not testify at the trial because he was recovering from a heart attack, although St. Amant later said that he suspected Albin simply did not want to testify.[19]

In his cross-examination of St. Amant, Kleinpeter asked about the television station's refusal to air the original film and the substitution with the film of St. Amant reading the transcript of his interview with Albin. Again, St. Amant emphasized that his target in the interview was his opponent, Russell Long, not Herman Thompson. When Kleinpeter asked, "Do you have any personal knowledge whatsoever of any improper activities whatsoever of Captain Herman Thompson?" St. Amant's answer was, "I have no personal knowledge of it, nor did I impute it, nor did I intend to."[20]

In other words, he was simply repeating Albin's allegations. But it is well established in defamation law that someone who repeats a defamatory statement is liable for damage to reputation caused by the statement, the same as the person who originally made the statement.

After St. Amant's testimony, the defense rested its case.

Kleinpeter then brought his client, Thompson, back to the witness stand.

At first, Thompson denied ever taking an envelope with cash from Smith, the secretary in the union's office. But then he added that he may have received the union's charitable contributions in an envelope once or twice, but he said that he gave these envelopes to the sheriff's secretary without opening them. Thompson also testified that he had never received cash from Partin or any other union member for any reason other than charity.

After Thompson's rebuttal testimony, the plaintiff rested.

THE VERDICT

Judge Blanche issued his verdict at the conclusion of the one-day trial. He found that St. Amant had libeled Thompson and awarded him $5,000.[21]

In his oral ruling from the bench, Blanche began with a review of Louisiana defamation law, relying on a 1958 decision of the Louisiana Supreme Court: "The test of whether a statement is libelous," he said, "is set forth in *Madison v. Bolton*, that the test of a libelous article is the effect the article is fairly calculated to produce, the impression it would naturally engender in the minds of the average persons among whom it is intended to circulate."[22]

Blanche said that by alleging a connection between Thompson and Partin, whom the judge said had been defined by St. Amant as "a crook of the highest order," St. Amant had "tended to impugn some dishonest motives to Captain Thompson."[23] Even if this was not St. Amant's intent, it was the effect that mattered. "Even though Mr. St. Amant may not have intended to impugn any dishonest motives to Mr. Thompson or injure or hurt his reputation," Blanche said, "nevertheless the fair inference to be drawn by what was stated to the average person had that exact effect."[24]

St. Amant's statements, Judge Blanche held, "inferred and attributed to Mr. Thompson dishonesty," and "under our law are injurious *per se*—unless the truth of the accusation is proved." But while it was literally true that Thompson had received money from Partin and the union, Judge Blanche added, it was clear that the money was for charitable purposes. "Mere fact of receiving that money is not proof of dishonesty on [Thompson's] part," he said. Thus St. Amant had indeed defamed Thompson.[25]

The harm done to Thompson's reputation was particularly acute because he was a policeman, Blanche said, "for there is nothing more vile to our system of justice as to believe our policemen are dishonest." The alleged association with Partin, he said, would likely haunt Thompson to his grave and even beyond. To buttress this observation Judge Blanche quoted Shakespeare's *Julius Caesar:* "The evil that men do lives after them. The good is oft interred with their bones."[26]

"I believe people remember bad things about you for a long, long time," Blanche said.[27]

Judge Blanche also included a revealing personal anecdote in his ruling:

> While not in evidence and having nothing to do with the case, while I was listening to the testimony, I have remembered that I had run out of money and needed some and had borrowed some money from a lawyer who had a case in my court. I gave it no thought, we were and had been friends, just as I am and have been with practically every member of the bar. I was just thinking to myself how that would look out in print or on T.V. I don't know whether the lawyer won or lost his case.
>
> I can't recall it, but I remember that I was out of money and rather than cash a check, I got it from him. I have no idea whether he won or lost the case or what case it may have been, but I sure realize the impropriety of it and what it could have done to me. I certainly had no dishonest motive. I just forgot to cash a check and borrowed money from a friend, which all of you lawyers are to me, and I can see right now that if somebody got on T.V. and put it out that money had passed between me and the lawyer and he had won the case, I really would have been in a fix. The more I would have tried to explain it, the worse it would have gotten.[28]

While Judge Blanche held that Thompson had been libeled, he also observed that Thompson did not seem to have suffered any economic damages from St. Amant's statement. So Judge Blanche ordered St. Amant to pay Thompson damages of $5,000.[29]

St. Amant later admitted that he received "a good licking" in the trial.[30]

The trial only resolved the claims against St. Amant and did not involve Thompson's claims against Albin or WLCS radio. The case against the radio station was eventually declared abandoned and was dismissed. There is no existing record of the lawsuit against Albin, but presumably it was dismissed as well.

(6)

Results Shift in Louisiana's Appeals Courts

While the U.S. Supreme Court's transformation of defamation law in *New York Times v. Sullivan* may have been an occasion for "dancing in the streets," as Alexander Meiklejohn called it,[1] as a practical matter it required courts considering defamation cases in its wake to give up their established standards and dance to a new, unfamiliar tune.

The trial judge in the *Thompson v. St. Amant* libel case was among those caught in this sea change. Although the trial had occurred after the *Sullivan* decision, Judge Fred Blanche had initially held that the *Sullivan* case did not apply to Herman Thompson's case against Phil A. St. Amant. But the judge reconsidered and later decided that it did, forcing him to reevaluate his verdict in Thompson's favor before affirming it. When the verdict was appealed, the Louisiana Court of Appeal and the Louisiana Supreme Court both had to reconsider the verdict for Thompson and their standards for defamation in the wake of the *Sullivan* ruling, with the courts reaching very different decisions that eventually brought the case to the U.S. Supreme Court, which had reshaped American defamation law by its decision in *Sullivan* and now had to deal with the aftermath.

SULLIVAN'S IMPACT

The trial and Judge Blanche's verdict in Thompson's case against St. Amant occurred two months after the U.S. Supreme Court released its opinion in *New York Times v. Sullivan*, which held that public officials had to show "actual malice" in order to win a defamation suit.

The *Sullivan* ruling had come up during the trial. Richard G. Van Buskirk, St. Amant's attorney, had argued that Thompson was a public official who, according to *Sullivan*, was properly subject to public criticism, and as such was required to show such "malice." It is unclear whether Van Buskirk meant "malice" in the pre-*Sullivan* sense or as a reference to *Sullivan*'s "actual malice" standard. But Robert L. Kleinpeter, Thompson's lawyer, countered that regardless of whether St. Amant's statement was intended to be criticism of someone who was arguably a public official, "[St. Amant] does not have the right to drop little names . . . and associate them with theft, conspiracy, etc."[2]

When he awarded the $5,000 in damages to Thompson at the conclusion of the trial, Judge Blanche said that the *Sullivan* ruling had no effect on the case since Thompson was a public employee, not an elected public official. Blanche also noted that when a statement is defamatory per se—when it "falsely accuses any person of being dishonest, a liar; being fraudulent, or of having unworthy motives, or to impute the same by insinuations or innuendo"—malice is inferred under Louisiana law.[3]

In reaching this conclusion, Judge Blanche used an analogy: "I was interested in Mr. Van Buskirk's remarks that they [St. Amant's statements] were not [defamatory] and the reasons why they were not but I wonder, Mr. Van Buskirk, what you would think if someone should reflect on your honesty as a lawyer in such a publication."[4] Ironically, two years later Van Buskirk himself was disbarred for misusing client funds.

But the error in Judge Blanche's initial ruling was that the "malice" he referred to was not "actual malice" as the U.S. Supreme Court defined it in its *Sullivan* ruling. Instead, by "malice" he meant general ill will toward the plaintiff. Such "malice" could, indeed, be presumed under Louisiana law. But since it was a new concept that had no history in Louisiana law, *Sullivan*'s "actual malice" could not.

St. Amant's lawyer filed a motion for a new trial in the case on May 18, 1964, thirteen days after the verdict. The motion argued that the "judgment is clearly contrary to the law and the evidence," and that "the interests of justice require that a new trial or a partial new trial be granted."[5] It took Judge Blanche seven months to rule on the motion, issuing an opinion stating the rationale for denying the motion on January 22, 1965. He issued the formal denial five days later.

In this ruling, Judge Blanche more comprehensively addressed the impact of *Sullivan* on Thompson's case. Citing Louisiana Supreme Court decisions from 1939 and 1955 that discussed deputy sheriffs as public officers, Judge Blanche concluded that Thompson *was* a public official and that the *Sullivan* "actual malice" rule actually *did* apply to Thompson's case, conclusions that were contrary to his own prior ruling. Based on these conclusions, Judge Blanche maintained that the standard he applied in his verdict, based on inferred "malice," was inadequate under the new *New York Times v. Sullivan* "actual malice" standard.[6] "The Court's [original] decision cannot stand on the basis that malice may be implied by the mere character of the statement in light of its holding that plaintiff is a public official," he wrote, "and that brings us to the final question of whether under the federal rule as enunciated in *New York Times Company v. Sullivan* the plaintiff has shown actual malice."[7]

Thus Judge Blanche reevaluated his prior verdict on the basis of the *Sullivan* standard. He focused on St. Amant's testimony that his primary target in the address was Russell Long, that Thompson wasn't "even in [his] mind" in making the statements in the television address, and that St. Amant did not know what the money that Partin gave Thompson was for. These admissions, Blanche held, showed that St. Amant had acted with *Sullivan* "actual malice" in making the statements.[8] "If he never gave any consideration as to what effect those remarks might have on Captain Thompson's reputation and character and was content to let the public draw whatever inference it desired concerning these remarks," Judge Blanche wrote, "then fairness dictates that despite defendant's avowed absence of ill will toward Captain Thompson or intent to do him harm or damage, he acted with reckless and wanton disregard for whether the statement was false or not."[9]

This fulfilled the *Sullivan* "actual malice" standard and led to the same result: Thompson won. Thus Blanche reaffirmed his prior verdict, denied St. Amant's motion for a new trial, and issued an order to that effect.[10]

A SHOOTING INCIDENT

While the new trial motion was pending, St. Amant was involved in an incident with the son of East Baton Rouge Parish sheriff J. Bryan Clemmons.

In the early morning hours of September 7, 1964, St. Amant claimed that he heard some noises on the driveway outside his home. Through the window he saw two men placing a paper bag on the aerial antenna of his car. It turned out that the bag had messages written on it that threatened St. Amant for his support of Barry Goldwater. When he went outside, the men jumped in their car and peeled away; St. Amant got in his own car and gave chase, eventually catching up with the car. The driver turned out to be the son of Sheriff Clemmons, also named J. Bryan Clemmons, who worked as a deputy in his father's office.

The younger Clemmons later denied any knowledge of the bag placed on

St. Amant's car, saying that he was just dropping off a colleague and his wife after a Labor Day barbecue.

After St. Amant caught up with the car, Clemmons got out and approached St. Amant's vehicle. St. Amant, who had his gun, let off what he intended as a warning shot, which hit the inside of the door of his own car. Both Clemmons and St. Amant reported the incident to Baton Rouge police, and the incident was reported in the local newspapers, but no charges were filed.

St. Amant did not see the incident as isolated from the libel case and the politics of the time. "They were out to get me," he recalled.[11]

LOUISIANA COURT OF APPEAL

Richard G. Van Buskirk, St. Amant's attorney, filed a notice of his client's appeal of the trial verdict on February 1, 1965, six days after Judge Blanche rejected the new trial motion. Van Buskirk filed the appeals brief itself with the Louisiana Court of Appeal the following day.

St. Amant's appeal was based on three arguments: that the statements that St. Amant made about Thompson were true and thus could not be libelous because truth is an absolute defense to libel; that the statements were protected by the qualified privilege for truthful comment and criticism of people in public life involved in matters of public concern; and that the statements were not made with "actual malice."

On the first point, the appeal argued that "it is beyond cavil that the plaintiff *did receive funds* as related by the union member [Albin] in his affidavit." Because "plaintiff admitted the truth of the statement [at issue]," St. Amant's appeal added, the case "presents the rather unusual situation where defendant was condemned and cast in damages for telling the truth."[12] This truth, according to the appeal, was as follows: "Plaintiff readily admitted collecting money from the named business agent [Partin], the Sheriff testified that he knew of and approved the practice, and a former secretary to the business agent testified as to $100.00 in cash which had been delivered by the business agent to the plaintiff."[13]

Of course, this does not address the distinction made by Judge Blanche in his trial court ruling that the defamation was not based on the money transfer itself but instead on the alleged implication that the cash was for Thompson's personal benefit. The appeal acknowledged that the plaintiff and his witnesses testified that the money was for charity and pointed out that "no one—and certainly not the defendant—has ever suggested to the contrary." But the trial court's ruling, the appellate brief continued, focused on St. Amant's inability to prove Thompson's lack of integrity, even though the appeal argued that St. Amant never questioned Thompson's integrity in his speech.[14]

The appellate brief also drew attention to Albin's statement about the Teamsters members who said that they were uncomfortable calling the sheriff's office after the theft of the safe from the union hall because of Thompson's friendliness with and receipts of funds from Ed Partin, regardless of the purpose of the funds.

The brief also addressed "actual malice." In addition to its decision in *Sullivan* establishing the concept, by the time of the appeal the U.S. Supreme Court had applied "actual malice" to criminal libel in *Garrison v. Louisiana*, holding Louisiana's criminal libel statute unconstitutional when used against statements about a public official because the statute did not require "actual malice" as an element of the crime. But since the statement that money had changed hands between Partin and Thompson was literally true, the brief argued, St. Amant could not have acted with reckless disregard for truth or falsity of the statement, and thus the trial court verdict finding "actual malice" was a legal error.

In his response to the appeal, Thompson requested an increase in damages from $5,000 to $12,000. He also argued that Judge Blanche's trial verdict was a correct application of the law, citing a number of Louisiana defamation cases.

The brief also made the argument, based on the common law and Louisiana conception of "malice," that such "malice" could be implied from the mere fact of publication of a defamatory and false statement. As for *Sullivan*'s new "actual malice" standard, the brief argued that it was applicable only to public officials and that Thompson did not fit in this category.

After the brief was submitted but before the case was argued, St. Amant's lawyer, Richard G. Van Buskirk, was arrested for writing a bad check. He was later disbarred for financial impropriety with client funds. "I went there [to the court of appeal] and my lawyer didn't show up," St. Amant recalled. "Finally, somebody brought me the word that he was in jail." Because Van Buskirk was unavailable, St. Amant argued his case himself, by reading to the appeals judges the brief that Van Buskirk had written.[15]

Despite the impromptu nature of his presentation, St. Amant convinced the judges. The First Circuit Court of Appeal issued its decision on February 28, 1966, and unanimously reversed the trial verdict.

Most of the appeals court's decision is a recitation of the relevant facts that Judge Blanche relied on in reaching his initial trial verdict and in ruling against St. Amant's motion for a new trial. But in describing the context in which the alleged defamation took place, the appeals court seems to criticize St. Amant's focus on Partin and others in his speech, rather than on his opponent in the Senate primary:

> The record shows that the political method used in this particular instance was one so frequently used, that is, to allege certain wrongdoings on the part of one individual or group of individuals and then allege a connection between that individual or group of individuals and a politician. In the present case it was sought to show a connection between Senator Long and one E. G. Partin, local leader of the Teamsters Union who was accused of all sorts of wrongdoings. . . . The affidavit by Mr. Albin was most broad in its accusations of various acts of commission and omission on the part of Mr. E. G. Partin, including his being involved or connected with Fidel and [Raúl] Castro, his misuse of Union funds, and his committing various acts of violence. It barely mentioned Mr. St. Amant's opponent.[16]

But the five judges of the appellate court reserved most of their criticism for Judge Blanche, particularly his failure to adequately address the impact of the U.S. Supreme Court's decisions in *New York Times v. Sullivan,* which was decided before the trial in Thompson's case, and *Garrison v. Louisiana,* which was decided after trial but before Blanche ruled on the motion for reconsideration: "In the Trial Judge's original reasons for judgment and in the briefs filed by counsel for plaintiff and for defendant much jurisprudence is cited and there is a great deal of discussion as to what does or does not constitute actionable libel or slander. However, since the rendition by the Supreme Court of the United States in the case of *New York Times Company v. Sullivan* and in *Garrison v. State of Louisiana,* most of what was discussed is now moot and of no relevancy."[17]

These two cases, the appeals court observed, are "relevant to the case at issue since it is clear from a reading of both cases that the rule for libel in cases regarding a public official's conduct is the same whether it be civil libel or criminal libel."[18]

Thus the appeals court proceeded to apply the *Sullivan* "actual malice" test to Thompson's claim. While noting that in *Sullivan* the U.S. Supreme Court had declined to determine "how far down into the lower ranks of government employees the 'public official' designation would extend," the appeals court agreed with Judge Blanche's conclusion (when denying the new trial motion) that Thompson was a public official. The court also rejected Thompson's contention that his collection of charitable donations should be considered an activity of his job responsibilities that did not implicate his government position, with the court saying that St. Amant's statement at issue in the case involved Thompson's trustworthiness as a deputy sheriff.[19]

Applying the *Sullivan* test to St. Amant's statement, the appellate court noted the vagueness of the "actual malice" standard, observing that "neither the *Garrison* case nor the *New York Times* case sets forth with any degree of clarity the steps the plaintiff must or must not take in order to determine whether or not statements were made with reckless disregard as to whether such statements were true or false."[20] Yet the court then proceeded to determine whether the statements had been made with such reckless disregard.

> The mere fact that criticism of the manner in which a public official performs his duties would tend to affect his private reputation as well as his public reputation would not render inapplicable the *New York Times* rule. It would certainly follow that if the statement made by the District Attorney of Orleans Parish and quoted in the *Garrison* case . . . is not libelous under the *New York Times* rule (the application of the civil rule of libel as announced by the [U.S.] Supreme Court in that case to criminal libel in Louisiana), then certainly the statements made by the defendant Mr. St. Amant in the present case would not be libelous under that rule.[21]

The only possible defamatory statement regarding Thompson, the appeals court said, was the one regarding "money that had passed hands between Ed and Herman Thompson, from Ed to Herman." But, the court added, since Thompson had been seen collecting money at the union hall, for whatever purpose, the statement "could not be said to have been used with reckless disregard as to whether false or true."[22]

Because Thompson was required to show "actual malice" and could not do so, the appeals court held that the trial court's award to Thompson must be reversed:

> It is . . . the opinion of this Court that prior to the decisions of the United States Supreme Court in the *New York Times* and the *Garrison* cases the words of the plaintiff would have been libelous under the Louisiana jurisprudence. However, in view of the U.S. Supreme Court's holding that the Constitution delimits a State's power to award damages for libel in actions brought by public officials against critics of their official conduct, as discussed above, this Court has no alternative but to hold that the judgment of the Trial Court is in error and should be reversed and there should be judgment in favor of the defendant dismissing plaintiff's suit at his cost.[23]

Eleven days after its decision, Thompson petitioned the appeals court for a rehearing, arguing that the court had erred in finding that he was a public official under *Sullivan;* that the statements at issue involved his official conduct; that the statements were not made with "actual malice"; and that the *Sullivan* "actual malice" rule should not even apply in this case. The appeals court denied the rehearing request three weeks later.

The message of the court of appeal was clear: *Sullivan* and *Garrison* had fundamentally changed the law of defamation as it applies to public officials. And in this new regime, Thompson was a public official who could not win a defamation case based on the comments about him in St. Amant's speech because there was no evidence that the statements had been made with "actual malice," which was now required by the U.S. Supreme Court's decision in *Sullivan.*

LOUISIANA SUPREME COURT

After the Louisiana Court of Appeal overturned the trial verdict and award in his favor, Thompson turned to the state's supreme court, filing an application for review of the case on May 3, 1966. The application argued that the appeals court had improperly substituted Judge Blanche's determination that St. Amant had not made his statement with "actual malice" with its own judgment that he had and that this question was an issue of fact—which the trial judge was in the best position to determine and which the appeals court had no power to overrule—rather than a question of law over which the appeals court had jurisdiction:

> While the Court of Appeal stated that the plaintiff was the victim of intemperate "mud-slinging," it nevertheless reversed the lower court's conclusion that the statements were made with reckless disregard for the truth. It would appear that the Court of Appeal's decision on this point was based on a comparison of the statements made to those made in other cases[,] and then [the court] substituted its judgment on this *question of fact* for that of the Trial Judge. There was no finding by the Court of Appeal that the conclusion of the lower court that the statements were made with reckless disregard of the truth was manifest error.[24]

The application also argued that the court of appeal was incorrect when it classified Thompson as a public official, saying that both the trial court and the appeals court based this ruling on Louisiana cases, not on the constitutional considerations that the *Sullivan* decision imposed on defamation cases.

In support of this notion, Thompson cited the same footnote from *Sullivan* that the appellate court had used to justify its use of state court decisions, as well as language from the U.S. Supreme Court's decision in *Rosenblatt v. Baer*, another case interpreting *Sullivan* that had been decided only ten weeks before submission of the application. In *Rosenblatt*, Justice William Brennan Jr.'s majority addressed the question of how to determine whether the libel plaintiff in that case—the supervisor of a county-owned recreation area—was a public official. Brennan rejected the notion that this should be answered by using state-law standards, saying that "states have developed definitions of 'public official' for local administrative purposes, not the purposes of a national constitutional protection. If existing state-law standards reflect the purposes of *New York Times*, this is at best accidental."[25]

The court in *Rosenblatt* then defined public officials as "government employees who have, or appear to the public to have, substantial responsibility for or control over the conduct of governmental affairs." Thompson argued that he did not meet this standard. "Mr. Thompson," the application for review asserted, "was a salaried employee of the parish, having no more responsibility for control of the conduct of governmental affairs than a bailiff of the Court or a Deputy Clerk of Court performing the most menial of tasks."[26]

The application also argued that the court of appeal erred in finding that St. Amant's statements involved Thompson's official duties and that they had not been made with "actual malice." Finally, the petition argued that the application of *Sullivan* was inappropriate because the language of that decision spoke of the importance of First Amendment protection for discussion of matters that were "major public issues of our time" and that the issue of Thompson's honesty did not rise to that level.[27]

The Louisiana Supreme Court granted review of the case on June 9, 1966. It was the first defamation case to come to the court since the U.S. Supreme Court's decision in *Sullivan* and thus was the Louisiana Supreme Court's first opportunity to consider the *Sullivan* standards in the context of Louisiana defamation law.

After the appeal was granted, both sides submitted briefs arguing their positions.

Thompson's brief claimed that St. Amant's campaign speech had involved Thompson in "everything from criminal conspiracy, burglary, robbery, Communism, and nefarious characters of all kinds and descriptions," while pointing out that St. Amant had admitted that he did not even know Thompson. But the brief did not argue that this showed that St. Amant had acted with "actual malice" in making his statements about Thompson. Instead, the brief put forward various arguments for the proposition that the *Sullivan* "actual malice" rule should not apply. Even if it did, Thompson argued, the trial court's retroactive finding of "actual malice" was proper and should not have been reversed by the court of appeal.[28]

Thompson's brief asserted that both the trial court and the court of appeal "fell into error in looking to State Court precedents in deciding whether Deputy Thompson was a public official within the *New York Times* rule." But the brief argued that because Thompson would not have been covered by the absolute privilege in defamation cases for statements by high-level government officials acting in their official capacity, he similarly was not a senior-enough public official to fall within the ambit of *Sullivan*'s heightened requirements for defamation plaintiffs. In support of this contention, an appendix to the brief included an article that outlined standards that courts could and had used to determine whether defamation plaintiffs were subject to the *Sullivan* requirements.[29]

Thompson's brief also argued that the heightened standards should not apply to St. Amant's statements about Thompson because Thompson was not even the target of the speech: the target was Senator Long. And even if the heightened standards did apply, the fact that Thompson was not the target of the speech showed that the statements regarding Thompson were made with "actual malice": "We submit to the Court that the statements had to be in reckless disregard for the truth, since they had no bearing whatsoever on the political race and there was nothing to be accomplished by the statements other than the possible (albeit unsuccessful) furtherance of the defendants' own political ambitions at the expense of an honest, hard-working deputy sheriff."[30]

Finally, Thompson argued that St. Amant had waived any constitutional defenses, including invocation of the *Sullivan* "actual malice" rule, by not raising them at trial. This may have been difficult for St. Amant to do, however, since the *Sullivan* decision had come down only two months before the trial in Thompson's case against St. Amant.

St. Amant was represented by a new attorney, Russell J. Schonekas of New Orleans. After the *St. Amant* case, Schonekas had other connections to players in the drama surrounding the *Thompson* libel case: he was a law partner with Jim Garrison in the early 1970s and represented Carlos Marcello in the early 1980s.

The brief that Schonekas submitted for St. Amant was much shorter than Thompson's and was filed with the court on November 4. The brief argued that Thompson was a public official subject to public scrutiny and discussion and that he needed to prove "actual malice" in order to prevail in a defamation action. "There can be no doubt that [Thompson], a deputy sheriff with the rank of Captain[,] is a public official," the brief argued, adding that "there is no evidence in the record that the statements were made with knowledge that they were false[,] and the [appeals] court so held." Quoting extensively from the appeals court's ruling, the brief argued that the decision of the court of appeal should be affirmed:[31] "Defendant-respondent respectfully submits that the statements which form the basis of this suit are privileged because the plaintiff-relator was a 'public official' under the law of Louisiana and of the United States; that there was no showing that these utterances were made with actual malice, that is with knowledge that they were false of with reckless disregard of whether they were false or not."[32]

The Louisiana Supreme Court issued its opinion in the case on February 20, 1967. The five-member majority of the court reversed the court of appeal, reinstating the trial verdict. Two of the Supreme Court's justices dissented.

The majority opinion, by Associate Justice Frank W. Summers, began with a recitation of the facts of the case, including the allegations in Albin's affidavit that St. Amant read on the air. "The speech," the opinion observed, "was unmistakably designed to disclose Albin's knowledge of illegal, unsavory and criminal actions by E. G. Partin, business agent of the local Teamsters' Union." While Thompson's name was mentioned in this context "only incidentally," the majority said, the statement still unmistakably accused him of impropriety:[33]

> St. Amant's presentation of this political address—the manner in which he expressed himself, the tone and theme of the speech, the obvious manifestation of his belief in the veracity of Albin's statements—was calculated to impress upon the reader or listener that he had confidence in Albin's charges against Partin and Thompson and that he believed them to be true. The publication was principally designed to malign the conduct of the incumbent United States Senator; but to do this it was necessary to show Partin's unsavory character and criminal record. Thompson's name was brought into the story only incidentally, yet, he was nonetheless unmistakably accused of criminal conduct.[34]

The initial question, the court majority said, was determining whether the statement at issue—that "money . . . had passed hands" from Partin to Thompson—was true, since "it is settled in Louisiana that the truth of a defamatory remark is generally a valid defense in a civil suit for defamation."[35]

The court then held that the statement was actually false. But even though the court characterized this as consistent with the trial and appellate court rulings, in both of those rulings the lower courts had actually held that the statement was literally true: that money had actually "passed hands" between Partin and Thompson. But the trial court held that this statement was false in its implication that Thompson received funds from Partin illicitly, while the court of appeal did not see any such implication.

Instead of viewing the implications of the statement as what should be determined to be true or false, Justice Summers's majority portrayed the implications as evidence of the harm to Thompson:

> Thompson admitted that checks passed to him from Partin as a solicitation for the Baton Rouge Kids' Baseball Clinic, but the remarks contained in St. Amant's publication say much more. Sheriff Bryan Clemmons, Thompson's employer, found it necessary to defend

> Thompson against the charges contained in the speech. For many citizens called the sheriff for an explanation because they believed that St. Amant had accused Thompson of taking a pay-off from Partin. A neighbor who heard the broadcast told Thompson that "some man" had called him "some kind of thief and all kinds of names." The meaning the controverted remarks convey to the average reader is utterly defamatory of Thompson.[36]

The majority then considered whether Thompson was a public official within the parameters outlined in *Sullivan*. The court said he clearly was, pointing out that the position of deputy sheriff had been created by the state legislature and that a deputy sheriff was sworn into office with an oath required by the state constitution. In addition, the majority opinion observed that "the deputy is a representative of the sheriff in his official capacity; he is a public officer or official whose authority and duty are regulated by law. So far as the public is concerned, the acts of a deputy are the acts of the sheriff himself." This finding was consistent with existing Louisiana law, which clearly established that "when a man places himself before the public as a candidate for public office, or is elected to public office, or assumes any other position of general interest to the public, he also places his every word or action before the community as a proper subject for fair comment and criticism."[37]

But the majority opinion cautioned that this was not the end of the inquiry. *Sullivan* "actual malice" does not, the court said, apply to all public employees, but under *Rosenblatt* it applies only to those government employees who have, "or appear to the public to have, 'substantial responsibility for or control over the conduct of governmental affairs.'" Because Thompson was a deputy sheriff with "'substantial responsibility for or control of governmental affairs,' at least where law enforcement and police functions are concerned," the majority held that he was a public official for the purposes of the *Sullivan* rule.[38]

The court then found that St. Amant's reliance on Albin's statement and his failure to give any regard to his allegations against Thompson showed that he had acted with reckless disregard in his statements about Thompson: "Having no personal knowledge of Thompson's activities, St. Amant relied upon Albin's sworn statement to verify the truth of the defamatory matter. . . . In his zeal to show a bad character and background in Partin and to link him to his opponent, he gave no consideration whatsoever to Thompson. He was heedless of the effect his address would have on Thompson or of the truthfulness or not of the statements concerning him."[39]

With "actual malice" established, the majority concluded that no proof of actual damages was required and the trial award was "not excessive." Thus the majority reversed the appeals court decision and reinstated the trial award of $5,000 to Thompson.

Chief Justice John B. Fournet and Associate Justices Joe B. Hamiter, Frank W. Hawthorne, and Joe W. Sanders joined in Summers's majority opinion. Associate Justices E. Howard McCaleb and Walter B. Hamlin dissented.

McCaleb's dissent started by noting that he agreed with the majority that Thompson was a public official to whom *Sullivan* "actual malice" applied, but he added that he disagreed with the majority on every other point. First, McCaleb wrote, St. Amant's statement about Thompson was substantially true, since "it makes no essential difference whether the payment was made in cash or by check. In either case the affidavit that money had passed between Partin and Thompson is an admitted fact." Albin's statement, repeated by St. Amant in the broadcast, was "fair comment, however erroneous, based on substantially true facts," McCaleb wrote. Justice McCaleb also concluded that there was no showing that St. Amant had made the comment with "actual malice":[40] "Surely St. Amant, having secured an affidavit to the facts set forth therein, can hardly be said to have been actuated by malice toward Thompson. Indeed no proof is shown here that St. Amant knew that any fact stated in the affidavit was false or that any conclusion drawn from a true fact stated in the affidavit was false."[41]

The majority's finding that St. Amant had acted with reckless disregard by relying on the truthfulness of Albin's affidavit and not independently investigating the allegations against Thompson, McCaleb concluded, was "exactly contrary to the view of the United States Supreme Court in the *New York Times* case."[42]

The other dissent was from Associate Justice Walter B. Hamlin, who stated only that "the result reached by the Court of Appeal is correct," and cited as support the U.S. Supreme Court's decision in *Time, Inc. v. Hill.*[43]

In that case, announced only six weeks prior to the Louisiana Supreme Court's release of the decision in *Thompson,* the U.S. Supreme Court reversed a finding that *Life* magazine was liable to a family who sued for invasion of their privacy after a situation in which they were held hostage was portrayed in the magazine as having been more violent than the actual event. The majority opinion was written by Justice Brennan—who had also written the majority opinion in *Sullivan*—joined by Justices Stewart and White. They justified their reversal by applying the *Sullivan* "actual malice" standard and finding that the magazine had not acted with reckless disregard for the truth.

Justice Black concurred in the *Time, Inc. v. Hill* case, in an opinion joined by Justice Douglas, stating that while the majority's ruling was consistent with the court's holding in *Sullivan*, he thought that the protection of free speech was much more expansive and expressed concern over the majority's acceptance of a claim of invasion of privacy against the press. Justice Douglas also wrote his own concurrence to express concern over First Amendment implications of the privacy claims in this case. Justice John Marshall Harlan II concurred in part and dissented in part, saying that because the article at issue had admittedly been fictionalized, it was not in his view a matter of public interest, and on remand a negligence rather than "actual malice" standard should apply.

Justice Abe Fortas wrote the dissent in *Time, Inc. v. Hill*, joined by Chief Justice Earl Warren and Justice Tom C. Clark. Fortas argued that the majority's reversal and remand were unnecessary, since the "the [jury] instructions in this case are acceptable even within the principles today announced by the Court":[44] "I do not believe that we must or should, in deference to those whose views are absolute as to the scope of the First Amendment, be ingenious to strike down all state action, however circumspect, which penalizes the use of words as instruments of aggression and personal assault. There are great and important values in our society, none of which is greater than those reflected in the First Amendment, but which are also fundamental and entitled to this Court's careful respect and protection. Among these is the right to privacy."[45]

Fortas also explained that after eleven years of litigation, "[the plaintiff] should not be subjected to the burden of a new trial without significant cause. . . . Perhaps the purpose of the decision here is to indicate that this Court will place insuperable obstacles in the way of recovery by persons who are injured by reckless and heedless assaults, provided they are in print and even though they are totally divorced from fact. If so, I should think that the Court would cast its decision in constitutional terms. Short of that purpose, with which I would strongly disagree, there is no reason here to order a new trial."[46]

By citing the *Time, Inc.* majority opinion in his dissent in the *Thompson* case, Justice Hamlin was arguing that the court should have affirmed the appeals court's reversal of the trial verdict for Thompson.

But the majority of the Louisiana Supreme Court disagreed with Hamlin and reinstated the trial verdict. St. Amant responded to the Louisiana Supreme Court's decision by seeking a rehearing, alleging several errors in the court's opinion. The court denied that motion on March 27, 1967.

(7)

The U.S. Supreme Court Sets a Standard

The shifting results in *Thompson v. St. Amant*—the trial verdict for Thompson, its reversal by the Louisiana Court of Appeal, and then the reinstatement of the trial verdict by the Louisiana Supreme Court—were largely the effect of uncertainty as to how to apply the *Sullivan* "actual malice" standard. Thus perhaps it was inevitable that the U.S. Supreme Court would have to resolve these questions by accepting review of the *Thompson* case. When it did, its decision again changed the outcome, finding for St. Amant. In reaching this decision, the Supreme Court also furthered the development of the "actual malice" standard that it had established in *Sullivan* and established once and for all that "actual malice" required a high level of irresponsibility by the defendant for a well-known plaintiff to prevail in a defamation case.

In the wake of the Louisiana Supreme Court ruling, it was again St. Amant's turn to seek review from a higher court, and the only remaining option was the U.S. Supreme Court. Requests for review of a case by the U.S. Supreme Court are made in the form of petitions of certiorari. But the odds were relatively long: the Supreme Court has almost complete discretion in deciding which appeals it will hear, and in its previous five annual terms, from the October 1962 term through the October 1966 term, the court had granted an average of only 11.6 percent of the nonindigent petitions for review that it had received. This increased slightly in the October 1967 term—the term in which St. Amant sought review—to 13.0 percent.

THE EARLY LEGACY OF *SULLIVAN*

The court had taken a special interest in defamation cases in the past several terms before St. Amant's certiorari petition. In the years following *Sullivan*, the court decided a number of cases that developed the contours of the defamation and First Amendment doctrines announced in that groundbreaking case.

In *Garrison v. Louisiana*, in a decision released six months after the ruling in *Sullivan*, the majority held that "actual malice" must be an element of a criminal defamation statute to be constitutional. Because Louisiana's criminal defamation lacked such a requirement, it was held unconstitutional. In *Rosenblatt v. Baer* (1966), the majority remanded for a determination whether the manager of a county-owned ski resort was a public official who had to show *Sullivan* "actual malice" in his defamation case. Later the same year, an eight-to-one majority held in *Sheppard v. Maxwell* that a guilty verdict in a murder case must be reversed because of extensive and intrusive media coverage of the case.[1]

The court decided three related cases in the months before the *St. Amant* certiorari petition. In *Time, Inc. v. Hill*, the case cited by Louisiana Supreme Court justice Hamlin in his dissent, the U.S. Supreme Court majority held that the "actual malice" requirement applied to a case alleging that a *Life* magazine article had given a false public impression of a family whose hostage ordeal had become a matter of intense public interest. The court further expanded the application of the "actual malice" standard in *Curtis Publishing Co. v. Butts*, holding that the standard applied to prominent individuals ("public figures"), not just public officials. Just two weeks before its first consideration of St. Amant's certiorari petition, the court remanded *Associated Press v. Walker*, a libel case involving a prominent former general, for reconsideration in light of the *Curtis Publishing* ruling.[2]

PETITION FOR CERTIORARI

St. Amant's petition for certiorari was filed with the U.S. Supreme Court on August 19, 1967, by his new attorney (his third), Moses C. Scharff of New Orleans. This was 180 days after the Louisiana Supreme Court's decision was issued, double the usual 90-day limit.[3]

The petition asserted that the primary issue in the case was simple: "Is there actual malice presented [in St. Amant's statements] or did the Court wrongfully imply it[?]"[4] The answer, the petition argued, was clearly the latter:

> Since at all levels the courts of Louisiana have concluded that Respondent, Thompson, was a public official, the case falls under the aegis of the New York Times rule of defamation. The only disputed fact, and the reason certiorari should be granted, is that these statements made by petitioner were uttered with actual malice or with reckless disregard of whether they were true or false. It is respectfully submitted that these statements were not made maliciously, and therefore under

> the public official rule of the Times case, the First and Fourteenth Amendments do guarantee the protection and privilege of free speech.[5]

The petition reduced the case to a single issue that remained unanswered in the aftermath of *Sullivan* and the cases that followed: "The sole question presented in this request for a writ of certiorari was whether the remarks admittedly made by St. Amant were made with actual malice, i.e., they were made with knowledge of falsity or in reckless disregard of whether they were true or false."[6]

After reviewing the history of the case, including the televised comments that led to the lawsuit, St. Amant's petition asserted that the "facts presented . . . were substantially true," since "the undisputed fact that some type of money did change hands still remains." But in addition to the defense of substantial truth, St. Amant also asserted an opinion defense: the reason for these money transfers, the petition asserted, "is a matter of individual opinions."[7]

The petition argued that "no proof was shown that petitioner St. Amant knew that any fact stated in the affidavit was false or that any conclusion drawn from these facts were false." Even if the statements were false, St. Amant should not be held liable, his petition argued, because "knowledge of falsity and ignorance of falsity cannot be held to be one and the same," and "there is no law or imposed legal duty to check, further than did petitioner, such a statement to avoid malice or recklessness." And the bottom line was that no proof had been shown that St. Amant made the statements about Thompson with reckless disregard for the truth, the requisite element of "actual malice."[8]

Because the court was on summer recess when the petition was filed, the certiorari petition was docketed for the court's following term, which began on October 2, 1967. This was also Justice Thurgood Marshall's first day on the court.

After submission of St. Amant's petition, bench memoranda were prepared by clerks for Chief Justice Warren and for Justices Fortas and Harlan.

The memorandum for Harlan, dated October 20 and apparently written by Harlan clerk Louis R. Cohen, was only two pages long. According to the memorandum, "The basis of the La. Sup. Ct.'s ruling was that there was no 'actual malice' but there was 'wanton disregard,'" so "what was required here was far below what *NY Times* [*v. Sullivan*] requires." After weighing the options, the memorandum opined, "The verdict in this case was for only $5,000 and I see no point in oral argument." A sentence in the memorandum that was blacked-out but could nevertheless be read stated, "There is no response, and I think one should be sought before summarily reversing." In line with this sentiment, the memorandum recommended that the court seek a response from Thompson to St. Amant's certiorari petition. A handwritten note at the end of the memorandum, apparently written by Justice Harlan, says, "I'd get a response, with a view to summary reversal."[9]

The memorandum prepared for Warren, dated October 23 and apparently written by clerk Larry Simon, is much more extensive. It summarized St. Amant's primary argument as being that since "it [was] an undisputed 'fact' that money passed [between Partin and Thompson]" and the imputation of devious reasons was Albin's opinion, St. Amant's repetition of this opinion did not constitute "actual malice." The memorandum dismisses this argument, saying it is "patently without merit" because it "seeks to draw a largely artificial distinction between fact and opinion, and in any event the statement [St. Amant] made was one of fact[,] not opinion."[10]

"In any event," the memorandum added, "it seems to me that a statement of opinion, just as one of fact, can be made with reckless disregard of its falsity."[11]

This presaged the Supreme Court's 1990 decision in *Milkovich v. Lorain Journal Co.* that there is no "wholesale defamation exemption for anything that might be labeled 'opinion,'" since "such an interpretation . . . would . . . ignore the fact that expressions of 'opinion' may often imply an assertion of objective fact." In *Milkovich*, the court held that a statement of opinion could be the basis of a defamation suit if it asserted or implied a "fact" that could be proven to be true or untrue.[12]

But despite the dismissal of St. Amant's primary argument, the memorandum by Warren's clerk still argued that "the judgment of the [Louisiana Supreme Court] was nevertheless erroneous and should be reversed." "I don't think," the memorandum continued, "the facts that [petitioner][13] never thought about Thompson and did not verify Albin's assertions, standing alone, can support a finding of reckless disregard." At most, the memorandum said, St. Amant made the statement negligently:[14] "I would think that reckless disregard must be proved by something more than a failure to check—namely, by proof that there was some reason the defendant should have checked. Proof of that sort might consist of a showing that the information came from a source reasonably far removed from the events described, or personally motivated to lie, or unwilling to swear to his description. None of these possibilities is present here."[15]

Concluding that "the judgment below cannot be reversed simply citing *Times* [*v. Sullivan*]," the memorandum recommends that the court either grant certiorari and then reverse in a two- or three-paragraph unsigned summary ("per curiam") opinion or request a response to the certiorari petition from Thompson.[16]

Clerk Peter L. Zimroth prepared a memorandum for Justice Fortas, dated October 25. The memorandum agreed with the others that the primary issue in the case was "whether the evidence can meet the test of *Times v. Sullivan*," but the Fortas memorandum disagreed with the other memorandum on whether it could:[17]

> No one claimed that [petitioner] had knowledge of the falsity of the statement. Therefore, under *Times*, [petitioner] would be liable only if he was made the statement in reckless disregard of its truth or falsity. The [Louisiana Supreme Court][18] held there was reckless disregard shown in the record. . . .
>
> I think the [Louisiana Supreme Court] has established a much too rigorous standard for [petitioner]. [Petitioner] had an interview with a member of the Teamster's local. It was reasonable, I think, for [petitioner] to believe that Albin knew what he was talking about. Further, [petitioner] went so far as to have Albin sign an affidavit attesting to the truth of everything he said in the interview. I don't think [petitioner] had to go any further to investigate the truth of Albin's statement.[19]

Zimroth's memorandum noted that an opinion—unsigned, but written by Justice Brennan—was then circulating in another case, *Beckley Newspapers Corp. v. Hanks*, in which a political candidate had sued a newspaper for libel. The per curiam opinion in *Beckley*, released November 6, reversed a judgment for the candidate after holding that a jury instruction in the case had not required *Sullivan* "actual malice" for the jury to find for the plaintiff. Since "actual malice" was now required in such cases, the instruction was erroneous and the jury verdict for the plaintiff had to be reversed.[20]

Like the memoranda by other justices' clerks, the memorandum to Fortas suggested that the court should eventually reverse the verdict in *St. Amant*, but not until first releasing the opinion in *Beckley* and perhaps after requesting a response from Thompson. But unlike the other memoranda, which concluded that the Louisiana Supreme Court had erred by imposing a standard less stringent than *Sullivan* "actual malice," the Fortas memorandum determined that the standard applied by the Louisiana court was actually too rigorous: "I think [petitioner] could rely on a sworn statement by someone who was a member of the union. If a newspaper is not required to make a 'special investigation' [as in *Beckley*], I certainly don't think the court should require a single person to make an investigation in addition to getting a sworn affidavit."[21]

At the top of the first page of the Fortas memorandum are handwritten comments, apparently written by Fortas himself. One of these, "I'd reverse summarily," is crossed out. Another, apparently written after the first, says, "I'd grant + ask to be noted," perhaps indicating a desire that the court grant certiorari so that the case could be heard on the merits.[22]

The Supreme Court considers certiorari petitions at conference meetings each Friday during its term. A "discuss list" of pending petitions and appeals is prepared for the meeting by the chief justice, who excludes cases that the chief justice believes do not merit any consideration by the conference. The associate justices also notify the chief justice of the cases they do not think merit consideration; they can also have cases added to the "discuss list." At the meeting, the justices—starting with the chief justice, then speaking in order of seniority—discuss their views of each case on the list, often based on memoranda prepared by their clerks. Each justice has a vote on whether to grant review. It takes four votes—the "rule of four"—to grant certiorari. Of course, this is less than a majority of the nine-member court.

Likely because of the backlog of accumulated petitions at the start of the October 1967 session, the court did not consider the *St. Amant* petition until its November 3 meeting.

At that meeting Justices Black, Douglas, and Warren apparently initially wanted to follow the recommendation of all three bench memoranda that the court grant certiorari and then summarily reverse the Louisiana Supreme Court's decision. As one scholar explained, such a summary reversal traditionally indicated that the "case was uncontroversial, obvious, and did not require a substantial opinion." But this changed. "Beginning in the mid-twentieth century, the Supreme Court expanded the role of the per curiam, fashioning it as a strategic device to resolve time-sensitive cases quickly, as a protective shield from controversial issues, and as a way to make new law by indirection. Through the per curiam, the Court at times also aimed to convey a message of consensus while engaging in more complicated and substantive decision making."[23]

In addition to a brief summary of the memorandum's recommendation, a handwritten note at the top of the Warren memorandum—apparently written by Chief Justice Warren himself—also says, "Related to *Times,*" apparently referring to the *New York Times v. Sullivan* decision, and "Ask WJB," an apparent reference to Justice William J. Brennan. Brennan wrote the majority opinion in *Sullivan* and was a champion of free speech under the First Amendment.[24]

Despite this notation, Justices Warren and Brennan differed in their votes on the *St. Amant* certiorari petition. Brennan, along with Justices Fortas, Harlan, Marshall, and White, initially called for the court to grant certiorari and allow the case to proceed normally by giving Thompson a chance to respond. For two justices, this position may have been broader than the *St. Amant* case. Justice Brennan had previously written that summary disposition must be "very clearly" justified "because our ordinary practice is not to reverse a state decision with oral argument," while Justice Marshall had criticized the practice of summary disposal of cases generally.[25]

Justice Harlan apparently changed his position after the initial vote. While he had favored a grant of certiorari and a full review of the case, he changed his position to instead favor summary reversal. This switch is interesting in light of his clerk's recommendation that the court should request a reply to the certiorari petition and then likely summarily reverse without oral argument, as well as Harlan's ambiguous attitudes toward summary dispositions in prior cases.[26]

Justice Potter Stewart was consistent in the two votes, favoring denial of certiorari both times.

Harlan's switch left four justices favoring granting certiorari and allowing the case to proceed normally, four favoring granting certiorari and summarily reversing, and one favoring that certiorari be denied. With both of the grant options meeting the "rule of four" standard, but the informal requirement of six votes for summary reversal not being met, the court decided to request that Thompson reply to the certiorari petition.[27]

Had the court mustered a consensus for summary reversal of the Louisiana Supreme Court's reinstatement of the verdict for Thompson, it would have been a clear, definitive statement that the Louisiana high court had incorrectly applied the *Sullivan* standard. As one observer wrote, "Summary reversal is a blunt tool . . . [which] represents a potent statement that the lower court's decision was so patently wrong that the court can reverse it without briefing on the merits or oral argument from the parties." But such summary reversals have also been criticized as threatening "the acceptability of the Court's decisions to lower courts and to the Bar as a whole."[28] Others have criticized the court's use of summary dismissal as a dereliction of the court's duty: "The summary opinion is one of various processes whereby the Court seeks to assure that time and effort of the Justices are allocated in relation to the importance and complexity of what is to be decided. As such, the summary opinion has obvious utility in the efficient functioning of the Court, and there can be no question of its propriety. There remains, however, the problem of its appropriate use, and, more specifically, whether the Court is extending the use of the summary opinion to cases where fuller exposition of views is warranted."[29]

OPPOSITION TO CERTIORARI

As requested by the court, Thompson filed his brief in opposition to a grant of certiorari on December 8, 1967. The short, five-page brief concisely summarized the primary argument that Thompson had made before the Louisiana Supreme Court: that the lower courts had fully considered the *Sullivan*, *Garrison*, and *Rosenblatt* precedents, so no review of the Louisiana Supreme Court ruling in Thompson's favor was necessary. The brief also argued that in the Senate campaign St. Amant "had engaged in mud slinging to the extent that he included any and everyone whose names may have come to him at the moment," including "[making] statements with utter disregard of whether they were true or false" of which Thompson—who "was as far removed from and unconnected with this political race as any other ordinary citizen"—was an innocent victim.[30]

A supplemental bench memorandum was prepared by Warren's clerk Larry Simon after submission of Thompson's opposition. After summarizing the submission, the memorandum makes the same recommendation as Simon's prior memorandum: the court should grant certiorari and reverse in a per curiam opinion: "My view is unchanged," Simon wrote. "Briefly, I think that failure to check, on the facts of this case, cannot as a matter of law constitute reckless disregard. I think it must be shown that there was some reason that [petitioner] should have checked. Therefore, I recommend granting cert[orari] and reversing in a per curiam [opinion]."[31]

A handwritten notation at the top of this memorandum, apparently written by Chief Justice Warren, summarizes this sentiment, and perhaps indicates agreement with it. The notation reads, "Grant & Reverse."

But the court did not follow this recommendation when the petition again came up for consideration at the January 15, 1968, conference. This time, unlike the split vote at the earlier session, all of the justices except Justice Stewart apparently now voted in favor of granting certiorari and proceeding with full briefing from the parties.[32] The court announced its grant of certiorari later that day.[33]

MERITS BRIEFS

The case then moved to the next stage: briefs from both parties on the merits of the case.

St. Amant's brief, filed on February 29, was virtually identical to his certiorari petition, with only minor edits to reflect the certiorari grant and add parallel citations to the case appendix. It reduced the case to the simple question of whether St. Amant's comments were made with "actual malice."

Thomson filed his more extensive reply brief on March 30, which made three arguments. The first was that St. Amant had not used the *Sullivan* "actual malice" defense at trial, even though "the instant case was heard on the merits during the month of May, 1964 and *New York Times Co. vs. Sullivan* was decided in March, 1964." Because St. Amant had not invoked the *Sullivan* standard at the trial two months after the watershed ruling, Thompson argued, St. Amant could not assert it on appeal.[34]

This argument was based on an error: St. Amant's attorney at trial, Richard G. Van Buskirk, had in fact invoked the *Sullivan* decision, arguing at trial that Thompson was a public official under *Sullivan* who was required, and had failed, to show "malice." It is unclear, however, whether Van Buskirk meant "actual malice" when he said "malice."

This was reported in the *Baton Rouge Morning Advocate* in its story on the trial verdict: "In his defense of the case, Van Buskirk argued truth as defense, and said the Supreme Court's recent decision [in *Sullivan*] upholds criticism of public officials. . . . 'The right of the public to know how their public officials are conducting public offices is so important that it precludes an action for libel unless malice is shown,' Van Buskirk said."[35]

Trial judge Fred A. Blanche Jr. had also specifically addressed the *Sullivan* decision in his original trial verdict, concluding that it did not apply because Thompson was not a public official, which Blanche said was limited to elected officials. In addition, St. Amant apparently made the *Sullivan* "actual malice" argument in support of his motion for a new trial, since Judge Blanche specifically addressed it in response to that motion. Although Judge Blanche ultimately held that his original verdict "[could] not stand" in light of *Sullivan*, he reached the same result as the original verdict after considering St. Amant's motion for rehearing because he held that the facts showed that St. Amant had indeed acted with "actual malice."

The second argument in Thompson's brief to the U.S. Supreme Court was that *Sullivan* "actual malice" did not apply because Thompson was not a public official. Nor, Thompson's brief argued, was he "a public man in whose public conduct society and the press had a legitimate and substantial interests," to which, the brief argued, "the application of the [*Sullivan*] rule appears to have been further extended" by the U.S. Supreme Court's ruling in *Associated Press v. Walker.*[36]

There was no evidence, Thompson's brief argued, that he was such a "public man": "The record is absolutely barren of any proof as to the activities, position, and duties of the plaintiff-respondent, Herman A. Thompson. Any and all conclusions drawn as to whether Herman A. Thompson was or was not a 'public official' or a 'public man' is based entirely upon assumptions since no facts were offered in support of the defense."[37]

The brief further argued that Thompson did not enjoy ready access to the media in order to respond to St. Amant's statements. This argument was based on language in *Time, Inc. v. Hill,* which would later be more fully developed by the Supreme Court in post–*St. Amant* cases, explaining that public figures usually had ready access to the media to refute false statements about them.[38]

Unlike St. Amant, who was "engaged in a state wide campaign for U.S. Senator and appeared on television to present his case and supposedly expose his opponent," Thompson was "a salaried employee without the means to purchase statewide television time." The brief pointed out that Thompson was not "a candidate himself or . . . involved in political activities," and asked, "How much attention would he draw [in the media] if time was made available to him?" "There must be an answer," the brief concluded on this issue, "and we submit that that answer lies in a limitation upon the applicability of the *New York Times* rule in such a situation as presented in the instant case."[39]

The third argument in Thompson's brief to the U.S. Supreme Court was that—despite the first argument that "actual malice" was not argued at trial and thus should not apply to the appeal—Judge Blanche had indeed found that St. Amant acted with "actual malice":[40] "We submit that a thorough review of the state court decisions, from the trial court through the Supreme Court, reflects that even though the federal rule was not properly asserted nor preserved, that the federal decisions were applied, properly considered and correct conclusions reached."[41]

Larry Simon, the clerk for U.S. Supreme Court chief justice, Earl Warren, again prepared a bench memorandum based on the submitted briefs. While the text of this memorandum largely repeated that of the earlier bench memorandum prepared at the certiorari stage, the new memorandum added a fundamental question that was presented by the case: "Whether an alleged defamatory statement made by [petitioner] about [respondent][42] is privileged under the rule of *New York Times v. Sullivan.*" It also added the notation to its summary of St. Amant's argument that "[petitioner] next argues that the court below erred in holding that the statement was made with 'actual malice'—that is, with knowledge of its falsity or reckless disregard of truth or falsity."[43]

The new memorandum also added a summary of the arguments made in Thompson's brief and expanded the discussion of the legal issues addressed by some of the arguments. But the conclusion was similar to before: the court should reject St. Amant's arguments that his statement about money passing was opinion—an argument that the original memorandum had judged as being "without merit"—but nevertheless reverse the Louisiana Supreme Court's ruling for Thompson because "reckless disregard must be proved by something more than a failure to check—namely, by proof that there was some reason the defendant should have checked."[44]

But the court could not simply summarily reverse, since doing so would not resolve the question of whether St. Amant's reliance on Albin constituted "actual malice" or "actual malice" was due to St. Amant's failure to independently investigate Albin's claim. If the U.S. Supreme Court were to summarily reverse the Louisiana Supreme Court, a lower court would still have to resolve this issue. "Accordingly," the memorandum concluded, "I would reverse the judgment below, and remand the case for further proceedings consistent with the Court's opinion."[45]

ORAL ARGUMENT

Oral argument in *St. Amant v. Thompson* before the U.S. Supreme Court was held on Thursday, April 4, 1968. (Later that same day, Dr. Martin Luther King Jr. was assassinated in Memphis, Tennessee, at 6:00 p.m. Central Time.) It was the third case on the court's argument schedule that day, after cases on whether the distribution of future rights to buy corporate shares at a discount was taxable income and whether prosecutors could use a murder defendant's testimony from the prior trial in a retrial when the first verdict was overturned for improper use of evidence.

When the *St. Amant* case was called, attorney Russell J. Schonekas of New Orleans, representing St. Amant, began his argument by explaining that "this case, unlike the two prior ones, I don't think is nearly as complicated, and presents very simple issues for a change. I say they're simple because they're singular and simple. It's just a question in why the Louisiana Supreme Court has absolutely refused to follow the instructions and law as laid down by this Court, and that's [the] sum and substance of the entire case."[46]

In his summary of the facts of the case, Schonekas repeated an error from St. Amant's merits brief, stating that the trial judge had held that the *Sullivan* decision did not apply to Thompson's claim against St. Amant. It was true that during the trial Judge Blanche had found the *Sullivan* decision inapplicable because Thompson was not a public official. But in ruling on St. Amant's motion for a new trial, Judge Blanche had modified the reasoning for his verdict in light of *Sullivan*, but not the end result.

Schonekas then began to explain to the justices what he said were the primary issues in the case: that Thompson was not a public official and that the *Sullivan* "actual malice" standard should therefore not apply. Even if the "actual malice" standard did apply, he argued, there was no evidence that St. Amant had acted with reckless disregard for the truth, which was the definition of "actual malice" that the court had provided in *Sullivan*.

Justice Brennan almost immediately interrupted and questioned Schonekas on the first point: "I guess perhaps I don't read your [Louisiana] Supreme Court opinion correctly. I thought the holding here was that, yes, he's a public official within the *New York Times* rule and therefore there's a burden to show malice in the sense of knowing falsity or reckless disregard. That while there was no showing of knowing falsity, there was sufficient evidence to show reckless disregard. Am I wrong about that?"[47]

Schonekas agreed that Brennan's understanding was correct, but added that the problem was the "manner in which this holding is applied."[48]

After a bit of back and forth, Justice White—who asked the most questions during the argument—asked Schonekas whether his position was that "whatever evidence there is in this record didn't amount to reckless disregard." Schonekas replied that it was. "In other words," Schonekas added, "St. Amant at worst could've been guilty of negligence, of not going further in doing something more."[49]

Schonekas explained that it was reasonable for St. Amant to rely on Albin in making the statements about Thompson, since Albin had been a union official and therefore presumptively knew the nature of the relationship between Thompson and Partin. In this way, he said, the situation "parallels the *Times* [*v. Sullivan*] case entirely." By this he meant that the *New York Times* had known the civil rights group that placed the advertisement at issue in that case and had not fact-checked the ad because the newspaper trusted the source. But it was Justice White who had to bring this point out explicitly.[50]

Schonekas went on to argue that *Sullivan* had set a very high bar for "actual malice." "You must practically come in and say, under the *Times-Sullivan* case, 'I hate you, I'm going to say it, I'm going to say it to hurt you and that's the only way it's malice,'" he explained to the justices. The only exception to this rule, he said in response to additional questioning from Justice White, was if the statement was in fact true: it was not enough, Schonekas said, that the speaker believed that it was true.[51]

Later on during Schonekas's argument, Justice Brennan stated the essential issue: "This really for us narrows down to the single question whether there was evidence upon which there could have been—a finding could be made that this was done with reckless disregard of whether it was true or false." Schonekas agreed, and after a bit more discussion with the justices rested his case.[52]

Robert L. Kleinpeter, who had represented Thompson since the case began, started his argument before the Supreme Court with a recitation of the facts, which he said had "been a little—I won't say misstated, but not properly stated" by Schonekas. His oration claimed that St. Amant's "scattershot" campaign speech had "defamed just all kinds of people," including Thompson.[53]

In a response to a question from Justice Marshall, Kleinpeter confirmed that Judge Blanche had used the *Sullivan* case in making his initial verdict and award for Thompson: "The trial judge had the *New York Times* decision completely in front of him, Your Honor. . . . And he mentioned it by name, yes sir."[54]

When asked by Justice Brennan if there was any issue for the Supreme Court to decide other than whether the evidence was sufficient to show "actual malice" by St. Amant, Kleinpeter said that the court should also decide whether Thompson was in fact a public official under *Sullivan* and the more recent cases that had defined the characteristics of public officials. And he had a proposal for a method for making this determination and the result: "My criteria, Sir, would be this: that if this man occupied a position that he is a public employee or public officer, and that his position was such that the public, as you said in *Rosenblatt* case, had such a particular interest. In other words, like in *Rosenblatt,* this man was in charge of running a resort and handed funds and things like this. Captain Thompson, true, was a public officer and the people had an interest in him as a sheriff, but not a particular interest above that they would have for all deputy sheriffs."[55]

After Kleinpeter agreed that Sheriff Clemmons, who was elected to his office, was clearly a public official under *Sullivan,* Justice Marshall asked how far beneath the sheriff himself would employees of the sheriff's office be considered public officials. "Mr. Justice Marshall," Kleinpeter replied, "I just have to tell you I don't know."[56]

But he explained that wherever in the office hierarchy this line fell, Thompson was beneath it: "This man occupied a position where he could not rebut anything that Mr. St. Amant said. Here's a man on statewide television taking out after Senator Long, and just incidentally defaming a few others. But here's a man who's a captain on the sheriff's force: How is he going to buy equal time? Would he be heard equally? Would his voice be as strong?"[57]

After reiterating his other points, Kleinpeter rested, and Schonekas said he saw no need for rebuttal. "I think Justice Brennan was very accurate," Schonekas added. "One simple problem, it's been decided previously, just applying to this case." "I see," replied Chief Justice Warren. "Case is adjourned."[58]

DELIBERATIONS AND RULING

After the Supreme Court hears argument in a case, the case seemingly disappears, only to reemerge with a written decision—along with any concurrences and dissents—anytime from several weeks to several months after the oral argument. But while the case disappears from public view, within the court the justices and their clerks are often involved in a convoluted process. Through this process they determine not only who should win a particular case but also why and how to explain that decision in a conclusive ruling that gives the rationale and sets a precedent that can be understood and applied in future cases.

The Justices Vote

After oral argument, the justices consider the case at their next conference meeting, usually held every Friday during the court's session. The justices considered the *St. Amant* case at their weekly meeting on Friday, April 5, the day after argument in the case. In accordance with custom, Chief Justice Earl Warren began the discussion, followed by the other justices in order of seniority. The justices' discussion is shrouded in secrecy: only the justices are present, without even their clerks there. But all nine justices at the meeting took notes that are now available among their papers in various archives. Collectively, these notes allow for a reconstruction of the meeting that is likely to be fairly accurate.

Chief Justice Warren began. He "seemed perturbed by St. Amant's conduct" and was initially reluctant to condone it. Warren also criticized Russell J. Schonekas, St. Amant's lawyer, saying that "he has not read the record." Justice Harlan spoke next and said that the issue in the appeal was not a question of evidence but that the trial judge had misconstrued the constitutional "actual malice" standard, a position consistent with the conclusion reached by Harlan's clerk in the bench memo. Justice Stewart, who was next, agreed that the trial court had applied the wrong test and noted that it is up to the plaintiff in a defamation case to prove reckless disregard.[59]

For Justice White, the only notation in Justice Warren's notes next to his name is "record," apparently meaning that White suggested that the court should summarily reverse in a per curiam opinion.[60]

According to his own handwritten notes, before argument Justice Fortas favored reversal of the Louisiana Supreme Court's ruling in *St. Amant*. His rationale for taking this action was likely the one outlined in his clerk's memorandum. This is reinforced by the notation "Affirm? Peter says otherwise" in Fortas's handwritten notes. But he changed his mind during or after the oral argument to favor either affirming the Louisiana Supreme Court's ruling, perhaps based on the rationale of his dissent in *Time, Inc. v. Hill*, or dismissing the case on the grounds that certiorari had been improvidently granted, a rare action that researchers have found is often to avoid particularly thorny legal issues.[61]

The Fortas notations also contain a short analysis of the case, in the form of two questions and answers and one comment which reveal the justice's thinking:

> 1. Is he [Thompson] a public official?—No
> 2. Was there malice?—Yes He [St. Amant] was not running against Thompson.[62]

After their discussion, the justices voted. According to Justice Douglas's notes, five of the justices—Justices Brennan, Harlan, Marshall, Stewart, and White—voted for reversal of the Louisiana Supreme Court's decision reinstating the award for Thompson. Justice Fortas immediately voted to affirm. Justices Black and Douglas have two marks next to each of their names, perhaps indicating that they changed their votes. But in the end, as indicated on both Douglas's and Warren's notations, eight justices voted to reverse in a full decision, while only Justice Fortas voted to affirm.

When the chief justice is in the majority, he has the prerogative to assign the task of writing the decision in the case. The following Monday, Warren assigned the task to Justice White. White got to work and circulated the first draft of his majority opinion to the other justices eleven days later, on April 19.

Several justices moved quickly to sign on to White's opinion, with Justices Brennan and Stewart agreeing to do so the same day as the draft was circulated and Justice Harlan and Chief Justice Warren doing so within a few days. Justice Marshall also agreed to join but appears to have disagreed with one sentence of the draft opinion. White changed the sentence in accordance with Marshall's wishes.[63]

Justice Black requested that he and Justice Douglas be noted as concurring with White's opinion "for the reasons set out in their concurrences in *New York Times Co. v. Sullivan* and *Garrison v. Louisiana*." In those concurrences Black and Douglas had explained their broad interpretation of the First Amendment as barring almost all restrictions or punishment for speech.[64]

Justice Fortas's copy of White's draft opinion contains notations in the margins, apparently written by Fortas clerk Peter L. Zimroth, disagreeing with White's rationale. These included comments that "there was anything to indicate to [petitioner] that Albin's statements were false"; thus he did not have to go further than submitting a sworn statement that the statements were true, which he had done, and that "perhaps it would be good to distinguish between the duty of a newspaper or magazine to investigate and the (lesser) duty of an individual like [petitioner]."[65]

White's second draft of the majority opinion, with stylistic changes from the first and the Black/Douglas concurrence language added, was circulated to the justices on April 24. None of the justices had any significant comments about the revised draft. The same day, Justice Fortas circulated a draft of his dissent. None of the justices commented on their copies of this opinion.

The revised majority opinion, and Fortas's dissent, became the final decisions in the case.

Majority and Concurrence

The final decision in *St. Amant v. Thompson*, with six justices joining with Justice White's majority opinion, was announced on April 29, 1968, just twenty-six days after the oral argument. Justices Black and Douglas concurred with the result, while Justice Fortas stood alone in dissent.

Despite the various issues addressed in the briefs and argument, Justice White's majority opinion distilled the case to a single issue at the very start of the decision: "The question presented by this case is whether the Louisiana Supreme Court, in sustaining a judgment for damages in a public official's defamation action, correctly interpreted and applied the rule of *New York Times Co. v. Sullivan*."[66]

The majority did not, for example, examine the question of whether Thompson was or was not a public official or if that issue was a matter of state or constitutional law. Instead, the court simply accepted the Louisiana courts' determination that Thompson was a public official, based on Louisiana state law, saying that the state courts' determination was adequate under *Rosenblatt v. Baer*.

The court also did not address St. Amant's argument that he could not be held liable for simply repeating a statement of Albin's expressing an opinion about Thompson.

In its recitation of the facts of the case, White's majority opinion incorrectly stated that "the case was tried prior to the decision in *New York Times Co. v. Sullivan.*" And the opinion glossed over Judge Blanche's reevaluation of the trial verdict in light of *Sullivan* while ruling on the motion for a new trial, stating that the trial court had found the *Sullivan* rule "no barrier to the judgment already entered."[67]

After reviewing the facts and the back-and-forth result of the case before the Louisiana appellate courts, White's majority opinion raced to its conclusion, simply declaring that "we cannot . . . agree with either the Supreme Court of Louisiana or the trial court that Thompson sustained [the] burden [of showing that St. Amant had acted with *Sullivan* 'actual malice']."[68]

The majority opinion then addressed the central question of the case and the concept for which the *St. Amant* case is most frequently cited: the definition of "reckless disregard," and whether St. Amant's behavior met the standard.

First, the majority acknowledged that "'reckless disregard,' . . . cannot be fully encompassed in one infallible definition. Inevitably its outer limits will be marked out through case-by-case adjudication." But White added, "Our cases, however, have furnished meaningful guidance for the further definition of a reckless publication," citing the majority opinions in *Sullivan* and *Garrison* and Justice Harlan's plurality opinion in *Curtis Publishing Co.*:[69] "These cases are clear that reckless conduct is not measured by whether a reasonably prudent man would have published, or would have investigated before publishing. There must be sufficient evidence to permit the conclusion that the defendant in fact entertained serious doubts as to the truth of his publication. Publishing with such doubts shows reckless disregard for truth or falsity and demonstrates actual malice."[70]

As media law scholar W. Wat Hopkins explains, this was a fundamental shift in the understanding of the *Sullivan* "actual malice" standard: "Actual malice, as applied in *Times v. Sullivan,* seemed to be an almost objective standard when compared to the emotionalism associated with the ill will rule of common law actual malice. . . . In *St. Amant,* however, the Court explained that actual malice was also a subjective test, emphasizing the importance of the publisher's state of mind—whether he entertained serious doubts as to the truth of the material."[71]

While this injected a subjectivity into the "actual malice" standard, "the publisher's state of mind could be established with objective evidence," Hopkins explains, as shown by the court's detailed description of St. Amant's preparation for the broadcast at issue in the case.[72]

In fact, White's opinion conceded, "It may be said that such a test puts a premium on ignorance, encourages the irresponsible publisher not to inquire, and permits the issue to be determined by the defendant's testimony that he published the statement in good faith and unaware of its probable falsity." But, he continued, "to insure the ascertainment and publication of the truth about public affairs, it is essential that the First Amendment protect some erroneous publications as well as true ones." The jury—or, in a bench trial, the judge—must assume responsibility, the majority said, for determining the veracity of such statements, including "whether the publication was indeed made in good faith."[73]

Thus if the plaintiff can show that the statement was not made in good faith, that would constitute serious doubt and thus "actual malice." As Hopkins explains, "The relevant issue in an actual malice case . . . is the publisher's state of mind toward the material he is publishing, rather than his attitude towards the subject of the publication." This is the difference between the ordinary legal concept of "malice" and the concept of "actual malice" as defined in *Sullivan:*[74] "*New York Times* and succeeding cases have emphasized that the stake of the people in public business and the conduct of public officials is so great that neither the defense of truth nor the standard of ordinary care would protect against self-censorship and thus adequately implement First Amendment policies."[75]

By finding that "St. Amant had broadcast false information about Thompson recklessly, though not knowingly," White said that the Louisiana Supreme Court had misapplied the "reckless disregard" element of the "actual malice" requirement. The Louisiana court's findings, he wrote, "fall short of proving St. Amant's reckless disregard for the accuracy of his statements about Thompson."[76]

After holding that neither Judge Blanche nor the Louisiana Supreme Court had applied the standard correctly, White's opinion applied what the majority said was the correct formulation of the standard to Thompson's claim against St. Amant. The conclusion was that there was no basis for the ruling that St. Amant had acted with "actual malice" in making the statement about Thompson: "By no proper test of reckless disregard was St. Amant's broadcast a reckless publication about a public officer. Nothing referred to by the Louisiana courts indicates an awareness by St. Amant of the probable falsity of Albin's statement about Thompson. Failure to investigate does not in itself establish bad faith."[77]

After citing several "other facts in this record [that] support our view," White's majority reversed and remanded the decision by the Louisiana Supreme Court, "because the state court misunderstood and misapplied the 'actual malice' standard which must be observed in a public official's defamation action."[78]

As they had requested, after reaching this result the majority opinion stated that Justices Black and Douglas "concur in the judgment of the Court for the reasons set out in their concurring opinions in *New York Times Co. v. Sullivan* and *Garrison v. Louisiana.*"[79]

Justice Fortas's Lone Dissent

Justice Fortas was alone in his dissent, which was based on his view that St. Amant had not "satisfied the minimal standards of care specified by *New York Times Co.* v. *Sullivan.*"[80]

While agreeing with the majority that Captain Thompson was a public official, Fortas argued that this did not mean that he could not be defamed: "The occupation of public officeholder does not forfeit one's membership in the human race. The public official should be subject to severe scrutiny and to free and open criticism. But if he is needlessly, heedlessly, falsely accused of crime, he should have a remedy in law. *New York Times* does not preclude this minimal standard of civilized living."[81]

Even though St. Amant made his statement in the midst of a political campaign, Fortas wrote, his "casual, careless, callous use of the libel cannot be rationalized as resulting from the heat of a campaign." And, he pointed out, Thompson "was not petitioner's adversary in the political contest."[82]

Thompson's public official status meant that the *Sullivan* "actual malice" standard applied, and Fortas concluded that St. Amant's accusation had been made with a level of recklessness that met this standard. "Under *New York Times,*" he wrote, "this libel was broadcast by petitioner with 'actual malice'—with reckless disregard of whether it was false or not. . . . Petitioner had a duty here to check the reliability of the libelous statement about respondent. If he had made a good-faith check, I would agree that he should be protected even if the statement were false, because the interest of public officials in their reputation must endure this degree of assault. But since he made no check, I agree with the Supreme Court of Louisiana that *New York Times* does not prohibit recovery."[83]

Such a holding, Fortas argued, was not contrary or offensive to the free speech provision of the First Amendment: "The First Amendment is not so fragile that it requires us to immunize this kind of reckless, destructive invasion of the life, even of public officials, heedless of their interests and sensitivities," he wrote. "The First Amendment is not a shelter for the character assassinator, whether his action is heedless and reckless or deliberate. The First Amendment does not require that we license shotgun attacks on public officials in virtually unlimited open season."[84]

Fortas had made a similar argument in his dissent in *Time, Inc. v. Hill,* in which he disagreed with the majority's imposition of the *Sullivan* "actual malice" requirement on a "false light" privacy claim:

> I fully agree with the views of my Brethren who have stressed the need for a generous construction of the First Amendment. I, too, believe that freedom of the press, of speech, assembly, and religion, and the freedom to petition are of the essence of our liberty, and fundamental to our values. . . . I agree with the statement of my Brother Brennan, speaking for the Court in *NAACP v. Button* that "[t]hese freedoms are delicate and vulnerable, as well as supremely precious in our society." But I do not believe that whatever is in words, however much of an aggression it may be upon individual rights, is beyond the reach of the law, no matter how heedless of others' rights—how remote from public purpose, how reckless, irresponsible, and untrue it may be. I do not believe that the First Amendment precludes effective protection of the right of privacy—or, for that matter, an effective law of libel. . . .
>
> The courts may not and must not permit either public or private action that censors or inhibits the press. But part of this responsibility is to preserve values and procedures which assure the ordinary citizen that the press is not above the reach of the law—that its special prerogatives, granted because of its special and vital functions, are reasonably equated with its needs in the performance of these functions. For this

> Court totally to immunize the press—whether forthrightly or by subtle indirection—in areas far beyond the needs of news, comment on public persons and events, discussion of public issues and the like would be no service to freedom of the press, but an invitation to public hostility to that freedom. This Court cannot and should not refuse to permit, under state law, the private citizen who is aggrieved by the type of assault which we have here, and which is not within the specially protected core of the First Amendment, to recover compensatory damages for recklessly inflicted invasion of his rights.[85]

But Fortas's opinion was the dissent in *St. Amant v. Thompson*, and the eight-justice majority reversed the award for Thompson and remanded the case to the Louisiana Supreme Court. The Louisiana Supreme Court received notice of the U.S. Supreme Court's ruling—a document known as a mandate—on May 28, 1968. And while there are no further available records in the case at the Louisiana Supreme Court, the Louisiana Court of Appeal, or the trial court, the trial verdict ordering St. Amant to pay $5,000 was presumably vacated, and Thompson was ordered to pay St. Amant $623 in court costs, as the U.S. Supreme Court ordered.

(8)

The Aftermath

There was little immediate response among legal scholars and observers to the U.S. Supreme Court's ruling in *St. Amant v. Thompson*. The decision was not even mentioned in the *Harvard Law Review*'s recap of the Supreme Court's 1967–68 term.

It was not until 1971 that scholar Clifton O. Lawhorne declared the importance of the ruling, only to pull back from this pronouncement several years later. Shortly after the decision, Congressman Lawrence G. Williams of Pennsylvania wrote a letter to each of the justices protesting the *St. Amant* ruling as a "disgraceful decision" that would "make every holder of elected public office fair game of any one who wants to slander and destroy the good name of a decent, respectable elective office holder" and would "have the effect of discouraging good men from running for public office." Justice Black wrote back, "I am confident . . . that it will not keep you from running next time."[1]

While the *St. Amant* case attracted little attention at first, within a few years it garnered more notice. But then the case was subsumed into the series of U.S. Supreme Court cases after *Sullivan* that explored and explained some of the intricacies of that ruling, including the applicability and definition of "public figure" and "actual malice."

THE PARTICIPANTS

After the mandate was issued and the damages and attorney fees paid, the participants in the case moved on.

After the trial, Herman Thompson continued in his position with the East Baton Rouge Parish Sheriff's Office. He played a bit role in the investigation of the assassination of Martin Luther King Jr. when King's killer, James Earl Ray, claimed that he had been given Thompson's phone number by an alleged co-conspirator in the assassination named Raoul, who had told him that Ray should call the number to arrange their next meeting. Ray claimed that he had called the number while passing through Baton Rouge in 1967, but no one had answered. Thompson was interviewed by and submitted a deposition to the House Select Committee on Assassinations, which rejected Ray's claims, concluding that "Ray's allegation was merely an attempt to gain credence for his Raoul story and to raise an implication of official complicity in the assassination."[2]

Thompson left the sheriff's office in 1971 after twenty-six years, later claiming that he was dismissed for political reasons when J. Al Amiss replaced Clemmons as sheriff in 1972. Thompson himself ran for sheriff in 1975 but withdrew from the crowded race after two months. After leaving the sheriff's office, Thompson worked as manager of safety and security with H. E. Wiese, Inc., an industrial construction company.

In 1971, Thompson was elected to the board of the Baton Rouge Kids' Baseball Clinic, the same organization to which the money from Partin that was at issue in St. Amant's political address and the resulting libel case was supposedly donated.

Thompson's attorney, Robert L. Kleinpeter, maintained his law practice until 2007 and died in 2013.

After losing the 1962 primary to Long, St. Amant vowed that he would "continue to fight for a government of law for free men who believe in free enterprise." So he established the Louisiana Governmental Association "to stimulate interest in Constitutional government."[3]

Two years later, in 1964, St. Amant ran for a seat in the U.S. House of Representatives but came in last among ten candidates. He was, however, elected to the Democratic State Central Committee. While he held the party position, St. Amant broke with the mainstream of the party when he supported the 1964 and 1968 presidential candidacies of Alabama governor George Wallace and became involved with Wallace's American Independent Party. He lost in a 1967 congressional primary and in a run for state representative in 1971.

St. Amant's political philosophy was perhaps best summed up in his comment after losing the primary to Long. He said, "I accept my obligation to the more than 100,000 voters who indicated their belief in the kind of America I would build, and will continue to fight for a government of law for free men who believe in free enterprise."[4]

Judge Fred A. Blanche Jr., who presided over the trial in *Thompson v. St. Amant*, served as a Louisiana district court judge until 1969, when he became a judge of the Louisiana First Circuit Court of Appeal.

As an appellate judge, Judge Blanche was involved in a number of defamation cases. In *State v. Time* (1971), he wrote a majority opinion affirming a trial court's dismissal of a libel suit filed by the state of Louisiana against *Life* magazine on the grounds that the state does not have a personal reputation that can be defamed.

In *Snowden v. Pearl River Broadcasting Corp.* (1972), the court majority upheld a verdict against a radio station that broadcast accusations by an anonymous caller who identified the plaintiffs as drug dealers and users. The majority held that the station's practice of putting anonymous callers on the air live, without any vetting or delay before broadcast, constituted "reckless disregard" and thus "actual malice": "Appellant [radio station] placed itself in a position fraught with the imminent danger of broadcasting anonymous unverified, slanderous remarks based on sheer rumor, speculation and hearsay, and just such a result actually occurred. Such an eventuality was easily foreseeable and likely to occur, as it in fact did. In our judgment, the First Amendment does not protect a publisher against such utter recklessness."[5]

But while Judge Blanche concurred with the majority's result, he wrote a separate concurring opinion in which he argued that *Sullivan* and its progeny, including the U.S. Supreme Court's standard for "reckless disregard" in *St. Amant*, did not apply to the case at all:

> The radio station picked out the subject which they believed to be a matter of public or general interest and invited private citizens to comment thereon. Thereafter, one private citizen took the opportunity to defame other private citizens while on the discussion of a topic of general public interest, i.e., narcotics abuse. Granted that the general subject of narcotics abuse is a matter of great public or general interest, how does it serve freedom of speech or freedom of discussion on such subject matter for one private citizen to accuse falsely another of being involved therein? In my opinion, the protection of one's right to speak freely on public issues is not involved in such cases, and the protection afforded by the First Amendment is inapplicable.[6]

While the use and sale of narcotics is clearly an issue of public interest, Blanche wrote, "[the plaintiffs'] individual involvement therein was not a matter of public or general interest until after the call." Because their alleged individual involvement was not a public issue, he concluded, *Sullivan* and its progeny should not apply; nevertheless, the award to the plaintiffs could be upheld on the basis of state law.[7]

The same argument could have been made in the *St. Amant* case, since Herman Thompson's receipt of funds was arguably not a matter of public concern until St. Amant repeated J. D. Albin's allegation that the funds were not just charitable donations.

In *Batson v. Time, Inc.* (1974), Blanche was a member of a panel that reversed the trial court's grant of summary judgment to a state official in his lawsuit against *Life* magazine over an article that connected him with Louisiana mob boss Carlos Marcello.

Ten years after joining the appeals court, in 1979, Blanche became an associate justice of the Louisiana Supreme Court. The court decided only three defamation cases during his tenure, and he did not write opinions in any of these cases. Blanche remained on the Louisiana Supreme Court until his retirement in 1986. He died in 1997.

J. D. Albin, whose affidavit made the accusations about Thompson that St. Amant read on the air, remained with Teamsters Local 270 in New Orleans until his retirement. He died in 2006.

SULLIVAN'S PROGENY

As the players moved on, so did the law. The reversal in fortune for Herman Thompson in his libel suit was the result of his getting caught up in major changes in defamation law that had begun with *Sullivan* and continued with the ruling in *St. Amant* and beyond. The conclusion that the *St. Amant* decision was intended as a vehicle for continuing the change in defamation law that had begun in *Sullivan* is explained by Clifton O. Lawhorne, who observed that the broad observations and guidelines for defamation claims by public officials in the U.S. Supreme Court's majority opinion in *St. Amant* "were not necessary to the determination of the case at issue. They were needed only to clarify the evolving law as it pertained to libeling public officials."[8]

The court took a short pause in pushing along this evolution after *St. Amant*, with Lawhorne noting in 1971 that "since the ruling in the *St. Amant* case, the Supreme Court has been very selective in the [defamation] cases it accepts for review."[9]

But this process soon resumed and continued through the 1980s. In the years following its decision in *Sullivan*, the court filled in several of the details of the application and nuances of the "actual malice" standard announced in that case—a line of cases and decisions that is universally referred to as "*Sullivan*'s progeny."[10]

As Anthony Lewis explained in his epic history of the *Sullivan* case, "With the decision in *New York Times v. Sullivan*, a sea change began in the law of the First Amendment. The Supreme Court increasingly gave the amendment's bold words their full meaning. . . . Then, in the years following the *Sullivan* decision, the Court resoundingly vindicated the promise of the First Amendment that in the United States there shall be 'no law . . . abridging the freedom of speech, or of the press.'"[11]

Only a few months after announcing its decision in *Sullivan*, the court extended the "actual malice" requirement to criminal defamation cases in *Garrison v. Louisiana*. In 1963, prior to the U.S. Supreme Court's decision in *Sullivan*, the Louisiana Supreme Court upheld the criminal libel conviction of New Orleans district attorney Jim Garrison for statements made about local judges in the midst of a political dispute, holding that the state's criminal law was valid under the First Amendment. The Louisiana Supreme Court discussed "actual malice" as a requirement for a criminal libel defendant to assert a qualified privilege, but to that court the term "actual malice" meant "personal ill will," not the meaning that the U.S. Supreme Court would later imbue the term with in *New York Times v. Sullivan*.

The U.S. Supreme Court agreed to review the case, and then first heard the case six weeks after announcing its decision in *Sullivan*. After holding over the case for reargument the following term, seven months later it reversed the Louisiana Supreme Court's ruling, holding that the *Sullivan* "actual malice" requirement must be met in criminal libel cases involving statements about public officials. "We must decide whether, in view of the differing history and purposes of criminal libel, the *New York Times* rule also limits state power to impose criminal sanctions for criticism of the official conduct of public officials," the court's opinion in *Garrison* stated. "We hold that it does."[12]

After establishing "actual malice" as the applicable constitutional standard for both civil and criminal libel involving public officials, the court then turned to the types of plaintiffs to whom the new standard applied. This was one of the unanswered questions that arose in the wake of *Sullivan:* Who qualifies as a public official whose actions the court declared to be subject to public scrutiny and debate, with that scrutiny and debate receiving heightened protection under the First and Fourteenth Amendments from liability for defamation? In two 1967 cases and a 1971 case, the court extended the "actual malice" requirement to another category of plaintiffs, public figures, which included a prominent college football coach, a retired high-level military official, and a candidate for public office.[13]

In *Rosenblatt v. Baer,* a 1966 case in which the plaintiff was the supervisor of a country recreational facility, the court crafted a test for determining whether a lower-level government official is subject to the "actual malice" requirement. The question, the court said, is whether "a position in government has such apparent importance that the public has an independent interest in the qualifications and performance of the person who holds it, beyond the general public interest in the qualifications and performance of all government employees."[14]

Robert L. Kleinpeter, Thompson's lawyer, used *Rosenblatt* in his oral argument before the U.S. Supreme Court in *St. Amant v. Thompson* to argue that as a deputy sheriff Thompson was not a public official and thus did not have to prove that St. Amant had acted with "actual malice" in order to win his defamation claim. The court majority apparently acknowledged this argument in a footnote in its ruling, in observing that the Louisiana Supreme Court had cited and followed *Rosenblatt* in holding that Thompson was a public official who had substantial responsibility for or control over the conduct of public affairs.

The next series of cases that the court considered involved the meaning of "actual malice." In 1967 a six-justice, per curiam opinion reversed a jury libel verdict for a court clerk, saying that "it cannot be said on this record that any failure of petitioner to make a prior investigation constituted proof sufficient to present a jury question whether the statements were published with reckless disregard of whether they were false or not."[15]

The court then further refined the meaning of the term the following year in its decision in *St. Amant.*

All of these decisions were part of a larger, tectonic shift in understanding of the First Amendment. By one count, during its sixteen years under Chief Justice Earl Warren, the court considered 128 cases involving free speech rights. Case by case, the court developed a new jurisprudence of free speech, with broader protections for expression and more limitations on restrictions of speech. These decisions also shifted the focus in defamation cases away from the truth or falsity of the statement at issue to the defendants' state of mind when the statement was made. This shift, and the litigation costs it engendered, led to calls for reform of defamation law in the 1980s and '90s.[16]

ST. AMANT AS *SULLIVAN'S* PROGENY

The U.S. Supreme Court's ruling in the *St. Amant* case was the next step in defining the *Sullivan* "actual malice" standard: "*St. Amant* provided the justices with their first real opportunity to attempt to clear up some of the confusion resulting from the multiple opinions in *Butts* and [its companion case] *Walker* and to shed some light on the meaning of the actual malice standard they had created in *Sullivan*."[17]

As we have seen, the court held in *St. Amant* that a defamation plaintiff must show "sufficient evidence to permit the conclusion that the defendant in fact entertained serious doubts as to the truth of his publication" and made the false, defamatory statement anyway. In doing so, the court set a very high bar for claims to survive the "actual malice" and "reckless disregard" requirements, so high that these standards have been criticized, even by some of the justices themselves, as unrealistic standards that cannot be met except in the most egregious cases.[18]

In 1971, three years after the Supreme Court's *St. Amant v. Thompson* decision, Clifton O. Lawhorne called it "the most important of the recent Supreme Court libel decisions." But a decade later, Lawhorne had a diminished view of the case, pointing out that many of the court's declarations in the *St. Amant* decision "were needed only to clarify the changing law as it pertained to libeling public officials." Still, First Amendment scholar Rodney A. Smolla calls the case "by far the most important Supreme Court explication of the 'actual malice' standard."[19]

The *St. Amant* decision was only one step in filling out the details left uncertain in the wake of *Sullivan*. In addition, the *St. Amant* ruling itself raised several issues that the courts had to resolve in future cases. As Lawhorne wrote in 1981, "The Supreme Court was not offering its restatement of the law [in *St. Amant*] as the final word on its public-official rule of libel. It had only defined that rule as it existed by mid-1968. Further development of the law on a case-by-case basis was predicted."[20]

SULLIVAN'S PROGENY AFTER *ST. AMANT*

Lawhorne's prediction of "further development of the law on a case-by-case basis" after *St. Amant* came to pass, with the Supreme Court addressing several of the issues left unresolved after the *St. Amant* ruling in subsequent decisions over the next several years.

One of the legal issues remaining after the *Sullivan* and *St. Amant* decisions was what evidence would be sufficient to show that a defamation defendant had acted with reckless disregard for the truth in making a statement. The court left this question unresolved in *Cantrell v. Forest City Publishing Co.*, a 1974 decision, even though it held that the standard had been met by the plaintiff in that case.[21] But the court began defining the scope of such evidence in its 1979 ruling in *Herbert v. Lando,* holding that since "*New York Times* and its progeny made it essential to proving liability that the plaintiff focus on the conduct and state of mind of the defendant, the thoughts and editorial processes of the alleged defamer would be open to examination."[22]

The court reinforced this five years later, reversing the libel award in *Bose v. Consumers Union* on the grounds that the plaintiff company had not shown "actual malice," since "the District Court did not identify any independent evidence that [the defendant author] realized the inaccuracy of the statement, or entertained serious doubts about its truthfulness, at the time of publication." In *Harte-Hanks Communications Inc. v. Connaughton* (1986) the court upheld an appellate court's finding of reckless disregard when a newspaper intentionally ignored information that called into question the accusations that the newspaper's source made about a court official. "Although failure to investigate will not alone support a finding of actual malice," the majority wrote in *Harte-Hanks,* "the purposeful avoidance of the truth is in a different category."[23]

Unlike the court's civil rights decisions, which encountered ferocious resistance by the public, government officials, and even courts in many areas of the country, trial and appellate courts generally endeavored to apply the U.S. Supreme Court's rulings on defamation law. But many of these rulings show confusion about what, exactly, constitutes "reckless disregard." The meaning of the term has been labeled as "somewhat subjective," with the degree of recklessness required rising along with the seriousness of the charge in the defamatory publication. Attempting to define the term, legal scholar Willard H. Pedrick concluded, "is to attempt the impossible." This does not mean that attempts have not been made. W. Wat Hopkins, for example, concludes that "the rule seems to be that the investigation must be extensive enough to support a publisher's belief in the truth of the material published."[24]

Lower courts applying this standard have held that mistakes, language giving a false impression that was not purposely chosen to do so, and errors based on reporters' misunderstandings do not meet the *St. Amant* standard. Even statements that were poorly chosen or timed or were made with ill will or spite, or in anger, do meet the standard.

The difficulty in defining "reckless disregard" after *St. Amant* also had the practical effect of leading to high litigation costs. These costs were particularly high for media defendants, especially when pretrial proceedings and post-trial appeals are considered. In addition, trial verdicts in several high-profile cases led many journalists and First Amendment attorneys to claim that defamation suits had become "a giant lottery system" in which "libel plaintiffs rarely win, but the successful ones often hit a jackpot of huge damages," and defendants face huge expenses for attorneys. This led to proposals for reform of defamation law, most prominently the "Annenberg Proposal" for "the creation of a no-fault, no-damages declaratory judgment proceeding for libel disputes" as an alternative to litigation, similar to proposals that had been advocated by the Hutchins Commission twenty years earlier. But neither the Annenberg Proposal nor other proposed reforms to lessen the burden on defamation defendants have ever been enacted into law.[25]

Another unresolved issue after *St. Amant* was how far down into government bureaucracy the concept of a "public official" went. In *Rosenblatt v. Baer*, the court rejected the use of state definitions of public officials for this determination, explaining that "states have developed definitions of 'public official' for local administrative purposes, not the purposes of a nation constitutional protection." So the court set its own threshold, based on whether a government employee has "substantial responsibility for or control over the conduct of governmental affairs."[26]

In *St. Amant* the court accepted the Louisiana Supreme Court's determination that Thompson was a public official under this definition but did not further explain or refine the *Rosenblatt* test. And it has not done so since. So lower courts have resorted to their own judgment of what types of public employees meet the definition of "public official," with inconsistent results. As commentator Kate M. Adams observed:

> Lower court applications of the *New York Times* conditional privilege are inconsistent from state to state and often inconsistent with the Supreme Court's mandate, because, in part, *New York Times* and its progeny have not provided clear guidance in defining these public plaintiffs. As a result, courts generally resort to a reexamination of the principles underlying the decision in *New York Times.*
>
> Unfortunately, lower courts do not evince consistent application of the principles either. Courts repeat the now familiar statements of *New York Times* in a myriad of combinations to lend support to whatever decision they reach—whether increasing constitutional protections of speech or preserving the state's power and laws of redress for reputational injury.[27]

In *St. Amant,* of course, all the courts that considered the case concluded or accepted that Herman Thompson was a public official. This is consistent with how other courts have ruled regarding police officers, with "law enforcement officers at virtually every level" being held to be public officials. As media attorney Bruce W. Sanford observes, "The courts have been fairly consistent in treating law enforcement officers as public officials . . . because law enforcement officials wield extensive authority," including the power of arrest.[28]

One federal appeals court saw another flaw with *St. Amant.* In *Edwards v. National Audubon Society* (1977), the federal Second Circuit Court of Appeal observed that the Supreme Court's ruling in *St. Amant,* which held that a reporter may entertain "serious doubts" yet still not act with "reckless disregard," conflicts with the "neutral reportage" privilege, which provides that a report of an accusation by one public figure against another public figure cannot be defamatory as long as the accuser is a responsible, prominent organization or individual; the charge is serious and on a matter of public interest; and the charge is reported accurately and disinterestedly. This was because the privilege has been held to apply even though the reporter entertains "serious doubts" about the veracity of the statement(s). This conflict has led some courts to reject the privilege.

Yet another issue left unresolved by *St. Amant* was whether the "reckless disregard" standard applied to other types of plaintiffs besides public officials. The year before *St. Amant,* the court had already applied the "actual malice" standard to a well-known football coach in *Curtis Publishing Co. v. Butts* and to a former general who became involved in the civil rights debate in its companion case, *Associated Press v. Walker:* "We consider and would hold that a 'public figure' who is not a public official may also recover damages for a defamatory falsehood whose substance makes substantial danger to reputation apparent, on a showing of highly unreasonable conduct constituting an extreme departure from the standards of investigation and reporting ordinarily adhered to by responsible publishers."[29]

In *Greenbelt Cooperative Publishing Association v. Bresler* (1970), the court held that this standard was applicable to a real estate developer involved in a public controversy over the rezoning of his land; he was also a state legislator from an adjacent district. In *Rosenbloom v. Metromedia, Inc.* (1971), a plurality of the court expanded the "actual malice" requirement to all matters of public concern, regardless of the nature of the plaintiff, but the court pulled back on application of the "actual malice" rule to plaintiffs not in the public eye only three years later in *Gertz v. Robert Welch, Inc.*

The plaintiff in *Gertz* was an attorney who represented the family of a man killed by a Chicago police officer in a civil suit against the officer. While the case received wide publicity, and Gertz had been active in civic and charitable activities, the Supreme Court held that the attorney was a private figure, not a public figure. The court also redefined the standard applicable to private figures, pulling back from the plurality opinion in *Rosenbloom:* "So long as they do not impose liability without fault, the States may define for themselves the appropriate standard of liability for a publisher or broadcaster of defamatory falsehood injurious to a private individual."[30]

The court concluded that this ruling "allows the States to impose liability on the publisher or broadcaster of defamatory falsehood on a less demanding showing than that required by *New York Times* [*v. Sullivan*]" in cases involving plaintiffs who do not meet the criteria to be declared public officials or public figures.[31]

In later cases, the court held that not only the nature of the plaintiff, but also the nature of the issue involved, and of the defendant, determine parties' required evidence and burden of proof in a defamation case.[32] The end result is that plaintiffs who are public officials or public officials suing over a matter of public concern must show that the statement at issue was false and must also show "actual malice" by clear and convincing evidence in order to receive any damages in a defamation case. In most such cases, the plaintiff must show actual damages as a result of the statement. If a public official or public figure is suing for defamation over a matter that is not a public concern (a private concern), the same falsity and "actual malice" requirements apply, but damages may be presumed and may serve as the basis for awarding compensatory damages. But a public official or public figure suing over a matter of private concern must prove "actual malice" in order to receive punitive damages, which are damages meant to punish the defendant rather than simply compensate the injured plaintiff.

State law has more sway when private figures sue for defamation. When a private figure sues over a matter of public concern, that plaintiff must prove falsity and must prove "actual malice" in order to recover punitive damages. But the state sets the standard of fault that the plaintiff must prove in order to receive compensatory damages. That standard must require at least negligence, and thus cannot be based on strict liability. Actual damage must be shown in order for such a plaintiff to receive compensatory damages, but a punitive damage award requires that the plaintiff show "actual malice." The same standards apply when a private figure sues over a matter of private concern, except that in such cases the defendant must prove the truth of the statement rather than the plaintiff having to prove that the statement is false. This last point is a remnant of British defamation law that was inherited by the American colonies but now is limited only to defamation suits by private figures suing over a matter of private concern.[33]

In short, the requirement for *Sullivan* "actual malice" applies in many types of defamation cases, in order for the plaintiffs to recover some or any form of damages, depending on the specifics.

ST. AMANT AS A PRECEDENT

U.S. Supreme Court

The U.S. Supreme Court cited *St. Amant* in nineteen cases from 1968 through 2017, with the most recent citation in 1991. In nine of these cases, 47.4 percent, *St. Amant* was cited for the definition of "reckless disregard." It was cited for the "actual malice" requirement in eight cases, 42.1 percent. The other legal principles in *St. Amant* were each cited in just one of the Supreme Court's opinions.

The first U.S. Supreme Court decision after *St. Amant* to cite the case was

Pickering v. Board of Education. Pickering was actually argued on March 27, 1968—eight days before the *St. Amant* argument on April 4, 1968—but the decision in *Pickering* was not released until June 3, 1968, five weeks after the *St. Amant* decision was released. *Pickering* cited *St. Amant*, along with *Sullivan*, as support for the rule that "a State cannot authorize the recovery of damages by a public official for defamatory statements directed at him except when such statements are shown to have been made either with knowledge of their falsity or with reckless disregard for their truth or falsity." This principle was cited as evidence of the First Amendment's strong support for speech on matters of public importance, in a decision reversing the Illinois Supreme Court's approval of the firing of a teacher after he wrote a letter to the editor, "absent proof of false statements knowingly or recklessly made by him."[34]

Justice Marshall wrote the opinion for the six-member majority in *Pickering*. Justices Douglas and Black concurred because of their expansive view of the First Amendment. Justice White dissented on the grounds that the case should be remanded for a determination of whether there actually were knowingly or recklessly false statements.

The Supreme Court's next citations of *St. Amant* were not until 1971, when it was cited in five cases.

Three of the decisions were released on the same day, February 24, 1971. In *Time, Inc. v. Pape*, the six-justice majority reversed the appeals court's ruling that the omission of the word "alleged" in a magazine story citing a government report of police brutality was not "actual malice." In doing so, the court quoted the *St. Amant* decision's discussion of the standards for determining whether a defamation defendant had acted with reckless disregard.[35]

In *Monitor Patriot Co. v. Roy*, the court quoted *St. Amant* in discussing the difficulty of discerning reckless disregard: "The mental element of 'knowing or reckless disregard' required under the *New York Times* test, for example, is not always easy of ascertainment. 'Inevitably its outer limits will be marked out through case-by-case adjudication, as is true with so many legal standards for judging concrete cases, whether the standard is provided by the Constitution, statutes, or case law.'"[36]

Despite this difficulty, the court held in *Monitor Patriot* that the *Sullivan* "actual malice" standard applies to candidates for public office.

In the third decision released on February 24, *Ocala Star-Banner Co. v. Damron*, Justice Stewart's majority opinion reversed damages against a newspaper that confused a mayor and the mayor's brother when the latter was arrested on perjury charges. Even though the report was erroneous, the majority said that it involved an important public issue—the mayor's fitness for office—so the mayor had to show "actual malice" in his lawsuit against the newspaper. *St. Amant* was cited in Justice White's short concurrence for the principle "that innocent falsehoods are sometimes protected [in a particular case] only to ensure access to the truth [more broadly]."[37]

The next U.S. Supreme Court case to cite *St. Amant* in 1971 was *Rosenbloom v. Metromedia,* in which the court applied the "actual malice" standard to a man who was acquitted of obscenity charges and then sued a radio station over its report on his arrest, because the plaintiff's arrest was a matter of public interest. *St. Amant* was cited in a footnote to the plurality opinion that listed the several rulings on the application of "actual malice" that the court had made since *Sullivan.*[38]

The final citation to *St. Amant* in 1971 was in a footnote to an opinion dissenting to a denial of certiorari in *Dun & Bradstreet, Inc. v. Grove.* The Third Circuit Court of Appeal had reinstated a jury defamation verdict against Dun & Bradstreet for an erroneous credit report on the plaintiff company, holding that "the doctrine of *New York Times v. Sullivan* does not extend to private subscription credit reports." The U.S. Supreme Court denied certiorari on October 19, 1971. But Justice Douglas dissented, based on his expansive interpretation of the First Amendment, and cited *St. Amant* and several other cases in a footnote showing that the court had frequently substituted a jury's judgment with its own in First Amendment cases.[39]

As to the question of application of the "actual malice" standard to defamation claims for erroneous credit reports, the court later resolved that issue in *Dun & Bradstreet, Inc. v. Greenmoss Builders, Inc.* (1985).

The next U.S. Supreme Court case to cite *St. Amant* was the major *Gertz* precedent in 1974, which drew the boundaries for application of the "actual malice" standard, holding that it did not apply to private figures not involved in matters of public concern. The *St. Amant* case was cited in a footnote discussing the meaning of "actual malice" and listing the court rulings since *Sullivan* focusing on the issue.

In the next U.S. Supreme Court case to cite *St. Amant*, the plurality in *Time, Inc. v. Firestone* held in 1976 that "actual malice" did not apply to a private figure in a matter of private concern—an heiress's divorce, in this case. But the court added that the First Amendment still required that the defendant have acted with some level of fault in such cases. In a dissent, Justice Brennan quoted *St. Amant* for the principle that "to insure the ascertainment and publication of the truth about public affairs, it is essential that the First Amendment protect some erroneous publications as well as true ones," and cited it in a footnote describing the "actual malice" standard.[40]

The next set of Supreme Court decisions citing *St. Amant* was a group of three cases in 1979. In *Herbert v. Lando*, the majority rejected the argument that the First Amendment barred investigation into a newspaper's editorial processes in order for a defamation plaintiff to establish "actual malice." Both the majority and Justice Stewart's dissent in *Herbert* cited *St. Amant* for its definition of reckless disregard. Justice Brennan's partial dissent also cited the case, for the principle that false information has no intrinsic First Amendment worth.

The court issued two decisions that cited St. Amant on June 26, 1979. In *Wolston v. Reader's Digest Association*, the court held that a plaintiff who was once a public figure for his involvement in an issue of public concern does not retain that status after leaving the limelight. In *Hutchinson v. Proxmire*, the court held that a U.S. senator was not immune from a defamation claim under the constitution's speech and debate clause for statements made at a press conference in his office. *Wolston* cited *St. Amant* for the "actual malice" principle. In *Hutchinson*, the *St. Amant* ruling was included in a list of cases decided since *Sullivan* that refined the "actual malice" standard: in other words, a listing of *Sullivan*'s progeny to that date.

In 1982, the court denied certiorari in *Lawrence v. Bauer Publishing & Printing*, a libel case in which the New Jersey Supreme Court reversed a plaintiffs' verdict on the grounds that it was required to undertake its own independent review of the facts of the case rather than relying on the jury's conclusions. Dissenting from the certiorari denial, Justice William H. Rehnquist cited *St. Amant*'s statement that "the finder of fact must determine whether the publication was indeed made in good faith" in support of the importance of respecting the jury's findings.[41]

The court addressed this issue squarely two years later in *Bose Corp. v. Consumers Union*, with the five-member majority holding that the appellate courts should indeed undertake such an independent review in First Amendment cases. *St. Amant* was cited to support this holding, as well as for its definition of "reckless disregard" and application of the "actual malice" standard to suits brought by public officials.

In 1985, the court denied certiorari in *Lorain Journal Co. v. Milkovich* on the issue of whether a high school wrestling coach was a public or private figure, after previously denying certiorari in the same case when presented with the question of whether there was adequate evidence of "actual malice." Justice Brennan dissented from the 1985 certiorari denial, joined by Justice Marshall, citing *St. Amant* in support of the idea that the First Amendment gives "breathing space" for speech, including even some falsehoods. The court finally granted certiorari in the case five years later when presented with the issue of the distinction between statements of opinion and statements of fact. On this question, the court decided that statements of opinion that implied facts could indeed be the basis of a defamation claim.

In *Philadelphia Newspapers v. Hepps* (1986), a five-justice majority of the court held that the First Amendment required that private-figure plaintiffs in defamation cases be required to prove that the statement at issue was false, rejecting the final vestige of the common law rule that falsity could be presumed. In his dissent from this ruling, Justice John Paul Stevens cited *St. Amant* for its definition of reckless disregard.

The court's denial of certiorari in a second case in 1986 gave Chief Justice Warren Burger and Justice Rehnquist the opportunity to question the result in *St. Amant*, as well as the entire defamation regime that began with *Sullivan*. The court denied certiorari in *Coughlin v. Westinghouse Broadcasting & Cable, Inc.*, a case in which a television investigative reporter was sued for libel for alleging that a police officer had accepted a bribe to overlook illegal operation of a bar after hours. The federal trial court had dismissed the case, citing *St. Amant* in finding that the defendant reporter had not acted with reckless disregard: "A jury could find that [the officer's] actions were due to inexperience, not corruption. An issue also exists as to whether the [defendant television station's reporters], with a minimum of effort, could have discovered the truth. The Supreme Court's mandate, however, is clear: 'Reckless conduct is not measured by whether a reasonably prudent man would have published, or would have investigated before publishing.'"[42]

The Third Circuit Court of Appeal affirmed the dismissal, and the plaintiffs sought certiorari. The U.S. Supreme Court denied review, meaning that the "rule of four" justices voting to review the case was not met. Chief Justice Burger wrote an opinion dissenting from the certiorari denial, which Justice

Rehnquist joined. *Sullivan* "should be re-examined," Burger wrote. He then quoted the circuit court's reference to the "mandate" that it saw in *St. Amant* and argued that the Supreme Court should have granted review of this case "to determine whether the Court's 'mandate' remains an appropriate one."[43]

In 1989, the majority opinion in *Harte-Hanks Communications Inc. v. Connaughton* cited *St. Amant* several times for its discussion of what constitutes reckless disregard. This included the principle that led the court to affirm the verdict for the plaintiff: that while it had held in *St. Amant* that "failure to investigate will not alone support a finding of 'actual malice,' the purposeful avoidance of the truth is in a different category." In *Harte-Hanks* the court held that even egregious departures from journalistic standards did not constitute recklessness sufficient for a finding of "actual malice," but it ultimately held that the evidence in this particular case supported the jury's finding that the defendant newspaper had acted with reckless disregard for the truth.[44]

The most recent U.S. Supreme Court decision to cite *St. Amant* was *Masson v. New Yorker Magazine* in 1991. In the course of deciding that a writer's alleged alteration of a source's quotes could be the basis of a defamation suit, Justice Anthony Kennedy's majority cited the *St. Amant* case in support of the statement that "mere negligence does not suffice" for a determination that a defamation defendant acted with "actual malice."[45]

While the U.S. Supreme Court has not cited *St. Amant* since 1991, the definition of "reckless disregard" that the court announced in the case remains an integral part of modern American defamation law.

Lower Courts

As the Supreme Court expanded and refined the application of the principles announced in *St. Amant*, so did the lower courts. The case has been cited by federal and state trial and appellate courts 1,657 times, with the largest number of citations occurring in the 1980s (figure 1).[46]

While it would be expected that *St. Amant* would be cited most often in the first years after the decision, it was actually cited more often in later years. From the date of the decision on April 29, 1968, through the end of 1978—a period of ten years and eight months—*St. Amant* was cited by 269 decisions: an average (mean) of 24.5 cases a year, with a median of 25 cases. But in the decision's second decade, from 1979 through 1988, *St. Amant* was cited in 444 rulings, an annual mean of 44.4 cases and a median of 46. The number of cita-

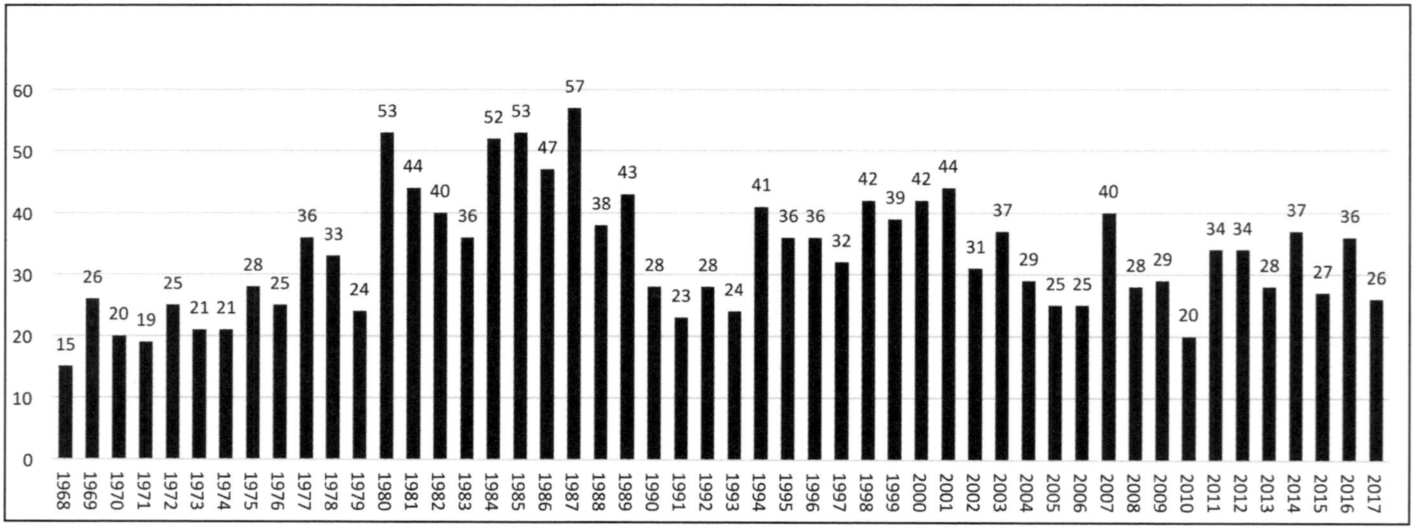

FIGURE 1. Number of federal and state trial and appellate court decisions citing *St. Amant v. Thompson*, by year

tions dropped to 333 in *St. Amant*'s third decade (1989 through 1998), a mean of 33.3 and median of 34. It was cited 340 times from 1999 through 2008, with the yearly mean and median both 34. In the latest period of data, from 2009 through 2017, *St. Amant* was cited 271 times, a mean of 30.1 a year and median of 29.

The spike in citations to *St. Amant* from 1979 through 1988 may be due to a trend of increasingly expensive defamation verdicts against major media outlets during that ten-year period. Because of these larger verdicts, "by the 1980s," Richard T. Kaplar and Patrick D. Maines complained, "it was clear that libel law was in disarray." These large trial awards were seen as a major threat. "Of the many troubling issues facing journalists in the 1980s," scholar Richard E. Labunski wrote in 1987, "none is more complicated and potentially damaging to their First Amendment rights than libel."[47] First Amendment attorney Bruce Sanford examined the reasons behind the large defamation awards in the 1980s:

> Time and again in the early 1980s, jury verdicts against the press seemed to be based not on a reasoned application of the constitutional requirements of proof but rather on an evaluation of whether a publisher or broadcaster had been "fair" to the libel plaintiff. . . . In the worst incidents, falsity was presumed, public figure determinations were thrown to a hopelessly confused jury, or the actual malice test was converted from a subjective inquiry as to whether the defendant in fact entertained doubts about truth prior to publication into a test of whether a reasonable man should have entertained such doubts. It was not uncommon to hear the lament from the press that the *New York Times* doctrine was not understood by juries and that it did not, in practice, give the press the protection from passion and prejudice in jury boxes that it was designed to provide.[48]

The U.S. Supreme Court's ruling in *St. Amant* is an example of this transformation of the "actual malice" test from a particularized, fact-specific determination of whether the real speaker in the case actually had doubts about a statement to a test based on whether a "reasonable man" in the speaker's position would have such doubts. This made it easier for plaintiffs to win defamation cases, since the essential issue was not whether the speaker *actually* had doubts about the accuracy of a statement but instead whether a reasonable person in the same situation would or should have had such doubts.

There was another smaller spike in citations to *St. Amant* from the mid-1990s through 2001. This may be the result of the U.S. Supreme Court's decision in *Harte-Hanks Communications Inc. v. Connaughton* (1989), which further explained and defined the legal standards for "reckless disregard" and "actual malice."

In the years following the Supreme Court's reformation of defamation law in *Sullivan*, critics have questioned the wisdom and validity of the entire *Sullivan* regime. Of course, these criticisms of *Sullivan* are also an implicit repudiation of the ruling in *St. Amant* and the other cases that refined the *Sullivan* "actual malice" standard. Yet of the 1,657 state and federal trial and appeals court decisions that cited *St. Amant* from when it was decided in 1968 through the end of 2017, none questioned the *St. Amant* ruling. In the vast majority of these cases (1,582, 95.4 percent), St. Amant was simply cited without any commentary: in majority opinions in 1,491 of these cases, in concurring opinions in 51 cases, and in dissents in 38 cases. In 163 of the cases, the courts explicitly stated that they were following the *St. Amant* precedent in making their rulings.[49]

In a small number of cases—fifteen rulings—courts went into some detail explaining the *St. Amant* decision and how it applied to the cases before them. In three cases, courts "harmonized" *St. Amant*, expanding the legal principles set by the Supreme Court's majority opinion in the case to apply to their current cases.

This record of *St. Amant* as a precedent that has not been questioned or contradicted is consistent with an observation by scholar Richard E. Labunski, who called the ruling "a rather confusing case, the details of which are less important than what the Supreme Court said about the standard of liability that should be applied in cases involving public officials and what constitutes 'reckless disregard' as first discussed in *New York Times v. Sullivan*."[50]

For example, in *Wylie v. Arnold Transportation Services*, a federal judge explained that *St. Amant* was different from the case before the court because

> the Supreme Court did not address [*in St. Amant*] the question of whether relying on an anonymous telephone call to inform those whose lives may be in danger, if the contents of that telephone call are true, and to advise the local police department about those contents

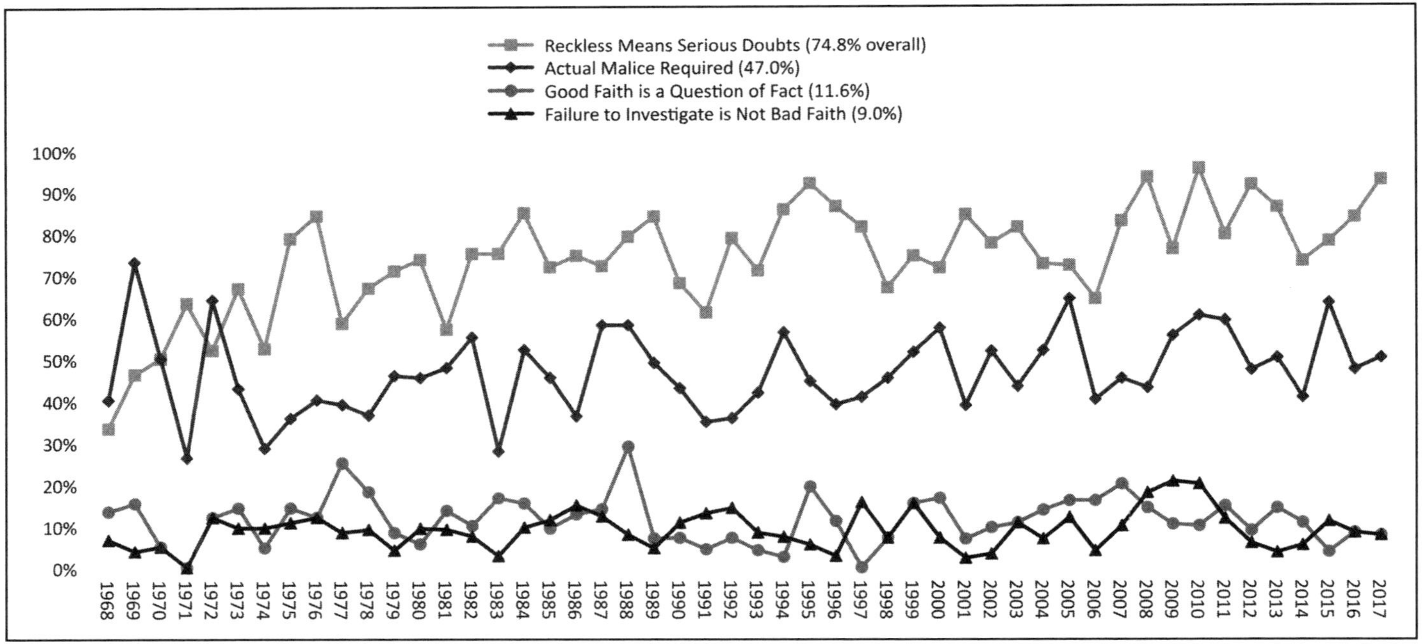

FIGURE 2. Percentage of federal and state decisions citing *St. Amant* principles, by year

> raises a genuine issue of material fact as to the defamation defendant's good faith or reckless disregard for the truth. Consequently, this Court concludes that relying on an anonymous telephone call, in and of itself, to provide warning to those who may be in harm's way and to the police department which could prevent a potentially dangerous situation from becoming deadly, does not raise a genuine issue of material fact as to either good faith or reckless disregard for the truth.[51]

Among all 1,657 decisions citing *St. Amant*, the most common reason for citing the case was its definition of "reckless disregard"—that the defamation defendant entertained serious doubts about the statement at issue—which was the reason for the citation in 74.8 percent of the cases. The second-most common reason for citing *St. Amant* has been for the application of the *Sullivan* "actual malice" requirement to public official plaintiffs, used in 47.0 percent of cases. The *St. Amant* case was less commonly cited for the point that whether the defendant acted in good faith is a question of fact to be determined by the jury (or the judge in a bench trial such as *St. Amant*), cited in 11.6 percent of the cases citing *St. Amant*, and the principle that a defamation defendant's failure to investigate does not itself show bad faith, cited in only 9.0 percent of cases. But a year-by-year analysis of decisions citing *St. Amant* shows that there has been some variation in the prevalence of these points (figure 2).

In the first few years after the *St. Amant* decision, the "actual malice" requirement and definition of "reckless disregard" jockeyed for the position as the most-often-cited principle from the case. But since 1973—the year before the U.S. Supreme Court decided *Gertz*, holding that the "actual malice" standard did not apply to private figures not involved in a manner of public concern—the meaning of "reckless disregard" has consistently been the leading reason for courts to cite *St. Amant*. This is also the reason why the case is most often cited in legal texts and treatises, with one scholar saying that Justice White's majority opinion in *St. Amant* "provided the most comprehensive guidelines for the [actual malice] standard."[52]

The other two principles from *St. Amant*—that whether the defendant acted in good faith is a question of fact and that a defamation defendant's failure to investigate does not itself show bad faith—have jockeyed for third and fourth place among citations in the years since the case was decided, and they have a difference of only 2.7 percent in their overall citation rates.

(9)

The Legacy of *St. Amant v. Thompson*

From their English antecedents, the American colonies developed a broad view of freedom of speech and thought that disdained government control via licensing and prosecutions for seditious libel. The American approach to speech evolved into political and legal philosophies that justified and explained a libertarian attitude toward ideas and expression, eventually leading to the adoption of the free speech and free press provisions of the First Amendment.

But tensions with the older attitudes remained, and the inclination of those in power to vanquish their opponents and their opponents' ideas fostered passage of and prosecutions under the 1798 Sedition Act. Such restrictions in the colonial and early independence periods fostered a robust debate over the meaning of the First Amendment and substantive changes in the law of defamation such as the establishment of truth as a defense.

Many years later, when Phil A. St. Amant gave his speech in 1962 and Herman Thompson filed his libel suit against St. Amant one week later, they faced a landscape of American defamation law that had not changed much since the early nineteenth century. But as it was in many other areas of law and of life, the period of the mid- and late 1960s turned out to be a turbulent era in defamation law, with *Sullivan* and subsequent decisions shifting the foundations of defamation law underneath Thompson and St. Amant as their case progressed through the courts. This is shown by the shifting results of the case. First, Thompson won at trial, and Judge Blanche sustained the verdict and award for Thompson in ruling on a motion for a new trial. Then the Louisiana Court of Appeal reversed, finding for St. Amant, only to be reversed itself by the Louisiana Supreme Court. And then the U.S. Supreme Court, after deciding not to follow its original inclination to summarily reverse, ended up ruling in favor of St. Amant after full briefing and argument, reversing the Louisiana Supreme Court's ruling and setting a standard for the "reckless disregard" component of the "actual malice" defamation requirement that it had established in *Sullivan*.

Procedurally, the path of the *St. Amant* case may have been a simple progression through ever-higher courts. But the case's journey was also through a landscape of evolving legal standards and rules that led to shifting outcomes at every level and eventually to new definitions and standards for *Sullivan* "actual malice."

The U.S. Supreme Court's ruling in *St. Amant* may have been the end of the journey for the principals in the case, but the dramatic evolution and changes in the American law of defamation continued through the 1960s, '70s, and '80s and took us to a destination that neither party likely could have foreseen at the start.

THE UNRESOLVED QUESTION OF *THOMPSON V. ST. AMANT*

Throughout *Thompson v. St. Amant*'s tumultuous journey through the courts, one fundamental issue that arose in the case was never actually resolved: What, exactly, was the purpose of the money that Thompson collected from the Local 5 union office? Was it a charitable contribution or some sort of payoff?

In his trial verdict, Judge Blanche concluded that although it was literally true that money had "passed hands" from Local 5 union boss Ed Partin to Thompson, St. Amant's statement was false in its implication that the money was evidence of a corrupt relationship between Thompson and Partin: "The only proof that this Court has is the fact that the money did pass, which was freely admitted by the plaintiff, and that is not sufficient evidence to attach any dishonest motive to Captain Thompson in view of the other testimony by him and as well as possibly the admissions of the defendant himself that he intended to attribute no dishonest motive to him."[1]

There is ample evidence, both from the *Thompson* case and other sources, that Ed Partin was deeply ensconced in the corruption of southern Louisiana and maintained connections to both Carlos Marcello's criminal operations and corrupt local officials. And he was, of course, a trusted aide to Teamsters president Jimmy Hoffa, at least until Partin testified against Hoffa in the jury tampering trial that finally sent the national union leader to prison. In fact, Ed Partin's brother revealed a fact that may give some indication that, while Teamsters Local 5 was paying bribes, it was not to Thompson. Instead, the payments were given to an emissary of Marcello's, and this ended as soon as Ed Partin went to prison. Doug Partin writes, "There was a man from New

Orleans, known to be one of Carlos [Marcello's] men, who would come by the [union] local office in Baton Rouge once a month to pick up an envelope. But after Ed went to prison, . . . that man stopped coming."[2]

Doug Partin does not discuss any other payments made by his brother Ed Partin or by Local 5. Of course, this does not mean that such payments did not happen. And Doug Partin does describe extensive shady dealings by his brother, including criminal activities.

So it is likely that Partin's union local—and perhaps Partin himself—paid bribes to local officials, possibly including members of law enforcement. After all, that is how Marcello continued to operate his illicit operations with seeming impunity; there is no reason that Partin would not have done the same in order to maintain his own shady practices.

But was Thompson one of Partin's recipients? The answer is likely no. Herman Thompson had a distinguished career in the sheriff's office, including training at the FBI National Academy and numerous other law enforcement training programs. He was subject to a lawsuit alleging improper behavior, but the suit ended in a verdict favorable to Thompson. And when he was offered what may have been perceived as a bribe, in the form of Partin's offer of a new suit upon Thompson's graduation from the FBI Academy, he flatly rejected the offer and reported it to his boss, Sheriff Clemmons.

Thompson was also involved in a number of Baton Rouge charitable organizations. These included the Baton Rouge Kids' Baseball Clinic, where he became a board member in 1971. So Thompson did legitimately raise money for the organization, and the funds in the envelope that he received from the secretaries in the Local 5 office were most likely for that purpose.

Without any other allegation or hint of bribes to Thompson, and considering Thompson's upright record, it seems pretty clear that the money that "changed hands" from Partin to Thompson was for charitable purposes.

The truth of St. Amant's statement was only one element of the libel case and, in the end, not the most important one. Instead, the overriding issues in the appellate courts' decisions were whether "actual malice" applied and, if it did, whether Thompson had proven that St. Amant acted with "actual malice" when repeating Albin's accusation. In the end, the U.S. Supreme Court majority ruled that "actual malice" did indeed apply but that St. Amant had not made the statement with such a level of fault. Legally, St. Amant's statement was not libelous.

OBSCURE NO MORE

The shifting results in Thompson's case as it proceeded through the appeals process show the turbulence and uncertainty of the legal waters in which the case was immersed. But when the case reached the U.S. Supreme Court, it reached the barrier that had been established in *New York Times v. Sullivan. Sullivan* was such a barrier to Thompson's claims against St. Amant that the U.S. Supreme Court initially considered summarily reversing the Louisiana Supreme Court's ruling for Thompson, without even giving him the opportunity to argue his case. After the court did allow such argument, only one justice was convinced that Thompson should prevail.

The *St. Amant* case came at a pivotal moment in the development of modern First Amendment principles. The Supreme Court had already revolutionized defamation law by holding in *Sullivan* and *Garrison v. Louisiana* that the First Amendment required that a high standard—actual malice—be applied in defamation cases involving public officials. Then the court had to actually define the terms it had introduced in these rulings: What characterizes a "public official"? What exactly constitutes "actual malice" and "reckless disregard"? And did these high standards apply to other types of plaintiffs, such as other prominent people? Did it matter why they were prominent? If they had faded from prominence, did it matter how, why, or how long ago the loss of stature had occurred? Did these new standards apply to all defamation cases or only under certain circumstances? Once the First Amendment was seen as a limitation on traditional defamation law, the court had to determine how far that limitation went.

These are the questions and issues that were to a greater or lesser extent, and with greater or lesser clarity, resolved and defined in the years following *Sullivan*, in the line of U.S. Supreme Court cases labeled as "*Sullivan*'s progeny."

These cases reshaped American defamation law, all but freeing it from its traditional British common law moorings. Some argue that this has gone too far and that it is too difficult—and may be practically impossible—for public officials and public figures to win a defamation case. But others point to a high number of defamation verdicts in the decades since *Sullivan* in arguing that it is not impossible for damages to be won—and affirmed on appeal—in legitimate cases where actual harm to reputation can be proven.

Because of the high "actual malice" threshold required for public officials and public figures to recover in a defamation case, there have been some calls for scaling back on the protections that *Sullivan* and its progeny provide the media. Some of these calls have even come from various Supreme Court justices. Yet the Supreme Court as a whole has taken no action to reverse or limit the *Sullivan* decision and in fact has cited it approvingly in recent rulings. Despite the criticism, *Sullivan* and its broad interpretation of the First Amendment are firmly ensconced in both American law and society, and any reversal or limitation on the legal principles of *Sullivan*'s progeny is not likely.

As a case falling under the rubric of *Sullivan*'s progeny, the Supreme Court decision in *St. Amant v. Thompson* was an integral part of the development of modern defamation law. By giving a definition and example of what the "reckless disregard" requirement of *Sullivan* "actual malice" really meant, the court's decision in *St. Amant* set a standard that protects those who are subject to genuine, malicious attacks while also preserving the robust protection that American media have fought for in their coverage of public affairs and matters of public interest, going back to the political philosophy of the pseudonymous sixteenth-century writer Cato.

While it has not received the attention that other landmark defamation cases have, the *St. Amant* decision was a significant step in the journey that began in *Sullivan* toward the robust protection that American courts provide to comment about public officials, public figures, and matters of public interest. *St. Amant v. Thompson* serves as an important part of the development of modern American defamation law and the rollicking discussion and debate that it sustains.

If the decision in *Sullivan* was an occasion for dancing, it was a dance with no established steps or even a familiar tune. As Lee Levine and Steve Wermiel put it, "When the dancing was over, the Supreme Court faced myriad questions about the scope and meaning of its decision in *New York Times Co. v. Sullivan* and the actual malice standard it had created."[3] For while the *Sullivan* decision revolutionized American defamation law, it did not eliminate libel or slander as legal claims.[4] And it left many unanswered questions that the lower courts and the Supreme Court had to address in subsequent cases.

Like Lester B. Sullivan, East Baton Rouge Parish deputy sheriff Herman A. Thompson likely thought that his libel case against political candidate Phil A. St. Amant would be an easy victory. But because of the timing of his case, he got caught in a period of tumultuous change to defamation law in the wake of the *Sullivan* decision, which shifted the legal standards of defamation under his feet and ultimately led to his loss before the U.S. Supreme Court.

At its root, the dispute between Herman Thompson and Phil A. St. Amant was a simple one: Had St. Amant unfairly accused Thompson of receiving bribes from a union official? But in the political, social, and legal context of the day, the case came to involve much more than that and grew to encompass union corruption at both the local and national levels; the involvement of Senator Russell Long and other government officials with the union and its leadership; and the proper application of the new standards of defamation law established in *New York Times v. Sullivan*. Like Lester B. Sullivan, Thompson had no intention of setting any sort of legal precedent. But because of the timing of his lawsuit, he ended up caught in a maelstrom of cultural, political, and social change, including significant changes in the law of defamation.

APPENDIX A

Text of Phil St. Amant's Campaign Address

This is an attempt at a verbatim transcript of the address that U.S. Senate candidate Phil A. St. Amant gave as a campaign advertisement on the evening of June 27, 1962, on WAFB-TV (channel 9) in Baton Rouge.

The address consisted primarily of St. Amant reading the transcript of his interview with J. D. Albin. Passages preceded by "[Q:]" are the questions that were posed by St. Amant, while those preceded by "[A:]" are Albin's answers. The address also included an introduction and conclusion by St. Amant, as well as some aside comments during his reading of the interview transcript.

Since no video or audio recording of the address was available for this research, this transcript is based on the three available transcripts submitted into evidence in the libel case stemming from the address. These included a transcript of the affidavit that was read by St. Amant during the June 27, 1962, broadcast on WAFB-TV (Plaintiff's Exhibit 1, designated as "P1" in the footnotes); a transcript of an audio recording of the televised address, which was played during the trial by the plaintiff and transcribed as part of the trial transcript (Plaintiff's Exhibit 2, designated as "P2" in the footnotes); and a transcript of a film of the speech—originally intended for broadcast but not actually used—which was also shown by the defense during the trial and transcribed as part of the trial transcript (Defendant's Exhibit 2, designated as "D2" in the footnotes).[1]

Of the three available versions of the speech, the transcript based on the audio recording (Plaintiff's Exhibit 2) seems to be the most complete and accurate, since it includes the introduction, interstitial comments, and conclusion that St. Amant testified were part of the address as televised. St. Amant also verified that the audio recording was what was broadcast on WAFB-TV on June 27, 1962.

While the audio recording transcript (Plaintiff's Exhibit 2) was used as the primary basis for the transcript below, differences from the other versions are noted.

1. While Thompson's attorney was a bit ambiguous in introducing this material at trial, he refers to it as "the source material for the actual statement" (Trial transcript, Thompson v. St. Amant, La. Dist. Ct. 1962 [hereinafter "Trial transcript"], 105) and "the film . . . from which the transcript for [St. Amant's] television broadcast was prepared." Trial transcript, 121. This is reinforced by the fact that this version lacks the introductory, interstitial, and concluding material included in the actual broadcast.

Grammar has been retained, with [sic] *annotations to indicate errors in the original and a few words inserted in brackets to maintain logic and word flow. Punctuation has generally been left intact as well, with any changes, including footnotes added to the transcript, enclosed in brackets.*

Fellow Americans, this is Phil A. St. Amant, your conservative candidate for the United States Senate in the July 28th primary. I have a story to reveal tonight which is so unusual that I have bought this time on the television to inform the public. This story involves a well-documented criminal, an ex-convict who became a labor chieftain. It involves a misuse and theft of union funds, dealings with Communist officials of Cuba, a criminal conspiracy to destroy evidence and the destruction of that evidence; death resulting from the commission of a felony and a second death by a hit and run by a union car. Neither death has been prosecuted. It includes abuse by this labor chieftain of the members of his union, to include brutal beating, forgery;[2] a shooting of the labor chief; the struggle of working men to properly use the provisions of the law to protect themselves, and their being thwarted by intervention of your junior United States Senator with no less than Jimmy Hoffa to give a good character and reputation for this criminal local chief, in order to protect his position while he continues to ride roughshod over American working men, and finally, just before justice can be done, a key witness who had given Grand Jury testimony died by a most unlikely accident. Ladies and gentlemen, this is not my story: this is the story of working men, who in their struggle for freedom from tyranny sought me out when they saw no other way to turn. This is the story of the little man against oppression and political influence. This is the story of politics in Louisiana today. I give you the American working man.

Ladies and gentlemen, I would like to tell you that at this time we have had to refilm this part because as filmed originally Mr. J. D. Albin appeared on the screen live and told his story in answer to the questions that I gave him. However, because of legal advice to the station and checking with the F.C.C. of their legal responsibility, at this time it was determined that the original film would not be used on this program. Instead, I will read to you the signed affidavit of Mr. J. D. Albin as the testimony exactly as given. I want you to know then that the original film has been shown to the press and will be available for such showings as is permitted to the public. I would

2. In the P1 transcript, the original word—which is difficult to determine but may be "intrigue"—is crossed out at this point and replaced with "forgery."

like also to call to your attention that Mr. Albin in making these statements has shown considerable courage. He has signed this statement, he has sworn to it and he is prepared to back up any of his statements.[3]

I read to you now from his affidavit the questions and answers as given by him:[4]

[Q:] Will you please tell us your name and occupation?

[A:] J. D. Albin, unemployed since January 7, 1962 and ex-member of Teamsters Union No.[5] 5.

[Q:] Mr. Albin, will you please tell us what you know about Mr. Ed Partin's trip to Cuba in November 1960?

[A:] Mr. Partin asked me on a Monday morning some time late in November to take him to Moisant Airport in New Orleans, which I did. I saw him board the Cuba flight, the Havana flight for Cuba. Later in the day I received a phone call at my home from Partin. He told me[6] he had been in touch with the office and he asked us to find out why Otis Tynes had quit; that the office girl had told him that Otis had resigned that day, which I did. A. G. Klein and myself then went to the hall late in the afternoon, reached Partin at the Plaza Hotel in Havana, Cuba and relayed the message to him that that he ha[d] asked for. The next day in the afternoon, we went down to the Moisant Airport to pick Partin up. We saw him as he departed from the Cuba flight with a coat over his arm.[7] He went through customs, came out, we went to the automobile where he taken [*sic*] a package out[:] out of his coat from under his arm somewhere and put it in the back of the trunk of the car and we proceeded on back to Baton Rouge.

[Q:] Anything you'd like to comment on Otis Tynes' explanation as to why he had quit the union?

[A:] Otis told me he had quit because he didn't want to be made the goat for Partin in the Louisiana Creamery contract. Ed had gave [*sic*] me a message that morning to[o?], in [*sic*] the Louisiana contract[,] and told me to take it back and tell Otis to go and renegotiate this contract. This is a contract that was voted on by the members on November the 21st and accepted; a contract proposal from the company, which we felt at that time was a fair contract. This contract was later renegotiated and signed,

3. This paragraph does not appear in the P1 transcript or the D2 portion of the trial transcript.

4. This paragraph does not appear in the P1 transcript or the D2 portion of the trial transcript.

5. Indicated as "No." in all three transcripts.

6. At this point the D2 transcript has "He asked me—told me."

7. D2 transcript has "arms" here.

giving up many benefits, wage, boys working longer hours and was signed without the ratification of the membership.

[Q:] Do you have any other indication of, ah, [*sic*][8] contract . . . Well, ah, you said a moment ago that Partin did go to Cuba and you gave the indication how you knew he was there. Did he tell you anything about his conversations there or whom he met with?

[A:] He told us he met with Fidel Castro and [Raúl][9] Castro, Fidel's brother. He said that Fidel spoke very broken English but his brother spoke much better English.

[Q:] Did he indicate whose business he was on down there with the Castros?

He told us when he left that he was going to Cuba to take care of business for Jimmy Hoffa.

[Q:] Did you see any other indications that he had contact with officials in Cuba?

[A:] Yes. We later saw a letter that was written to Partin from Lopez . . . Ernesto Lopez of Cuba, and we taken [*sic*] this letter and put it in the form of a handbill and put it out to the membership at the time.

[Q:] Do you know anything unusual about the handling of the union funds during this period?

[A:] Yes. It was too numerous [*sic*] to relate here in the time allotted. He had used union funds for his own personal benefit, to pay house notes, he rented a car for his girlfriend in—Mildred Kelly, in Childressville, Alabama. I would also take numerous [*sic*] amounts of money out of the cash drawer during the week and at the end of the week he made this up by making out a check to someone else who would endorse it and they would deposit it into the union fund.

[Q:] Did you or any other members of the Teamsters' Union who were aware of this take any sort of action to correct it?

[A:] Yes. Frank L. Doughty on March the 21st wrote a letter to Arthur Goldberg with a copy being sent to James R. Hoffa, asking for an investigation of Teamsters' Local No.[10] 5. On the 25th, Frank L. Doughty received a reply from James R. Hoffa, asking for information, any and all information concerning these charges. On Mon-

8. "Ah" appears in both the P1 and P2 transcripts. While it is possible that the word "a" was intended, it appears that this is a pause in the sentence, particularly because the same "ah" pause appears elsewhere in the transcripts, and because "a" does not appear in the D2 transcript.

9. Raúl Castro's name is misspelled in all three transcripts: as Raoul in the P1 transcript, and as Roual in the P2 and D2 transcripts. The correct spelling is used here, in brackets to indicate a change from the originals.

10. "No." in all three transcripts.

day morning, Frank L. Doughty, which was the 27th of March, he mailed this information to Jimmy Hoffa. Later in the day, I found out that he had had, on the letter from[11] Hoffa, it said on the bottom a notation "copy sent to Teamsters' Local No.[12] 5." Now Ed received this copy on Monday. He became pretty riled up about it and in the afternoon. A. G. Klein, who was still working at that time as an assistant and an organizer for Ed at Teamsters' Local No.[13] 5[,] told me that Johnny Birch had stopped him on the Airline Highway and told him Ed wanted him to help get rid of the safe that night, that there was going to be an investigation of the local union and the records had to be destroyed. It was going to take four men to do it. He told me[14] who all was supposed to be in on it and that they were supposed to take it to Bruce Hunt's Shop. That's the man that owns Triple A Construction and cut it open that night, that it had been okayed with Bruce. Klein didn't want to be involved in this, so he got his brother in New Orleans to send him a telegram so he could get out of it and still stay in Ed's good graces because at this time he still felt that it was further information that could be derived from his employment in Teamsters' Local No.[15] 5. And we knew something had to be done if we were to ever straighten out the local union, and the onliest [*sic*][16] way to straighten it out was the removal of E. G. Partin. Now, we knew that this safe was gonna[17] be removed that night, but imagine our predicament, knowing of Ed's connections with the Sheriff's office through Herman Thompson—

I am breaking now in the reading of this affidavit by Mr. J. D. Albin to explain to the public that this material I am reading is a signed affidavit by Mr. J. D. Albin. It was originally given on film by Mr. J. D. Albin and has been so shown to the press. But because of legal admonitions given by their legal counsel to the station it is being presented here over this station by me and read directly from the affidavit. The language used here is exactly from the affidavit, such language as is used by Mr. Albin in the affidavit which he has signed and presented on film. I continue the affidavit of Mr. J. D. Albin:[18]

11. Transcript D2 has "letter coming from."
12. "No." in all three transcripts.
13. "No." in all three transcripts.
14. Transcript D2 has "He told him."
15. "No." in all three transcripts.
16. "Onliest" appears in all three transcripts.
17. "Gonna" appears in all three transcripts.
18. This paragraph does not appear in the P1 or D2 transcripts.

[A:] Now, we knew that this safe was gonna [*sic*][19] be removed that night, but imagine our predicament, knowing of Ed's connections with the Sheriff's office through Herman Thompson, who made recent visits to the Hall to see Ed. We also knew of money that had passed hands between Ed and Herman Thompson, from Ed to Herman. We also knew of his connections with State Trooper Lieutenant Joe Green. We knew we couldn't get any help from there and we didn't know how far that [*sic*] he was involved in the Sheriff's office or the State Police Office through that, and it was out of the jurisdiction of the City Police.

[Q:] What did you do then?

[A:] Well, we rode around a while trying to decide what to do. Finally, we decided that we would go to the Hall ourselves to see if there was any way we could stop them if we caught them coming out with the safe. We arrived a little too late. Somewhere in the neighborhood of nine o'clock the safe was gone. The next morning there was an investigation. Brother Herman Thompson came out and investigated it and I understand that Lieutenant Joe Green showed up. They seemed to think it was a job by a professional. I agree with them.

[Q:] Ah, this, ah[,] safe being gone—did this destroy the evidence?

[A:] No. Klein and myself had taken pictures of the checkbooks previous to this and photostated other documents that we thought would help in the case.

[Q:] Did the safe ever show up?

[A:] Yes. The safe turned up a few months later when a young man by the name of Forman dived off the river bridge and hit his head on this safe and killing [*sic*] himself.[20]

[Q:] This sounds to me like a death resulting from the commission of a felony. That's murder, isn't it?

[A:] That's the way we feel about it, but so far, nothing's been done.

[Q:] Now, after you sent this information to, ah, Hoffa, that had been photographed from the safe, did he take any kind of action?

[A:] Yes. He sent a panel in here to hear Frank L. Doughty's charges. When they came in, they told him they had something like an hour or forty-five minutes to hear these charges then and they had to catch a plane out of here, so Doughty[21] knew

19. "Gonna" appears in all three transcripts.

20. Contrary to the implication here that the death was caused by hitting the safe, news reports at the time said that George L. Forman Jr. died of a broken neck when he dove into an area of the Amite River that contained driftwood and bridge pilings. The safe was found by a diver searching for Forman's body. *See* "Safe Stolen Here in March Found in River," 1.

21. In the P1 transcript, "Doty" was originally typed here, then Wited-Out, with an insert mark indicating "Doughty," typed above the removed word, belonged in its place.

that no one could hear these charges in that short a time, so he more or less got out of it and let it go at that.[22] At a later date, an auditor was sent in from the International to audit the books, a Mr. Charlie Farrell. We felt this man was just and he found the books in terrible condition; in fact, he said a three year old child could run that local union better than Ed Partin was running it. He made his notations and comments back to the International Union and we felt at that time that something was fixing to happen. During this period, then, we found out from the office secretary that numerous telephone calls had been made to local politicians and two politicians in Washington. They were all supposed to meet in Washington to try to cement Ed's relations with James R. Hoffa.

[Q:] Would you like to comment on the names of the politicians in Washington who were called?

[A:] Well, two that was supposed to be in Washington was Jimmy Morrison and Russell Long. They had two or three from here. Ossie Brown, Apple Sanders (at the last minute for some reason or another decided not to make the trip).[23] Exactly why, I don't know.[24]

[Q:] Now, what happened as a result of these telephone calls?

[A:] Well, nothing was done after that[25] so we figured that these people must have intervened. Now, at a later date, Klein and I then filed charges through the local union, through the local union executive board, got up a petition with something like—a little over three hundred names on it and we made a trip to Washington to see Jimmy Hoffa.

[Q:] Who else went with you?

[A:] A. G. Klein, myself, Prentiss Moak and A. D. Burris.[26]

[Q:] Did you get to see Mr. Hoffa?

[A:] Yes. We saw Hoffa late that afternoon. We presented the petition to him and told him our story. He said it was hard for him to understand this about Brother

22. In the P1 and D2 transcripts, this sentence ends, "and let it go at that *time*" (emphasis added).

23. This is the grammar as it appears in the trial transcript. See Trial transcript, 26–27. But the grammar is ambiguous, and it is unclear whether both Ossie Brown and Apple Sanders decided not to go to Washington or only Apple Sanders declined to go. Based on a statement below, it seems that neither Ossie Brown nor Apple Sanders made the trip.

24. The D2 transcript has the closing parenthesis here, rather than after "trip."

25. The P1 and D2 transcripts have this as "after they—after that."

26. This statement confirms the reading of the prior statement regarding Ossie Brown and Apple Sanders not traveling to Washington.

Partin. He said that nice young Senator from down there, Brother—Senator Russell Long—that he was in my office and he praised Brother Hoffa [*sic*].[27]

(And there is a correction here in the affidavit and it should read "Brother Partin.")

I repeat:[28]

[A:] he praised Brother Partin to the highest and his standing in the community as being very good. He said, "I—I don't understand this."[29] We told him that[30] we felt that Brother Partin had his political pull through some unscrupulous employees, that he was[31] selling out his membership[32] so he promised to send somebody in here to investigate it and do something about it, which never did happen.[33]

[Q:] What did you men do then, when you returned to Baton Rouge?

[A:] We came back to Baton Rouge, we contacted, ah, the parties involved. Some of them we didn't even get an answer from. We did get[34] an answer from Russell Long. We asked—we told Russell what in the telegram—we told him in the telegram we sent him what Jimmy Hoffa had told us.[35] We also told him—about[36] having positive proof of his dealings—[37] (of Partin's) dealings with Fidel Castro and the

27. Based on the context, it appears that the first "he," in the phrase "He said that," refers to Hoffa. The second and third "he"s, in the phrase "he was in my office and he praised Brother Hoffa,'" refer to Long, relating comments that Hoffa said Long made in Hoffa's office. As noted in the next sentence, the reference to praise of "Brother Hoffa" is an obvious misstatement and should refer to "Brother Partin." P1 has an asterisk at this point, with a footnote indicating "intended to be Partin."

28. This statement and the parenthetical statement above are included in the P2 transcript, but not in the P1 or D2 versions. It seems that St. Amant said this in the broadcast as an aside.

29. Again based on the context, it appears that the first "he," in the phrase "he praised Brother Partin," refers to Senator Long and is paraphrasing Hoffa's comments to those who traveled to Washington: Albin, A. G. Klein, Prentiss Moak, and A. D. Burris. The second "he," in the sentence, in "He said, 'I—I don't understand this,'" refers to Hoffa.

30. P1 and D2 have "how" in place of "that."

31. At this point the P1 version of the transcript has an "ah," pause.

32. P1 and D2 have this phrase as "selling his membership out."

33. P1 has "which, ah, didn't happen" here.

34. "Get" is missing from the P1 version.

35. P1 and D2 have this sentence as "We asked—we told Russell what in the telegram that we sent him what Jimmy Hoffa had told us."

36. P1 and D2 have no pause and have the word "that" instead of "about."

37. P1 does not have the first "dealings," or the pause.

Communist regime in Cuba, that we felt it would be to [*sic*] his interest and ours if he would cease supporting[38] E. G. Partin. We received a telegram from Russell Long[,] which I have here, and I will read the contents:

(Quote from the telegram:)[39]

[A:] "Your information concerning E. G. Partin and James R. Hoffa is completely erroneous. I have never met James Hoffa personally and I have not undertaken to give him any estimate of the standing of Mr. Partin or any of his officers. Neither Hoffa, Partin[,] nor anyone else have asked me to express my opinion in a matter of this sort. (Signed,) Russell Long."

Klein and I contacted Russell Long, a little later on the telephone. He was not the distinguished speaker on that telephone,[40] he was pretty well shook. He finally admitted that he had talked to Brother Hoffa for Ed Partin but only as he would do for any other employee for their employer,[41] go to any other employer for an employee. What he didn't understand was this[:] that Ed Partin is not an employee of James R. Hoffa; he is employed by the members of Teamsters' Local Union No.[42] 5 for their benefit.

[Q:] Do[43] you know anything else about Mr. Partin's background and public record?

[A:] Yes.[44] I have what is known as a rap sheet here on Brother Partin. Just[45] a few of 'em [*sic*][46]—here is one in Roseburg, Oregon—robbery and auto theft—and was released at the Cisco County, California [*sic*]—there's about eighteen of 'em [*sic*][47] here. Another one here in Vancouver, Washington, investigated breaking and entering and pending.[48] Another one in Monroe, Washington, second degree burglary from Clark County, seems like about fifteen years[.] I don't know how much he served, and then you've got one here I understand was a colored girl up in Woodville, Mississippi, raped and robbed with firearms.

38. P1 has an "ah" pause at this point.
39. P1 lacks this parenthetical statement. It seems that St. Amant said this in the broadcast.
40. P1 has an ellipsis pause here.
41. P1 has an ellipsis pause here.
42. "No. " in all three transcripts.
43. D2 has an "ah" pause before the word "do."
44. P1 and D2 have an "ah" pause at this point.
45. D2 has an "ah" pause before the word "just."
46. "'em" appears in all three transcripts.
47. "'em" appears in all three transcripts.
48. The D2 transcript has "left pending."

[Q:] Have you heard anything recently in [*sic*] trouble he had in Cuba, Alabama?

[A:] Yes.[49] But before I mention this, I would like to go back a little bit to a recent hearing that we had here where some fifteen or twenty people jumped A. G. Klein and myself at the local union hall. We were told before we went into the hearing by one of the members, Emmett Tucker, that we were gonna [*sic*][50] get worked over as soon as we came out of that hall, so during the process of the hearing, I[51] approached Mr. Charles Winters, Secretary-Treasurer, Joint Council 93 and Business Manager of Local Union 270, New Orleans, and told him what had been said, so he told us that something would be done about it and there would be protection outside the hall when we left, and I don't mind telling you that when I stepped out of that hall and saw Lieutenant Joe Green standing there with a riot gun I had cold chills[52] running up and down my spine. I wasn't so much worried about those fifteen or twenty members that jumped us,[53] I was worried about Joe Green, and I would like to say at this time that he made no attempt to help relieve the situation that was going on. Now, you mentioned another thing here, this Cuba, Alabama, deal. On[54] December the 25th of 1961,[55] Partin was involved in a hit and run auto accident in Cuba, Alabama, killing a young soldier, an Air Force boy. There was three of 'em [*sic*][56] in the car,[57] two of 'em [*sic*][58] were injured and this boy was killed.

[Q:] How did this come to your attention?

[A:] It came to our attention through some more of Mr. Partin's meddling with[59] one of his members' family troubles, where two of the children that he—[60] he got 'em hid off somewhere—[61] for this boy—.[62] He's in jail and his wife has been trying to find the children for something like two months, and they were witnesses to this thing that had taken place in Cuba, Alabama.

49. P1 and D2 have an "ah" pause at this point.
50. "Gonna" appears in all three transcripts.
51. P1 has an "ah" pause at this point.
52. The P1 transcript has "a cold chill."
53. P1 has an ellipsis pause here.
54. P1 and D2 have a pause in place of the word "on."
55. P1 has "'61" instead of "1961."
56. "'em" appears in all three transcripts.
57. P1 has an ellipsis pause here.
58. "'em" appears in all three transcripts.
59. P1 and D2 have an "ah" pause at this point.
60. P1 has an ellipsis pause here.
61. P1 has an ellipsis pause here.
62. P1 has an ellipsis pause here.

[Q:] And has prosecution occurred as a result . . .

[A:] No.

[Q:] . . . of this accident?[63]

[A:] No. There was found upon—[64] well, immediately upon return to Baton Rouge, that[65] Partin got in touch with Lieutenant Joe Green[66] and[67] it was cover up from the word go, even to the extent of having a union car repaired in Lutcher, Louisiana, in the name of Bruce Hunt.[68]

[Q:] Can you tell us why Mr. Klein is not here testifying today?

[A:] Mr. Klein met with an accident in St. Francisville, Louisiana, where a truck had dropped on top of him loaded with about ninety thousand pounds of sand. This happened just a short while after he had testified in front of the Federal Grand Jury in New Orleans, and it's to my sorrow that I lost one of the, one of my closest and dearest friends, and . . .

[Q:] I believe Mr. Klein was a family man, wasn't he?

[A:] He sure was. He had five children, the youngest one about a year old, a year and a half old, and the oldest one about ten years old.

[Q:] Was this the sort of an accident you would expect for an experienced Teamster to become involved in?

[A:] Well, no, I wouldn't.

[Q:] As a working man, what is your reaction to Mr. Long's intervention into an affair of this sort?

[A:] It is very much unappreciated. We feel, right, that this was,[69] that he was meddling with the working men's affairs in this local union.

This is the end of the affidavit.[70]

I have been reading from an affidavit of J. D. Albin giving you on television, the public, the affidavit that Mr. J. D. Albin has testified to himself in person on film and which has been shown to the press but which has been read by me over this station because of legal admonition by their counsel to the station that it should be read by

63. It is unclear how St. Amant read this in his address, but the interruption appears this way in all three transcripts.

64. P1 has an ellipsis pause here.

65. P1 has an "ah" pause at this point.

66. D2 has the word "again" here.

67. P1 and D2 have an "ah" pause at this point.

68. The P1and D2 versions have "in Bruce Hunt's name."

69. P1 has an ellipsis pause here.

70. This paragraph is missing from the P1 and D2 versions.

me, Phil St. Amant, rather than given in person by Mr. Albin. Mr. Albin was quite willing to give it to the public and will do so in the future as soon as a legal decision can be made in this matter. It is on film and it will be available for a later showing, and I wish to comment here once more that Mr. Albin has shown great courage in this matter, and I respect him for it.[71]

And so, ladies and gentlemen, you have[72] here a true story of why the ordinary little man has no protection under our laws[:][73] political influence for notorious criminals. I want a public statement by Mr. Long on why he felt justified in giving a good character [reference] to Mr. Partin and then lying about it. I demand that he tell us of any other deals and influence he may have had with Jimmy Hoffa. I demand that he explain his philosophy to the public on voting against the rights of the working man to have a secret ballot to determine union fund expenditures and recall of union officers. I believe that you, the people, should ask him these questions. You have a right to know.

This is Phil St. Amant, your conservative candidate for the United States Senate. Thank you.

71. This paragraph is missing from the P1 and D2 versions.

72. D2 has the word "heard" at this point.

73. D2 reads, "true story of the ordinary little man, why he has no protection under our laws."

APPENDIX B

Court Opinions in *St. Amant v. Thompson*

TRIAL COURT VERDICT

Thompson v. St. Amant, No. 88,779 (La. Dist. Ct., 19th Dist. [Baton Rouge Parish]). Reasons for Judgment [Verdict], May 5, 1964.

The law with reference to libel and slander is that any publication, whether in writing, on television, radio, or in pictures or otherwise, which exposes any person to hatred, contempt, ridicule or which causes him to be shunned or which has a tendency to injure him in his reputation or occupation is a libelous statement. That has been our law and was recently stated in the case *Miller, Smith & Champagne, et al[.] v. Capital City Press*, 142 So. 2d 462,[1] but that is a hornbook law definition of libel and slander. The foundation of the law of libel and slander is the protection of a person's reputation, and as stated in *Kennedy v. Item. Co.*[,] 213 La. 347, 34 So. 2d 886,[2] the right to a good name and fame is absolute and is as essential to the pursuit of happiness as is the right to life, liberty and property.

The test of whether a statement is libelous is set forth *Madison v. Bolton*, 234 La. 97, 102 So. 2d 433,[3] that the test of a libelous article is the effect the article is fairly calculated to produce [*sic*], the impression it would naturally engender in the minds of the average persons among whom it is intended to circulate. As has been pointed out here, some statements are privileged when they involve public officials, and I believe the law stated by Mr. Van Buskirk with regard to its application to public officials was correct. Public officials are fair game, so to speak, but statements with regard to them are only actionable as being libelous when it can be shown that the maker of such a statement acted with malice, and that must be particularly alleged and proved.

The case of *Smith v. Lyons*, 142 La. 975, 77 So. 896,[4] with regard to the question of damages, and others there cited, are to the effect that when one falsely accuses any person of being dishonest, a liar; being fraudulent, or of having unworthy motives, or

1. 142 So. 2d 462 (La. App., 1st Cir. 1962).
2. 34 So. 2d 886 (La. 1948).
3. 102 So. 2d 433 (La. 1958), *reh'g denied* (La. May 26, 1958).
4. 77 So. 896 (La. Feb. 25, 1918) (on rehearing).

to impute the same by insinuations or innuendo, such action renders the individual publishing the same responsible for the consequences. In such instances the law implies malice and will award substantial damages without the showing of any special damages. Of course, a defense to any such libelous statement would be the truth. It is not libelous to make statements about another person or accuse him of being dishonest or accuse him of having unworthy motives which reflect on his character if they are true, but the one who makes such statements also has the burden of proving the truthfulness of the same.

I have gone over the statement again, the statement made by Mr. J .D. Albin in his affidavit and repeated by Mr. St. Amant in his Speech on WAFB-TV as follows: "We knew something had to be done if we were to ever straighten out the local union, and the onliest way to straighten it out was the removal of E. G. Partin." Prior to this statement, many statements had been made in the speech with reference to Mr. Ed Partin, business agent of the Teamsters Union, accusing him of such things as trafficking with the Castros in Cuba, being a criminal, in fact, referring to his rap sheet and criminal convictions, and also Mr. St. Amant in his speech and through Albin's affidavit painted Partin as abusive of these particular members in the union, abusive of the membership in the union, mishandling union funds, committing murder, and possibly other dishonest motives and acts which escape my memory. However, considering the whole tenor of the speech, I got the idea that Mr. Partin was a crook of the highest order. Following these remarks quoted by Mr. St. Amant, Mr. Albin stated that certain efforts were made by them to get help or relief from Mr. Partin, and they had gone to Washington to ask James Hoffa to aid them, and as a result of their efforts Mr. Partin had good reason to expect that an investigation of the union was imminent. The affidavit further reflects that they had received knowledge that Mr. Partin was going to remove the safe from the union hall, and as a person of average intelligence, I would draw the inference that Mr. Partin would only do this in order to hide any wrongdoing on his part with regard to his handling of union funds or otherwise, and he therefore had to get rid of the safe. The affidavit goes on to show how they had thought about what action they could take to prevent this, and it occurred to them that perhaps they should call the law, but that they were afraid to call the law, especially the Sheriff's office, because they knew of Captain Thompson's connections with Ed Partin, that they had known that money had passed hands, and the inference that I got was that this statement tended to impute some dishonest motive to Captain Thompson such as taking a payoff from Ed Partin. It also insinuated and inferred that he, Thompson, rather than do his duty and enforce the law or help them prevent the commission of a crime might aid and abet the wrongdoer[,] Mr. Ed Partin[,] since Partin had connections with Thompson. The statement did not infer, it charged that they should not go to him because if they did they would not get any help and did not know how far he was involved in the Sheriff's office or State Police office. There is no doubt in my mind that a person of average intelligence hearing that speech would figure that Captain Herman Thompson was in cahoots with Ed Partin, especially after all of these other dishonest motives and accusations made as to Mr. Ed Partin that previously thereto and [so?][5] linking Mr. Thompson' s name in the fashion stated, he couldn't help but imply to the average person that Captain Thompson was involved with Partin in a dishonest way.

I heard from Mr. St. Amant today that he intended no malice toward Captain Thompson. He was in a political fight with Senator Russell Long, that it was true that money had passed between Ed Partin and Captain Thompson, and that he had also been out at the Union Hall and that Partin and Thompson addressed each other by their first names. All of this was also admitted by the plaintiff. Plaintiff has stated that he had plenty of business at the Union Hall but the same was in connection with burglaries or[6] union activities involving strikes which made it necessary for him to confer with Mr. Partin from time to time. Mrs. Smith, Mr. Partin's secretary[,] stated that money was left in an envelope from Mr. Partin to Mr. Thompson and that he picked up the same. The Sheriff testified and so did Mr. Thompson that any money that he received from Mr. Partin was purely in connection with drives put on by some charitable institution such as the Baseball Clinic, Elks Club or other [7] charitable drives, and that any money that he ever received from him was soley [*sic*] for that purpose and was turned over to the Sheriff's receptionist[,] who would account for the same.

Even though Mr. St. Amant states that he did not intend to impute any dishonest motives to Mr. Thompson and did not intend to injure or hurt him in his reputation, nevertheless, the fair inference to be drawn by what was stated to the average person had that exact effect.

Having already held that the statement itself inferred and attributed to Mr. Thompson dishonesty, such statements are under our law injurious per se unless the truth of the accusation is proved. The only proof that this Court has is the fact that the money did pass, which was freely admitted by the plaintiff, and that is not sufficient evidence to attach any dishonest motive to Captain Thompson in view of the other testimony by him and as well as possibly the admissions of the defendant himself that he intended

5. A stain in the microfilmed copy of the original transcript obscures this word. But it can only be two characters long, and "so" makes sense in this spot in the sentence.

6. This word incorrectly rendered as "of" in the U.S. Supreme Court Appendix (hereinafter U.S. App'x.), 145.

7. The microfilmed copy of the original transcript ends at this point. The remainder of the opinion comes from the U.S. Supreme Court appendix.

to attribute no dishonest motive to him, but nevertheless, that mere fact of receiving that money is not proof of dishonesty on his part. It is not proof of his taking a payoff, nor proof that because of his connections with Partin he would not do his duty as a law officer. Proof of those charges, which are implicit in the language of the statement, would be his only defense under our law . . .[8]

I know of nothing more important to a police officer; or for that matter to any man, than his reputation. I know it is more important than money. The natural experiences of life teaches [*sic*] that regardless of a man's wealth it never takes the place of his good reputation and character. It is especially so of police officers, for there is nothing as vile to our system of justice as the belief that our police are dishonest. They are to enforce the law, and their professional reputation depends a great deal on their honesty and integrity. Of course, it is hard to show how far such a statement has injured Captain Thompson. Captain Thompson, as far as the Court knows and from listening to the Sheriff and others, has a fine reputation, but the statement was circulated all over the parish to many, many persons who have no knowledge of Captain Thompson, and as Shakespeare said, "The bad that men do lives after them and the good is oft interred with their bones."[9] The public will often not remember good things about people but remembers the bad things that have been said about them, and it is not unreasonable to assume that if Captain Thompson's name is discussed among the general public that it could be associated with taking some payoff from Ed Partin, the Teamsters agent, and that these union members were afraid to go to the police because they knew of Ed Partin's and Captain Thompson's connection. They will remember that long after they have forgotten how much education he has as a law officer, long after they have forgotten that he was a graduate of the F.B.I. School. Long after his many faithful years of service in the Sheriff's office, they will remember that.

It is my opinion that to have made a speech outlining in detail and charging Ed Partin with such great criminal activity and then to link Partin and Captain Thompson together with a statement that money had passed hands between them is a statement which is libelous per se. I was interested in Mr. Van Buskirk's remarks that they were not and the reasons why they were not, but I wonder, Mr. Van Buskirk[,] what you would think if someone would reflect on your honesty as a lawyer in such a publication.[10] You could have been a good lawyer, which you are, for years, and yet you would

8. The Supreme Court appendix indicates "torn copy" at this point. U.S. App'x., 147.

9. *Julius Caesar*, act 3, scene 2.

10. Ironically, two years later Van Buskirk was disbarred for misusing client funds. *See* Louisiana State Bar Ass'n v. Van Buskirk, 191 So. 2d 497 (La. 1966).

be put up to public ridicule and contempt, and damage would result not only to your reputation but indeed to your business, and if the same were not true and if the defendant could not prove it is true, I know that you should feel that you were damaged.

I was looking at the case of Deshotel v. Thistlethwaite, 240 La. 12, 121 So. 2d 222.[11] I don't know what would be the more injurious to reputation. I don't know whether it would be more injurious to be referred to as a coward or whether it would be more injurious to be referred to as a thief or a dishonest officer of the law.

On that point and with regard to what you stated about Section 315 of the Federal Communications Act,[12] it is my opinion that that act does not apply to Captain Thompson because I do not believe him to be a public official, though I know he is a public employee, like Mrs. Dobbs, my clerk, and countless others that we have enforcing the law, but I do not think that was intended to apply to other than public officials. If I am wrong about that, you will have to straighten me out, because if he is a public officer, so to speak, then the rules may be entirely different.

While not in evidence and having nothing to do with the case, while I was listening to the testimony, I have remembered that I had run out of money and needed some and had borrowed some money from a lawyer who had a case in my court. I gave it no thought, we were and had been friends, just as I am and have been with practically every member of the bar. I was just thinking to myself how that would look out in print or on T.V. I don't know whether the lawyer won or lost his case. I can't recall it, but I remember that I was out of money and rather than cash a check, I got it from him. I have no idea whether he won or lost the case or what case it may have been. But I sure realize the impropriety of it and what it could have done to me. I certainly had no dishonest motive. I just forgot to cash a check and borrowed money from a friend, which all of you lawyers are to me, and I can see right now that if somebody got on T.V. and put it out that money had passed between me and the lawyer and he had won the case, I really would have been in a fix. The more I would have tried to explain it, the worse it would have gotten.

Mr. Thompson states he gets money for a contribution to a charity, and, of course, to those people there money was passing hands between him and Ed Partin. Yet, I know unions, management and everybody else contributes to those drives. Dishonest motives can be attributed to an entirely innocent act. I will tell you one thing; from now on, if I run out of money, I am going to borrow money from the bank or go find a place to cash a check or do without.

This brings up the amount of the award, and that is the hardest thing about being

11. 121 So. 2d 222 (La. 1960), *reh'g denied* (La. June 29, 1960).

12. *See* 47 U.S.C. § 315(a) (as amended by Pub. L. No. 86-274, § 1, 73 Stat. 557 [1959]).

a judge, to determine what is a fair award. If I am not mistaken, where the damages are libelous per se and are of such a nature as to injure and degrade the character of a person, malice is inferred. While the damages are not punitive, the Court can only in its discretion make an award which I believe may at the best be arbitrary. Like I said before, I don't know who is talking about Captain Herman Thompson and believes he and Ed Partin are crooks together, and there is no way of knowing, except to say that if you are a lawyer and you get written up as being dishonest or you are a policeman and the inference from the remarks made is that you are not honest or would engage in some conspiracy, you just cannot recover from that without some damage, because I believe people remember bad things about you for a long, long time. Also, I don't know, it is not in evidence, and I only know this by hearsay, but I don't know what Mr. St. Amant makes. I know he is a retired Army officer. You have to balance that also against Captain Thompson and the damage to his reputation. I don't think that he has been harmed insofar as any monetary loss is concerned. His employers think as much of him today as they did at the date of this speech. He has lost no money. If I was fooling with WAFB-TV or with the Item Publishing Company, as in the *Kennedy* case[13] and others, the award would be considerably higher than I am going to give.

I fix the award in favor of Captain Thompson and against Mr. St. Amant at the Sum of $5,000.00.

Mr. Van Buskirk, we will furnish you with all of my remarks made in court today, and I will hold Mr. Kleinpeter off, and I know that he will do so voluntarily, from getting the judgment signed until you can examine them, and if you have any other argument that you wish to make and have found me incorrect in the law in any way, then you will have that opportunity.

I will sign a judgment accordingly in favor of plaintiff as stated.

Baton Rouge. Louisiana, this 8th day of May, 1964.
s/ Fred A. Blanche, Jr.
JUDGE, 19th JUDICIAL DISTRICT
COURT

(FILED: May 8, 1964.)

13. This is apparently a reference to Kennedy v. Item Co., 34 So. 2d 886 (La. 1948), reh'g denied (La. March 22, 1948), in which the Louisiana Supreme Court reversed a trial court ruling dismissing a lawyer's libel claim against a newspaper and, deciding that the article was not protected by the fair comment privilege, awarded the plaintiff lawyer $7,500.

TRIAL COURT RULING ON MOTION FOR RETRIAL

Thompson v. St. Amant, No. 88,779 (La. Dist. Ct., 19th Dist. [Baton Rouge Parish]). Reasons for Judgment [on Motion for Retrial], January 22, 1965.

The Court rendered oral reasons for judgment in favor of the plaintiff in the sum of $5,000.00 on a finding that defendant had libeled plaintiff in a political address which was subsequently printed and distributed by the defendant.[1] The Court has no misgivings about its decision that the remarks made by defendant were libelous but has entertained the motion for a new trial to consider the case in the light of the holding by the United States Supreme Court in the case of *New York Times Company v. Sullivan,* 84 S.Ct. 710 (1964).[2] That case held that:

> "The constitutional guarantees require, we think, a federal rule that prohibits a public official from recovering damages for a defamatory falsehood relating to his official conduct unless he proves that the statement was made with 'actual malice'—that is, with knowledge that it was [*sic*][3] false or with reckless disregard of whether it was false or not."[4]

Therefore, in light of the above quoted case, an inquiry into (1) whether or not the plaintiff is a public official and (2) whether the statement made by defendant was made with "actual malice"—that is, with knowledge that it was false or with disregard of whether it was false or not[—]is pertinent to a decision in this case.

The case of *State v. Mayeux*, 81 So. 2d 426,[5] had considered the status of a deputy Sheriff [*sic*] such as the plaintiff Captain Thompson:

> "A deputy sheriff is a state officer created by the Legislature and his appointment is provided for in LSA—R.S. 33:1433. Williams v. Guerre, 182 La. 745, 162 So. 609,[6] and the authorities cited therein [*sic*]."[7]

1. This is incorrect; St. Amant actually printed and distributed the address at a press conference *before* the address was broadcast.

2. 376 U.S. 254 (1964).

3. It is unclear why this ellipsis is here. There is no omission from the text of the U.S. Supreme Court opinion.

4. 376 U.S. at 279–80.

5. 81 So. 2d 426 (La. 1955).

6. 162 So. 609 (La. 1935), *reh'g denied* (La. June 7, 1935).

7. 81 So. 2d at 427.

In *Gray v. De Bretton*, 188 So. 722, 724 ([La.] 1939), further reference to a deputy sheriff as a public officer is made in the following language:

> "The relation between a sheriff and his deputy is an official and not a private relation. *The deputy is not a representative of the sheriff in his individual capacity, but he is a public officer whose authority and duty are regulated by law.* As to the public, whose servants these officers are, the acts and omissions of a deputy sheriff are the acts and omissions of the sheriff himself."[8] (Emphasis added)[9]

Further evidence that he is a public officer is found in the fact that Article 19, Section 1, of the Constitution of 1921 provides that "All officers shall take the following oath or affirmation . . . ," and R.S. 33:1433 under the title of "Public Officers" provides for the office of deputy sheriff and requires the taking of the oath and for the filing of a bond.

Having found plaintiff to be a public officer, the rule enunciated in *New York Times Company v. Sullivan, supra,* is applicable, namely, that malice may not be implied in the case of a public official (officer) and that actual malice must be shown, that is, with knowledge that it (the statement) was false or "with disregard of whether it was false or not."

Previously, the Court in its oral decision from the bench applied the Louisiana law which was just recently stated in the case of *Lamartiniere v. Daigrepont*, 169 So. 2d 373 [*sic*][10] (October 27, 1964), La. App., 3d Cir.:

> " . . . the defendant states, as a witness, that he entertained neither malice nor ill will against the plaintiff at the time it was uttered; yet; in such case, the law imputes malice to the act, on account of its character, for the use of opprobrious epithets implies malice when they are slanderous per se. It suffices to maintain an action to recover damages without proving special injury to the party defamed."[11]

Thus the Court's decision cannot stand on the basis that malice may be implied

8. 188 So. at 724 (La. 1939) (emphasis added by Thompson trial court).

9. The court added the emphasis to the quotation from the *Gray v. De Bretton* case and added "(Emphasis added)" to clarify this.

10. The court's citation is incorrect. The correct citation is 168 So. 2d 370.

11. 168 So. 2d at 372 (La. App., 3d Cir. 1964) (quoting Savoie v. Scanlan, 9 So. at 919 [La. 1891]).

by the mere character of the statement in light of its holding that plaintiff is a public official, and that brings us to the final question of whether under the federal rule as enunciated in *New York Times Company v. Sullivan* (*supra*) the plaintiff has shown actual malice.

Mr. St. Amant stated that he intended no malice toward Captain Thompson, that he was in a political fight with Senator Russell Long and had no interest in Captain Thompson. In reply to a question by plaintiff's counsel as to whether he gave any consideration to what effect the statement in the affidavit of Mr. Albin would have on Captain Thompson, he replied that Captain Thompson was not even in his mind. He further testified that he did not consider that Captain Thompson would be harmed by the statement and that he did not know what the money was for and that for all he knew the same could have been for Thompson's favorite charity. Finally, he admitted that as far as he was concerned he would let the public draw whatever inference it liked with regard to his reference to Captain Thompson.

Therefore, if Mr. St. Amant did not even know Captain Thompson or have any interest in him and if he did not know what the money was for, which is evidence that he made no attempt to investigate whether there was any relationship between Mr. Partin and Captain Thompson, to justify his charge that Captain Thompson was being paid off, and if he never gave any consideration as to what effect those remarks might have on Captain Thompson's reputation and character and was content to let the public draw whatever inference it desired concerning these remarks, than fairness dictates that despite defendant's avowed absence of ill will toward Captain Thompson or intent to do him harm or damage, he acted with reckless and wanton disregard for whether the statement was false or not and in the language of the Sullivan case "with disregard of whether it (the statement) was false or not."

The Court is satisfied that its original opinion was correct, and for the reasons here stated the motion for a new trial is denied and judgment will be signed in favor of the plaintiff as originally rendered herein.

Baton Rouge, Louisiana. this 22nd day of January, 1965
s/ Fred A. Blanche, Jr.
JUDGE, 19th JUDICIAL DISTRICT COURT

(FILED: January 22, 1965)

Thompson v. St. Amant, 184 So. 2d 315 (La. App. 1966) (No. 6571) (reversing trial verdict), rehearing denied (La. App. April 4, 1966).

Plaintiff in this action, Captain Herman A. Thompson of the East Baton Rouge Parish Sheriff's Department, alleges he was libeled and slandered by the defendant, Phil A. St. Amant, in a television address made by the defendant and a subsequent printed news release prepared by the defendant.

The case was tried on May 5, 1964 and for written reasons assigned [on] May 8, 1964, judgment was rendered against the defendant awarding the plaintiff the sum of $5,000 damages. Judgment was signed May 13, 1964. A motion for a new trial was filed [on] May 18, 1964, and for written reasons assigned [on] January 22, 1965, judgment was signed January 27, 1965 denying the motion for new trial and decreeing the judgment of May 13, 1964 [as] the judgment of the District Court as originally rendered. It is from that judgment that defendant has lodged this appeal.

The undisputed facts of this case show that the defendant, Phil A. St. Amant, had qualified as a candidate for United States Senator against the incumbent, Senator Russell B. Long, in the Democratic Primary of 1962, and on June 27, 1962, the defendant made an appearance on WAFB-TV, Channel 9, Baton Rouge, Louisiana, during which certain remarks were made about the plaintiff. The general context of the speech was made available to the press and given wide publicity by the press.

The record shows that the political method used in this particular instance was one so frequently used, that is, to allege certain wrongdoings on the part of one individual or group of individuals and then allege a connection between that individual or group of individuals and a politician. In the present case it was sought to show a connection between Senator Long and one E. G. Partin, local leader of the Teamsters Union[,] who was accused of all sorts of wrongdoings.

Insofar as the record here is concerned, the alleged slanderous and libelous material is contained in an affidavit by a Mr. J. D. Albin, an ex-member of the Teamsters Union, which was read by the defendant Mr. St. Amant during his television program. It appears that while the television station would be protected from statements made by Mr. St. Amant as a political candidate under the equal time provision of the Rules of the Federal Communications Commission, it would not be protected from statements made by Mr. Albin if those statements were made by St. Amant over the television. For that reason the television station personnel required that the defendant read the entire affidavit, which was in the form of questions and answers. The affidavit by Mr. Albin was most broad in its accusations of various acts of commission and omission on the part of Mr. E. G. Partin, including his being involved or connected with Fidel and Raoul [*sic*] Castro, his misuse of Union funds, and his committing various acts of violence. It barely mentioned Mr. St. Amant's opponent. That portion of the affidavit which plaintiff contends was slanderous is set forth below:

"Mr. Albin: Yes, Frank L. Doughty on March 21st, wrote a letter to Arthur Goldberg with a copy being sent to James R. Hoffa, asking for an investigation of Teamsters Local Union #5. On the 25th, Frank L. Doughty received a reply from James R. Hoffa asking for information, any and all information concerning these charges. On Monday morning, Frank L. Doughty, which was the 27th of March, he mailed this information to Jimmy Hoffa. Later in the day, I found out Ed had, in the letter coming from Hoffa, it said on the bottom of it a notation, copies sent to Teamsters Local Union #5. Now Ed received this copy on Monday. He became pretty riled up about it and in the afternoon, A. G. Kline, who was still working at that time as an assistant and an organizer for Local Teamsters Union #5, told me that Johnny Birch had stopped him on the Airline Highway and told him Ed wanted him to help him get rid of the safe that night, that there was going to be an investigation of the local union and the records had to be destroyed and it was going to take four men to do it. He told him who all was supposed to be in on it and that they were supposed to take it to Bruce Hunt's shop. That is the man that owns Triple A construction, and cut it open that night, that it had been okayed with Bruce. Kline didn't want to be involved in this so he got his brother in New Orleans to send him a telegram so he could get out and still stay in Ed's good graces, because at this time, we still felt that there was further information that could be derived from his employment in Teamsters #5 and we knew something had to be done if we were ever to straighten out the local union. The only way to straighten it out was the removal of E. G. Partin. Now we knew that this safe was going to be removed that night. *Imagine our predicament knowing of Ed's connection with the sheriff's office through Herman Thompson who made recent visits to the hall to see Ed. We also knew of money that had passed hands between Ed and Herman Thompson, from Ed to Herman. We also knew of his connections with State Lieutenant Trooper Joe Green. We knew we couldn't get any help from there and we didn't know how far he was involved in the sheriff's office or the State Police office through that and it was out of the jurisdiction of the City police.*[1]

"Col. St. Amant: What did you do then?

"Mr. Albin: Well, we rode around awhile trying to decide what to do. Fi-

1. The court added the emphasis to this paragraph of the transcript.

nally, we decided that we would go to the hall ourselves and see if there was any way we could stop them if we saw them coming out with the safe. We arrived a little too late, somewhere in the neighborhood of 9:00, the safe was gone. The next morning there was an investigation. Brother Herman Thompson came out and investigated and I understand that Lieutenant Joe Green showed up. They seemed to think it was a job by a professional. I agree with them."

The above quoted portion contains the sole reference upon which plaintiff's case is based.

In the Trial Judge's original reasons for judgment and in the briefs filed by counsel for plaintiff and for defendant much jurisprudence is cited and there is a great deal of discussion as to what does or does not constitute actionable libel or slander. However, since the rendition by the Supreme Court of the United States in the case of *New York Times Company v. Sullivan*, 376 U.S. 254, 84 S. Ct. 710, 11 L. Ed. 2d 686, and in *Garrison v. State of Louisiana*, 379 U.S. 64, 85 S. Ct. 209, 13 L. Ed. 2d 125, most of what was discussed [in the trial court ruling] is now moot and of no relevancy.

Before discussing the effects of the above cited decisions on actions of libel and slander in Louisiana, we feel we should point out certain factual matters, some contested and some uncontested, which are relevant to the issues herein and which will determine whether or not the issues in this case fall within the rule laid down by the United States Supreme Court in the recent decisions cited above.

It is undisputed that the plaintiff, Herman A. Thompson, is a well qualified, experienced law enforcement officer, having graduated from the F.B.I. National Academy, Southern Police Institute of Louisville, Kentucky, and is also a graduate of all phases of the Louisiana State University's law enforcement training program and of the East Baton Rouge Parish Sheriff's Department's own training school. He has the complete confidence of his employer, Sheriff Bryan Clemmons. Sheriff Clemmons testified that it was part of plaintiff's duties to participate in various fund-raising drives for East Baton Rouge Parish, including the Baton Rouge Kids' Baseball Clinic, the Mothers' March, March of Dimes, Elk's Christmas Funds Baskets, and others.

The undisputed facts also show that the plaintiff, Herman A. Thompson, was acquainted with the said E. G. Partin; that they were on first name basis; and that plaintiff was a frequent visitor to the Union Hall. Captain Thompson admitted this in his testimony:

"Q. Isn't it true that you were a rather frequent visitor at the Union Hall and used to drop in once a week or maybe every ten days:

A. That's right.

Q. To pass the time of day?

A. To pass the time of day and just to talk to the two secretaries, to use the phone and different things like that."

He also admitted that he collected charitable contributions from Ed Partin for the Baton Rouge Kids' Baseball Clinic.

With regard to the stolen safe referred to in the quoted portion of the affidavit, the plaintiff testified that he investigated the matter with Chief Criminal Deputy George LeBlanc, who made the report, and that the Crime Lab from the State Police also assisted, and he added: "I will have to admit that there was not as much effort put out as should have been for the simple reason the night before someone had burglarized Food Town of over fifteen thousand dollars and a lot of drugs were involved and it had every one of us tied up on that."

Both the plaintiff and Sheriff Clemmons admitted that various members of the Union might be aware that Mr. Partin on occasion gave Mr. Thompson money for some purposes, and while they both insisted that these funds were charitable contributions collected by the plaintiff for the Sheriff's office to be distributed to the proper charities, it is not inconceivable that some union members might have been suspicious of this exchange of funds.

Mrs. Marjorie Ann Smith was called as a witness in behalf of the defendant. She had been employed as a secretary for Teamsters Local No. 5 from September of 1958 to August of 1961. She testified that the latter part of February or the first part of March, 1961, she received instructions from Mr. Ed Partin and "called Mr. Herman Thompson at the Sheriff's office and he wasn't in, so I left word for him to call the Union, that we had something down there for him, and he was gone on a fishing trip and so a couple of days later Mr. Thompson came by the Union Hall and he said he wanted to pick up the envelope, and so Jeanette handed it to him out of her desk drawer and he folded it and put it in his pocket." She further testified that before Captain Thompson came to pick up the envelope she and Jeanette, another secretary working with her, opened the envelope and found that it contained five twenty dollar bills. She was asked what they did after they opened the envelope and she said:

"A. We put it in another envelope and sealed it up.

Q. Now, what type of an envelope was it in, Mrs. Smith, in the first place?

A. It was a legal size envelope, one of the Teamsters', with the Teamsters' emblem and address on it.

Q. Was it addressed to anyone?

A. It just had Herman Thompson's name on the front of the envelope.

Q. Are you familiar with the handwriting in which the name 'Herman

Thompson' was written?

A. Yes, sir, it was Mr. Partin's."

When asked what prompted them to open the envelope she said they knew Mr. Partin was under investigation and they were just wondering what was in the envelope. She could not, however, remember whether she ever reported this incident to the law enforcement officers and said "I have been before the Federal Grand Jury and I can't remember if that was brought out or not." She also admitted that she knew Captain Thompson had picked up some checks for Kids' Baseball; that it was not unusual for Mr. Partin to give money for all the major campaigns in the area, but that this was the first cash she had ever seen. She said Captain Thompson came by the Union Hall more frequently than other officers, usually while on duty and dressed in a suit, but sometimes when he was off duty and dressed in casual clothes and that sometimes he brought his little boy with him.

The testimony of the defendant, Mr. St. Amant, is, of course, also relevant and we quote below the pertinent portion thereof:

"Q. Now, sir, at the time you made your speech, did you give any consideration whatsoever or anything at all to what effects the reference to Captain Herman Thompson's name in this speech might have upon him?

A. Actually, when the original tape was made, and understand that when I read the affidavit I did not feel that I had any right to read parts of an affidavit or to just take sections from it. I do not understand the law on this, but I believe if I am going to give a document or affidavit, I should give the whole thing, and as I asked the question, I never mentioned the name of Herman Thompson. Herman Thompson wasn't even in my mind. I didn't even ask anything concerning the Sheriff's office. I asked quite an entirely different question, as you will see from the transcript, and out of this came a long story in which Mr. Thompson's name was used as explanation of why he felt there was a close personal relationship there that would keep him from going to the Sheriff's office. I neither elicited his name nor did I anticipate his name. Now, when I read the affidavit, I knew the name was in there and I did not consider that this was going to do anything to Mr. Thompson. In fact, I believe it has not. He was a Captain and is a Captain. I don't believe he has been suspended for five minutes and I don't believe he has lost any pay.

Q. Mr. St. Amant, with that knowledge and knowing that this reference to Captain Thompson was in this speech, you then permitted this very speech that we have listened to be transcribed and circulated to the members of the press?

A. I certainly did. I don't know what this money was for, Mr. Attorney. I did not suggest what the money was for, nor has— did Mr. Albin suggest what it was for. This could have been for his favorite charity for all I know, but as Mr. Albin explains, he couldn't go to him because he was contributing to this man, for whatever purpose. A close personal relationship existed. . . .

Q. So you left, you made the remarks, and left the inferences for the public to draw what they might, is that right?

A. I made the remark and let the public draw the conclusion that they might from the remark, which I believe was properly made at the time. I think you will find that Mr. Thompson's name, except from in quoting Mr. Albin, was never mentioned by me and no inference was drawn by me in further questioning that followed this. I had no interest at the time in Mr. Thompson. I had interest in Senator Russell Long, and I wanted to establish that here is a man in the public eye in a most disreputable fashion, and I am sure Mr. Thompson did not think I was speaking of him. I was speaking of the business agent who was notoriously in trouble at the time and was being helped out by a United States Senator to the detriment of his men, to the detriment of the working people of this parish. I believe this was true and I presented it as such. I have had no suits or opposition on this score from anybody else.

Q. In other words, Mr. St. Amant, you were after the big shot, so to speak, Senator Russell Long, and were not worried about the smaller individual, so to speak, that might have been involved down the way, is that correct?

A. Let's not draw an inference from my answer on that. I was not concerned with them. I did not think it concerned them."

It is clear that the Trial Judge was aware of the effect of the *New York Times* decision, *supra*, upon actions of this type for he granted a rehearing in order to consider the effect of that case upon the case at issue. The *Garrison* case, *supra*, was decided after the *New York Times* decision and was not considered by the Trial Judge in his reasons for judgment on rehearing. Although the *Garrison* case dealt with the Louisiana defamation statute, LSA-R.S. 14:47, it is also most relevant to the case at issue for in the *Garrison* case the rule of the *New York Times* case on libel was applied to the Louisiana statute and the comments and explanations of the rule in the *Garrison* case are therefore relevant to the case at issue since it is clear from a reading of both cases that the rule for libel in cases regarding a public official's conduct is the same whether it be civil libel or criminal libel.

We quote below the Trial Judge's Reasons for Judgment on rehearing:

"The Court rendered oral reasons for judgment in favor of the plaintiff in the sum of $5,000.00 on a finding that defendant had libeled plaintiff in a political address which was subsequently printed and distributed by the defendant. The Court has no misgivings about its decision that the remarks made by defendant were libelous but has entertained the motion for a new trial to consider the case in the light of the holding by the United States Supreme Court in the case of *New York Times Company v. Sullivan* [376 U.S. 254], 84 S. Ct. 710, 11 L. Ed. 2d 686 (1964). That case held that:

> "'The constitutional guarantees require, we think, a federal rule that prohibits a public official from recovering damages for a defamatory falsehood relating to his official conduct unless he proves that the statement was made with 'actual malice'—that is, with knowledge that it was . . . false or with reckless disregard of whether it was false or not.'
>
> "Therefore, in light of the above quoted case, an inquiry into (1) whether or not the plaintiff is a public official and (2) whether the statement made by defendant was made with 'actual malice'—that is, with knowledge that it was false or with disregard of whether it was false or not[—]is pertinent to a decision in this case.
>
> "The case of *State v. Mayeux* [228 La. 6], 81 So. 2d 426, had considered the status of a deputy sheriff such as the plaintiff Captain Thompson:
>
> "'A deputy sheriff is a state officer created by the Legislature and his appointment is provided for in LSA-R.S. 33:1433. Williams v. Guerre, 182 La. 745, 162 So. 609, and the authorities cited therein.'

"In Gray v. DeBretton [192 La. 628], 188 So. 722, 724 (1939), further reference to a deputy sheriff as a public officer is made in the following language:

> "'The relation between a sheriff and his deputy is an official and not a private relation. The deputy is not a representative of the sheriff in his individual capacity, but he is a public officer whose authority and duty are regulated by law. As to the public, whose servants these officers are, the acts and omissions of a deputy sheriff are the acts and omissions of the sheriff himself.'

"Further evidence that he is a public officer is found in the fact that Article 19, Section 1, of the Constitution of 1921 provides that 'All officers . . . shall take the following oath or affirmation . . .,' and R.S. 33:1433 under the title of 'Public Officers' provides for the office of deputy sheriff and requires the taking of the oath and for the filing of a bond.

"Having found plaintiff to be a public officer, the rule enunciated in *New York Times Company v. Sullivan, supra,* is applicable, namely, that malice may not be implied in the case of a public official (officer) and that actual malice must be shown, that is, with knowledge that it (the statement) was false or 'with disregard of whether it was false or not.'

"Previously, the Court in its oral decision from the bench applied the Louisiana law which was just recently stated in the case of Lamartiniere v. Daigrepont, 168 So. 2d 373 (October 27, 1964), La.App.3rd Cir.:

"'. . . the defendant states, as a witness, that he entertained neither malice nor ill will against the plaintiff at the time it was uttered; yet, in such case, the law imputes malice to the act, on account of its character, for the use of opprobrious epithets implies malice when they are slanderous per se. It suffices to maintain an action to recover damages without proving special injury to the party defamed.'

"Thus, the Court's decision cannot stand on the basis that malice may be implied by the mere character of the statement in light of its holding that plaintiff is a public official, and that brings us to the final question of whether under the federal rules as enunciated in *New York Times Company v. Sullivan* (*supra*) the plaintiff has shown actual malice.

"Mr. St. Amant stated that he intended no malice toward Captain Thompson, that he was in a political fight with Senator Russell Long and had no interest in Captain Thompson. In reply to a question by plaintiff's counsel as to whether he gave any consideration to what effect the statement in the affidavit of Mr. Albin would have on Captain Thompson, he replied that Captain Thompson was not even in his mind. He further testified that he did not consider that Captain Thompson would be harmed by the statement and that he did not know what the money was for and that for all he knew the same could have been for Thompson's favorite charity. Finally, he admitted that as far as he was concerned he would let the public draw whatever inference it liked with regard to his reference to Captain Thompson.

"Therefore, in [*sic*] Mr. St. Amant did not even know Captain Thompson or have any interest in him, and if he did not know what the money was for, which is evidence that he made no attempt to investigate whether there was any relationship between Mr. Partin and Captain Thompson, to justify his charge that Captain Thompson was being paid off, and if he never gave any consideration as to what effect those remarks might have on Captain Thompson's reputation and character and was content to let the public draw whatever inference it desired concerning these remarks, then fairness dictates that despite defendant's avowed absence of ill will toward Captain Thompson or intent to do him harm or damage, he acted with reckless and wanton disregard for whether the statement was false or not and in the language of the Sullivan case 'with disregard of whether it (the statement) was false or not.'

"The Court is satisfied that its original opinion was correct, and for the reasons here stated the motion for a new trial is denied and judgment will be signed in favor of the plaintiff as originally rendered herein."

We feel that the definition of a public official as set forth in the Judge's reasons for judgment on rehearing clearly answers the question as to whether or not the plaintiff is or is not a public official, and therefore the plaintiff's contention, as set forth in his brief, that he is not a public official has no merit, and the rule of the *New York Times* case does apply to plaintiff. We make this statement fully aware that in footnote 23 in the *New York Times* decision the Court said: "We have no occasion here to determine how far down into the lower ranks of government employees the 'public official' designation would extend for purposes of this rule, or otherwise to specify categories of persons who would or would not be included." Nor do we agree with the contention that as the Court in the *New York Times* case did not define official conduct, that the conduct herein was not official but of an extracurricular activity, that is, solicitation of money for civic charities. This position is also without merit because it is not that conduct which is criticized in the affidavit. The affidavit deals with the fears of the affiant concerning the manner in which the plaintiff would or would not discharge his duties if the mentioned safe was stolen. It is the relationship of Mr. Partin and the plaintiff in his official capacity that is the subject of the affidavit, not the reason for the plaintiff's appearances at the Union Hall.

In the *New York Times* case the [U.S. Supreme] Court held that the Constitution limits state power in a civil action brought by a public official for criticism of his official conduct to an award of damages for a false statement "made with 'actual malice'—that is, with knowledge that it was false or with reckless disregard of whether it was false or not." *Garrison v. State of Louisiana, supra.* Therefore, the central issue in this case is whether the facts bring it within the rule of the *New York Times* case, which rule was further enunciated in the *Garrison* case, and that is, were these statements made with "'actual malice'—that is, with knowledge that it was false or with reckless disregard of whether it was false or not." The record does not show that the statements made by the defendant about the plaintiff were made with knowledge that they were false. Therefore, we are not concerned with that portion of the definition of actual malice that deals with "knowledge that it was false" but there is no proof, but are concerned with whether or not, in view of the facts in the case, the statements made by the defendant were made "with reckless disregard of whether it was false or not." It should be pointed out that the proof of actual malice is on the plaintiff, *New York*

Times Company v. Sullivan, supra, that is, the plaintiff must prove that the statements were made with the knowledge that the same were false or with reckless disregard as to whether such statements were false or not.

Neither the *Garrison* case nor the *New York Times* case sets forth with any degree of clarity the steps the plaintiff must or must not take in order to determine whether or not statements were made with reckless disregard as to whether such statements were true or false. Mere negligence in determining whether or not a statement is correct is not a showing of actual malice. *New York Times Company v. Sullivan,* 376 U.S. 254, 288, 84 S. Ct. 710, 730, 11 L. Ed. 2d 686. Nor does speaking out of hatred mean actual malice under the *New York Times* and *Garrison* rule. In the *Garrison* case the Court said:

> "Moreover, even where the utterance is false, the great principles of the Constitution which secure freedom of expression in this area preclude attaching adverse consequences to any except the knowing or reckless falsehood. Debate on public issues will not be uninhibited if the speaker must run the risk that it will be proved in court that he spoke out of hatred; even if he did speak out of hatred, utterances honestly believed contribute to the free interchange of ideas and the ascertainment of truth. Under a rule like the Louisiana rule, permitting a finding of malice based on an intent merely to inflict harm, rather than an intent to inflict harm through falsehood, 'it becomes a hazardous matter to speak out against a popular politician, with the result that the dishonest and incompetent will be shielded.' Noel, Defamation of Public Officers and Candidates, 49 Col. L. Rev. 875, 893 (1949). . . ."

A study of the *New York Times* case and the *Garrison* case makes it clear that there must be more than an inference drawn before a statement can be said to fall within the rule of those cases. The mere fact that criticism of the manner in which a public official performs his duties would tend to affect his private reputation as well as his public reputation would not render inapplicable the *New York Times* rule. *Garrison v. State of Louisiana,* 379 U.S. 64, 77, 85 S. Ct. 209, 217, 13 L. Ed. 2d 125. It would certainly follow that if the statement made by the District Attorney of Orleans Parish and quoted in the *Garrison* case to the effect that

> "The judges have now made it eloquently clear where their sympathies lie in regard to aggressive vice investigations by refusing to authorize use of the DA's funds to pay for the cost of closing down the Canal Street clip joints,"

is not libelous under the *New York Times* rule (the application of the civil rule of libel as announced by the Supreme Court in that case to criminal libel in Louisiana), then certainly the statements made by the defendant Mr. St. Amant in the present case would not be libelous under that rule.

There is only one statement in the affidavit involved in this case which could possibly have damaged Captain Thompson and that was the statement "we also knew of money that had passed hands between Ed and Herman Thompson, from Ed to Herman." Since the facts show that the plaintiff was well acquainted with Mr. Partin and had been seen by the Union people collecting money at the Union Hall (which could conceivably make a discontent Union member who was opposed to the Union leadership suspicious of the relationship)[,] the use of the quoted statement could not be said to have been used with reckless disregard as to whether false or true.

The statement of the Trial Judge that Mr. St. Amant did not have any interest in Captain Thompson and did not know what the money was for, which the Judge said is evidence that he made no attempt to investigate whether his statements were true in order to justify his charge that Captain Thompson was being paid off and that he gave no consideration as to what effect the remarks might have on Captain Thompson's reputation and character but was content to let the public draw whatever inference it desired, would not place the case under the *New York Times* rule of proving he acted with reckless and wanton disregard for whether the statement was false or not. This actually was another way of applying the rule of Lamartiniere v. Daigrepont, La. App., 168 So. 2d 373, quoted by the Trial Judge, in that the Trial Judge was imputing malice to the act on account of its character.

It is clear from the record in this case that the reputation of Captain Thompson, who is highly regarded and a well respected police official, was injured by the statements made, which statements had no relevancy whatsoever to the issue which the plaintiff was attempting to get across to the public, and that Captain Thompson was the victim of intemperate "mud slinging." It is also the opinion of this Court that prior to the decisions of the United States Supreme Court in the *New York Times* and the *Garrison* cases the words of the plaintiff would have been libelous under the Louisiana jurisprudence. However, in view of the U.S. Supreme Court's holding that the Constitution delimits a State's power to award damages for libel in actions brought by public officials against critics of their official conduct, as discussed above, this Court has no alternative but to hold that the judgment of the Trial Court is in error and should be reversed and there should be judgment in favor of the defendant dismissing plaintiff's suit at his cost.

Reversed.

Thompson v. St. Amant, 250 La. 405, 196 So. 2d 255 (1967) (No. 48184) (reversing Louisiana Court of Appeal), rehearing denied (La. March 27, 1967).

This action for $150,000 in damages for an alleged libel was instituted by Herman A. Thompson, a deputy sheriff of the parish of East Baton Rouge, against Phil A. St. Amant, a retired Army officer and business man of that parish.

The trial court found that the plaintiff, Thompson, had made out his cause of action and, accordingly, condemned the defendant, St. Amant, to pay $5,000 as damages. Upon proper and timely application, a new trial was granted to reconsider the case in the light of *New York Times Co. v. Sullivan*, 376 U.S. 254, 84 S.Ct. 710, 11 L.Ed.2d 686 (1964), which had been handed down in the meantime. After reconsideration the trial judge reinstated his original judgment. On appeal the First Circuit reversed, and we granted review on Thompson's application.

The petition alleges that, on June 27, 1962, St. Amant, who was then a candidate for the office of United States Senator, appeared on a television program in Baton Rouge and delivered a political campaign address which was also reduced to writing and distributed to the press and other news media.

In the beginning of his speech St. Amant said:

> "I have a story to reveal tonight which is so unusual that I have bought this time on the television to inform the public. This story involves a well-documented criminal, and ex-convict who became a labor chieftain. It involves misuse and theft of union funds, dealings with Communist officials of Cuba, a criminal conspiracy to destroy evidence and the destruction of that evidence; death resulting from the commission of a felony and a second death by a hit and run by a union car."

The address thereafter consisted principally of the reading by St. Amant of a transcript of an interview which he had previously had with one J. D. Albin, a member of the local Teamsters' Union. The interview was in question and answer form, with St. Amant asking the questions which Albin answered. At St. Amant's urging, Albin had sworn to the correctness of the facts he recounted, and St. Amant had possession of the affidavit in written form.

By its content the speech was unmistakably designed to disclose Albin's knowledge of illegal, unsavory and criminal actions by E. G. Partin, business agent of the local Teamsters' Union. In the speech St. Amant claimed Senator Russell B. Long, his opponent and the incumbent United States Senator, had recommended Partin to James Hoffa, the union president. By this disclosure he sought to disparage his opponent.

Included among Partin's activities, according to Albin's statements which St. Amant read, was a visit by Partin with Fidel and Raoul [*sic*] Castro in Cuba during November 1960. St. Amant quoted Albin as saying that Partin was responsible for the negotiation of a labor contract in Baton Rouge, giving up many wage benefits and surreptitiously continuing a practice of longer working hours contrary to the interest of union members. Partin was accused of using union funds for his personal benefit, to pay house notes and the rent for his girl friend's car.

Albin related that Partin took "numerous amounts of money out of the cash drawer during the week and at the end of the week he made this up by making a check out to someone else who would endorse it and they would deposit it into the union fund." Albin then relates, in response to St. Amant's questions, that these practices prompted a local union member to write a letter to Arthur Goldberg, then Secretary of Labor, with a copy to James Hoffa, asking for an investigation of Partin's local union by the union hierarchy. According to Albin, when Partin learned of this he became "pretty riled up" and enlisted four members of the union to "help him get rid of the safe" which contained the union records. Albin continued:

> "Now, we knew that this safe was gonna be moved that night, but imagine our predicament, knowing of Ed's connections with the Sheriff's office through Herman Thompson, who made recent visits to the Hall to see Ed. We also knew of money that had passed hands between Ed and Herman Thompson . . . from Ed to Herman. We also knew of his connections with State Trooper Lieutenant Joe Green. We knew we couldn't get any help from there and we didn't know how far that he was involved in the Sheriff's office or the State Police office through that, and it was out of the jurisdiction of the City Police."

In his narrative Albin asserted that the safe disappeared that night and that Thompson and Lieutenant Joe Green of the State Police investigated the case but nothing happened. The safe turned up "a few months later, Albin said, when a young man by the name of Forman dove off the river bridge and hit his head on the safe . . . killing himself." This death St. Amant and Albin characterized as "a death resulted [*sic*] from the commission of a felony." They concluded Forman's death was a "murder" for which, they implied, Partin was responsible.

Then followed statements by Albin, all of which were likewise read by St. Amant, purporting to give information from Partin's "rap sheet," revealing that Partin had been either arrested, charged or convicted for robbery, auto theft, breaking and entering, "second degree burglary," rape, and robbery with firearms. Albin charged that Partin was responsible for the death of a young soldier in Alabama, killed in a hit-and-run automobile accident while Partin was driving the offending vehicle.

St. Amant continued to read the transcript of his interview with Albin, quoting Albin's story of why A. G. Klein, a good friend and a union member, was not "testifying today." He quoted Albin as saying that Klein, who had knowledge of the "safe incident" and other illegal activities of Partin, testified before a Federal Grand Jury in New Orleans, and that shortly thereafter Klein met his death in St. Francisville when a truck "dropped on top of him loaded with about ninety thousand pounds of sand."

St. Amant's presentation of this political address—the manner in which he expressed himself, the tone and theme of the speech, the obvious manifestation of his belief in the veracity of Albin's statements—was calculated to impress upon the reader or listener that he had confidence in Albin's charges against Partin and Thompson and that he believed them to be true. The publication was principally designed to malign the conduct of the incumbent United States Senator; but to do this it was necessary to show Partin's unsavory character and criminal record. Thompson's name was brought into the story only incidentally, yet, he was nonetheless unmistakably accused of criminal conduct.

In his petition Thompson alleged that the publication by St. Amant was false, libelous, scurrilous and malicious and was intended to belittle, degrade and ridicule him. Clearly, he alleged, the publication reflected a design and intent on the part of the defendant, St. Amant, to defame, slander and libel Thompson's good name, reputation and character before his friends, the courts and the public in general. From St. Amant's remarks, the petition alleges, the false and defamatory imputation arises that Thompson was guilty of gross misconduct of a nefarious nature.

In his answer St. Amant admitted making the speech but denied that he defamed or intended to defame Thompson. He alleged that the context in which the remarks concerning Thompson were made shielded those remarks from any defamatory imputation. In the alternative, he alleged that the utterances concerning Thompson were true and their publication was for the public good. Even if not true, he alleges, there was no malice on his part.

As it is settled in Louisiana that the truth of a defamatory remark is generally a valid defense in a civil suit for defamation, it becomes necessary to decide initially if the remarks concerning Thompson were true. If they are shown to be true that would ordinarily end the case. If the utterances are false, however, we must then proceed to determine if they are defamatory and actionable. La.R.S. 13:3602; *Deshotel v. [Thistlethwaite]*, 240 La. 12, 121 So. 2d 222 (1960). Both the trial court and the Court of Appeal decided that the statements were not true, and we agree.

By his testimony at the trial, Thompson acknowledged that he first knew Partin in connection with labor disputes—to which Thompson had been assigned for duty. He got to know Partin better, he said, while investigating burglaries at the union hall. In fact, because he had been designated for special duty by the sheriff, he was required to come in contact with almost all of the union business agents in Baton Rouge. He knew them all by their first names and readily conceded that he received funds from Ed Partin when he picked up a check every year for the Baton Rouge Kids' Baseball Clinic. The United Mine Workers, pipefitters', electricians', carpenters', and other unions and several civic and charitable organizations were also solicited by him.

Other duties assigned to him included supervising a bell-ringing campaign for the Salvation Army, soliciting for the Volunteers of America, the March of Dimes, the Cystic Fibrosis Fund, the Elks Club and the Lions' Club. He assisted in these civic and charitable undertakings as a public service. And except for such solicitations, he had no connection with Partin other than as a law enforcement officer.

An effort was made to discredit Thompson's testimony that he had only received "checks" from Partin in the solicitations. Partin's former secretary, Marjorie Ann Smith, testified that Partin once gave her an envelope for delivery to Thompson. She stated that she and Jeanette Fletcher, another employee in the union office, opened the envelope and saw five twenty-dollar bills. According to Marjorie Ann Smith's testimony, Jeanette Fletcher handed the money to Thompson in a sealed envelope. Thompson, however, categorically denied having received any cash. The trial judge and the Court of Appeal rejected the Smith woman's testimony and accepted Thompson's version that no money passed from Partin to him, other than checks representing donations by the union to charitable and civic organizations. Since Marjorie Ann Smith's testimony was rejected and Jeanette Fletcher did not testify, there is no evidence to support the charge that "money passed" from Partin to Thompson. On this vital issue of fact, which bears so heavily on our decision, we agree with the trial court and the Court of Appeal.

Moreover, as the determination of this issue involves the credibility of the witnesses Thompson and Smith and because there is no other evidence upon which a contrary result could be reached, the record will not support reversal of the findings of both the trial court and the Court of Appeal. Not only do we find that the remarks about Thompson were false, we find that the record reflects impressively his integrity and good character.

Thompson admitted that checks passed to him from Partin as a solicitation for the Baton Rouge Kids' Baseball Clinic, but the remarks contained in St. Amant's publication say much more. Sheriff Bryan Clemmons, Thompson's employer, found it necessary to defend Thompson against the charges contained in the speech. For many citizens called the sheriff for an explanation because they believed that St. Amant had accused Thompson of taking a pay-off from Partin. A neighbor who heard the broadcast told Thompson that "some man" had called him "some kind of thief and all kinds of names." The meaning the controverted remarks convey to the average reader is utterly defamatory of Thompson.

Preceded and followed as the remarks about Thompson were by the numerous charges of criminal conduct on the part of Ed Partin, linked as those words were with the sequence of events concerning the theft of union funds and the destruction of the safe, it is difficult to ascribe to the words "We also knew of money that had passed hands between Ed and Herman Thompson . . . from Ed to Herman" any meaning except that they charged Thompson with taking a criminal pay-off from Ed Partin. Charging that "we knew we couldn't get any help from there," in the context in which it was used, was a charge that Thompson would aid and abet the wrongdoer rather than perform his duty and enforce the law or otherwise help prevent the commission of a crime. And it is fair to conclude that the defamatory character of these words was in all probability heightened by a dramatic oral presentation.

These are statements of fact. They cannot be said to be expressions of opinion or comments within the rule of "fair" comment. 1 Harper & James, Torts § 5.26 and § 5.28 (1956).

It is one thing to state an innocent fact; it is another to state it in such a manner that it charges criminal conduct to the average listener and to a significant segment of the community. In the latter instance, the party who utters the words bears the burden of establishing either their truth or some justification sanctioned by law; otherwise he must bear the legal consequence of his indiscretion and the injury suffered by the victim of his remarks. In a civil suit those consequences are damages measured in money. *Lewis v. Louisiana Weekly Publishing Co.*, 189 La. 281, 179 So. 315 (1938).

In keeping with this principle, this court in recent years said that:

> "A mere insinuation is as actionable as a positive assertion, if the meaning is plain; and if the words used, when taken in their ordinary acceptation, convey a degrading imputation, no matter how indirectly, they are libelous—it matters not how artfully their meaning is concealed or disguised." *Madison v. Bolton*, 234 La. 997, 1010, 102 So. 2d 433, 437–438 (1958).

The guarantees of freedom of speech and of the press embodied in our state and federal constitutions, though designed to assure broad freedom for the expression of opinion, do not permit unrestrained license or confer the right upon an individual to speak or print whatever he chooses without bearing the responsibility for the utterance. Where the published matter is false, malicious and injurious, full responsibility for the damage it may cause is exacted by the law, unless a proper defense or justification is established. *Kennedy v. Item Co.*, 213 La. 347, 34 So. 2d 886 (1948); *Fitzpatrick v. Daily States Publishing Co.*, 48 La.Ann. 1116, 20 So. 173 (1896).

Realizing that these propositions would establish his legal responsibility for false and defamatory utterances, St. Amant asserts that, if we find the remarks to be false, then his defense is that Thompson was a "public official." Thus, he is prohibited from recovering damage for a defamatory falsehood relating to his official conduct, unless he proves the statement was made with "actual malice"—that is, with knowledge that it was false or with reckless disregard of whether it was false or not. He relies upon the ruling in *New York Times Co. v. Sullivan,* 376 U.S. 254, 84 S.Ct. 710, 11 L.Ed.2d 686 (1964) to support this contention.

In the *New York Times* [c]ase, the United States Supreme Court held that, in a civil action brought by a public official for criticism of his official conduct, the First and Fourteenth Amendments to the Federal Constitution limit state power to an award of damages for a false statement "made with 'actual malice'—that is, with knowledge that it was false or with reckless disregard of whether it was false or not." *See Garrison v. State of Louisiana,* 379 U.S. 64, 85 S.Ct. 209, 13 L.Ed.2d 125 (1964).

Thus the issue is clearly formed. At this phase of our deliberation we must decide whether Thompson, a deputy sheriff, is a "public official" within the meaning of the rule announced in the *New York Times* [c]ase. We hold that he is.

A deputy sheriff is a state officer whose position is created by the legislature. His appointment is provided for by Title 33, Section 1433, of the Revised Statutes of this State. *State v. Mayeux,* 228 La. 6, 81 So. 2d 426 (1955); *Williams v. Guerre,* 182 La. 745, 162 So. 609 (1935). Article 19, Section 1, of the Louisiana Constitution of 1921 requires that all officers of the State shall take the prescribed oath. This constitutional mandate has been implemented by the legislature to require deputy sheriffs to take that oath (La.R.S. 33:1433). The relation between a sheriff and his deputy, then, is an "official" and not a "private" relation. The deputy is a representative of the sheriff in his official capacity; he is a public officer or official whose authority and duty are regulated by law. So far as the public is concerned, the acts of a deputy are the acts of the sheriff himself.

However, because Deputy Sheriff Thompson is technically a "public official" under Louisiana law, it does not follow that the rule announced in the New York Times [c]ase applies to this case. The real test is whether the official has, or appears to the public to have, "substantial responsibility for or control over the conduct of governmental affairs." *Rosenblatt v. Baer,* 383 U.S. 75, 85, 86 S.Ct. 669, 15 L.Ed.2d 597 (1966). See also Bertlesman, *Libel and Public Men,* 52 A.B.A.J. 657 (1966).

The deputy acts for the sheriff, and his acts are the acts of the sheriff. The sheriff's position in government vests him and his deputies with "substantial responsibility for or control of governmental affairs" at least where law enforcement and police functions are concerned. The New York Times rule applies, therefore, to this deputy sheriff. Gilligan v. King, 48 Misc.2d 212, 264 N.Y.S.2d 309 (1965); cf. Henry v. Collins, 380 U.S. 356, 85 S.Ct. 992, 13 L.Ed.2d 892 (1965) and *Pape v. Time, Inc.,* 354 F.2d 558 (7th Cir. 1965).

It remains, in the light of the conclusions we have already reached, to determine whether the false and defamatory remarks concerning Thompson were uttered by St. Amant with "reckless disregard" of whether they were false or not.

The most important witness to the crucial fact in this regard was Marjorie Ann Smith. It was she who testified that, following Partin's instructions, Jeanette Fletcher gave an envelope containing five, twenty-dollar bills to Thompson. Her testimony is relied upon to establish the truth of the statement that "pay-off" money passed from Partin to Thompson or, at least, to relieve St. Amant of any charge that his utterances were in "reckless disregard" of whether they were false or not. Yet the first time St. Amant contacted her to verify this occurrence was after the lawsuit was filed and, of course, long after the political address had been televised and otherwise widely disseminated. Jeanette Fletcher, the only other witness to the occurrence, was not called to testify on this vital issue, and her failure to do so was not explained.

Having no personal knowledge of Thompson's activities, St. Amant relied upon Albin's sworn statement to verify the truth of the defamatory matter. Albin, however, did not testify. (St. Amant explained that he was ill and in the hospital.) Nowhere in the record is the reliability or the reputation for truth or veracity of Albin shown.

Although St. Amant testified that he had other affidavits to support some of the facts detailed in his address, none were produced. When asked if he gave any consideration to the effect the speech would have on Thompson, he replied that Thompson "wasn't even on my mind." Partin was his main concern; and in his zeal to show a bad character and background in Partin and to link him to his opponent, he gave no consideration whatsoever to Thompson. He was heedless of the effect his address would have on Thompson or of the truthfulness or not of the statements concerning him.

St. Amant's testimony indicates that he was laboring under the mistaken impression that because the words concerning Thompson were not in themselves defamatory he could not be involved in what might be implied from those words, such as the charge of criminal conduct which was implicit in them because of the context in which they were used. St. Amant felt he would be shielded from any responsibility because he was quoting Albin. In his own words, "Herman Thompson wasn't even on my mind." It was reckless error for him to take this position. Such a faulty assumption was in utter disregard of whether the remarks about Thompson were true or false.

We think the record contains adequate proof of actual malice on the part of St. Amant—that is, a reckless disregard as to whether the statements concerning Thompson were true or not.

Although "public men are, as it were, public property,"[1] we do not feel that the free-

1. Beauharnais v. People of State of Illinois, 343 U.S. 250n18, 72 S.Ct. 725, 96 L.Ed. 919 (1952).

dom of "uninhibited, robust, and wide-open"[2] debate on public issues guaranteed by the First Amendment to the Federal constitution can "sensibly be turned into an open season to shoot down the good name of any man who happens to be a public servant."[3]

No proof of damages was necessary, and we do not regard the verdict as excessive.

For the reasons assigned, the judgment of the Court of Appeal is reversed, and the judgment of the trial court is reinstated and made the judgment of this court.

McCALEB, J., dissents with written reasons.

HAMLIN, J., dissents, being of the view that the result reached by the Court of Appeal is correct. See also *Time v. Hill*, 385 U.S. 374, 87 S.Ct. 534, 17 L.Ed.2d 456.

McCALEB, Justice (dissenting).

I am in disagreement with all factual and legal conclusions of the majority opinion save one—that is, that plaintiff, Thompson, is a public official whose activities come within the rule laid down by the Supreme Court of the United States in *New York Times Co. v. Sullivan*, 376 U.S. 254, 84 S.Ct. 710, 11 L.Ed.2d 686 (1964).

In the first place, it is my view that the evidence in this case clearly discloses that the *facts* related in the sworn affidavit of J. D. Albin (which affidavit was read by St. Amant on television) are substantially true. Thompson admits in his testimony that he was a good friend of the labor leader, Partin (he called him Ed and Partin called him Herman), and was a rather frequent visitor at the Union Hall. He says that he regularly visited the Hall once a week or every ten days to pass the time of day and talk to the two lady secretaries, also to use the phone and "different things like that." He received contributions from Partin for the Baton Rouge Kids' Baseball Clinic but insists that he was given checks, vehemently denying that any payments were made in cash. At first, he denied that these checks were delivered in envelopes but later admitted that, on one or two occasions, the contribution had been placed in an envelope. He said: "Once or twice there has been an envelope but I never opened it. I would bring it in and give it to Polly."[1] He testified

2. New York Times Co. v. Sullivan, 376 U.S. 254, 84 S.Ct. 710, 11 L.Ed.2d 686 (1964).

3. Tucker v. Kilgore, 388 S.W.2d 112 (Ky. 1965).

1. Polly, to whom he refers, is Mrs. Coxe, the sheriff's secretary, who, Thompson and the sheriff say, kept the record of the collections made by Thompson (he was specially assigned for this extra curricular activity by the sheriff and he solicited, besides the Teamsters, the Electricians, Carpenters, Pipefitters, United Mine Workers and several other labor unions operating within the Baton Rouge area) in the fund-raising drives for various organizations—Baton Rouge Kids' Baseball Clinic, the Baton Rouge Mothers' March, March of Dimes, Elks' Christmas Fund Baskets, the Eagles Christmas Baskets, Lions Club Light Bulb Sale, the Volunteers of America, Cystic Fibrosis and the Shrine

further that he never received anything other than the contributions from Partin and that, when he graduated from the F.B.I. School and had successfully cleared certain burglaries at the Union Hall, Partin sought to reward him by offering him a suit of clothes and a check as a present. However, he says he rejected the offer and reported the matter to the sheriff.

It is thus seen from Thompson's testimony that Albin's statement in his affidavit—that "We also knew of money that had passed hands between Ed and Herman Thompson . . . from Ed to Herman" was true unless it be that there is a technically factual difference in payment by check or by cash.[2]

True, the affidavit states that "money had passed hands" but in usual parlance the term is broad enough to cover payment by check as well as cash. Yet the majority opinion attaches much significance to the evidence on this score. The opinion relies heavily on the statement of Thompson, an interested witness, and rejects as false and unreliable, the testimony of Mrs. Marjorie Ann Smith, one of the secretaries at the Teamsters' Hall, an apparently disinterested witness, who stated unequivocally that Partin had placed five $20.00 bills (which she saw) in an envelope which was delivered by the other secretary, Jeanette Fletcher, to Thompson under Partin's instructions.

For my part, I perceive no valid reason for the rejection of Mrs. Smith's evidence. The deduction that her testimony is unworthy of belief seems to be founded in part on the failure of St. Amant to call Jeanette Fletcher, the other secretary, who Mrs. Smith says also observed the $20.00 bills in the envelope, to corroborate Mrs. Smith's statement. But I know of no law placing such burden on St. Amant. It is not shown that he was acquainted with or had any control over Miss Fletcher who, as the record shows, was acquainted with Thompson and presumably available to him as a witness. Actually, since this phase of the case reduces itself to the affirmative statement of Mrs. Smith that cash was passed and the denial of Thompson that he received cash (the payment being made by check) it is to be wondered why Thompson did not call his friend, Partin, to the stand to verify his statement. Also, he could have called Mrs. Coxe to whom he allegedly delivered all checks from the Teamsters, but no cash, according to Thompson and the sheriff.

Circus. According to Sheriff Clemmons, it came as no surprise to him that some of the members of the Teamsters' Union (evidently meaning Albin and others) might be aware that Partin was giving Thompson money for some purpose, and he further testified that Thompson had received cash as well as checks in his solicitation activities from other sources but not from Partin.

2. Indeed, Thompson indicates that he did not know whether the payments enclosed in envelopes were made by check or cash, for he testified in rebuttal that, when the payment was in an envelope, ". . . I just brought the envelope in and gave it to Polly and didn't bother to open it."

Moreover, I note that the majority opinion states that "The trial judge and the Court of Appeal rejected the Smith woman's testimony and accepted Thompson's version that no money passed from Partin to him, other than checks representing donations by the union to charitable and civic organizations." I have carefully examined the opinions of the trial judge and the Court of Appeal (see 184 So. 2d 314) and find no ruling by either court rejecting the verity of Mrs. Smith's evidence.[3]

But, be this as it may, it makes no essential difference whether the payment was made in cash or by check. In either case the affidavit that money had passed between Partin and Thompson is an admitted fact. The only suggested difference is that Albin, the author of the affidavit, after relating that Partin withdrew money from the Union funds for his own use and later assertedly arranged for the disappearance of the safe containing the Union records (the accuracy of this part of Albin's affidavit is not challenged), expressed the opinion that, because of Partin's connection with a certain State Trooper, there would be no help obtained from the state police office for an investigation of the irregularities and that probably no assistance would come from the sheriff's office, in view of the close relationship between Partin and the plaintiff, Thompson. If Albin was incorrect in this deduction, this, under the *New York Times Co. v. Sullivan* rule, would not have warranted recovery even as to Albin (who, of course, is not a party defendant in this case) because the First Amendment to the Federal Constitution, which delimits by operation of the 14th Amendment the State's right to award damages for civil libels in matters involving public officials, applies only to those matters in which the injured official proves actual malice, i.e., that the publication is made with knowledge that it is false or in reckless disregard of whether it was false or true.

The *New York Times* rule, as I understand it, authorizes civil libel recovery by public officials for defamatory remarks based on facts known to be false. It does not extend this right of redress to the free expression of opinion, no matter how erroneous, when such conclusion is drawn from true statements of fact. In other words, in view of the fact that the statement that money had passed from Partin to Thompson is true, the

3. The trial judge rested his original opinion on the predicate that the affidavit of Albin was libelous per se. His only reference to Mrs. Smith's testimony is that she stated that money ". . . was left in an envelope from Mr. Partin to Mr. Thompson and that he picked up the same." As to this, the judge ruled, in effect, that it was immaterial whether the payments were made in cash or by check since all money paid was received ". . . purely in connection with drives put on by some charitable institution . . .," as avouched by the sheriff and Thompson. The court of appeal recited the substance of Mrs. Smith's testimony but made no finding as to her credibility. Indeed, such a finding would have been superfluous, in view of the court's conclusion that Thompson could not recover under the rulings in the New York Times and Garrison cases.

circumstance that Albin might have been mistaken, in implying that the money or check was given for Partin's or the Union's protection by the sheriff's office, would not afford a legal ground for holding the publication actionable. For this was fair comment, however erroneous, based on substantially true facts and to hold otherwise, according to the *New York Times* case, would unconstitutionally trench upon the right of free speech. As was stated in *Beauharnais v. People of State of Illinois*, 343 U.S. 250, 72 S.Ct. 725, 96 L.Ed. 919, and many times repeated, ". . . public men are, as it were, public property" and, in the absence of *actual* malice, an action for libel may not be maintained. *See also Garrison v. State of Louisiana*, 379 U.S. 64, 85 S.Ct. 209, 13 L.Ed.2d 125 (1964) and discussion in *Time v. Hill*, 385 U.S. 374, 87 S.Ct. 534, 17 L.Ed.2d 456 (1967).

What I have heretofore said would apply only if Albin, the author of the affidavit, was the defendant in this case. But this suit is not against Albin but against St. Amant for publishing the alleged libelous affidavit. Insofar as St. Amant is concerned, the case is exactly parallel with the New York Times decision. Surely St. Amant, having secured an affidavit to the facts set forth therein, can hardly be said to have been actuated by malice toward Thompson. Indeed no proof is shown here that St. Amant knew that any fact stated in the affidavit was false or that any conclusion drawn from a true fact stated in the affidavit was false.

However the majority opinion, in holding St. Amant liable for damages, deduces that the alleged defamatory remarks concerning Thompson were uttered by St. Amant with ". . . a reckless disregard as to whether the statements concerning Thompson were true or not." In reaching this conclusion the majority feels that St. Amant could not rely on the verity of the statements of fact contained in the affidavit; that it was incumbent on him to make an investigation of the truth of the statements before publication and that his failure to do so renders him liable as he necessarily utters the defamatory statement with reckless disregard of its truth or falsity. This pronouncement effectually implies malice for it places ignorance of falsity on a parity with knowledge of falsity and in the same category with actual malice by holding that failure to make an independent investigation of truth constitutes a reckless disregard of truth or falsity. But this is exactly contrary to the view of the United States Supreme Court in the *New York Times* case.

Under the Times doctrine a qualified privilege extends to misstatements of facts in a publication relating to a public officer if other conditions of a qualified privilege (absence of actual malice) exists. There, it was held that a statement attacking the official conduct of a public officer does not forfeit the protection of the constitutional guaranty of free speech by the falsity of some of its factual statements and by the alleged defamation of the public official or by a combination of these two elements and that a defense must be allowed for erroneous statements honestly made. The court found that actual malice had not been shown on the part of the signers or sponsors of a newspaper advertisement describing the maltreatment in Alabama of negro students protesting segregation, where there was no evidence whatever that they were aware of any erroneous statements or were in any way reckless in that regard.[4] With respect to the newspaper, it was held that a statement by its secretary that he thought the advertisement was substantially correct afforded no constitutional warrant for inferring actual malice from his ignoring the falsity of the advertisement, where his opinion was at least a reasonable one, and actual malice on the part of the newspaper was not shown by its failure to retract, upon plaintiff's demand, even though it later retracted upon the demand of the Governor of Alabama. It was found that there was no duty on the part of the newspaper to check the accuracy of the defamatory statement against the news stories in its own files which would have shown its falsity. This dereliction on the part of the newspaper was regarded as mere negligence and constitutionally insufficient to show the recklessness that is required for a finding of actual malice.

In the case at bar, the majority opinion places a much greater burden on St. Amant—for the Court implies actual malice, contrary to the *New York Times* case, by concluding that, because he testified that he gave no thought to Thompson, this ". . . was reckless error for him to take this position . . . a faulty assumption . . . in utter disregard of whether the remarks about Thompson were true or false."

In my view, St. Amant was justified in regarding the affidavit of Albin to be accurate. Further inquiry was not essential; the most that can be said is that, perhaps, he was negligent but negligence alone will not support a finding of actual malice.

The judgment of the Court of Appeal should be affirmed.

4. This holding clearly supports the view I have above stated with regard to the author of the affidavit.

U.S. SUPREME COURT

St. Amant v. Thompson, 390 U.S. 727 (1968) (No. 67-517).

MR. JUSTICE WHITE delivered the opinion of the Court.

The question presented by this case is whether the Louisiana Supreme Court, in sustaining a judgment for damages in a public official's defamation action, correctly interpreted and applied the rule of *New York Times Co. v. Sullivan*, 376 U.S. 254 (1964), that the plaintiff in such an action must prove that the defamatory publication "was made with 'actual malice'—that is, with knowledge that it was false or with reckless disregard of whether it was false or not." 376 U.S. at 279–280.

On June 27, 1962, petitioner St. Amant, a candidate for public office, made a televised speech in Baton Rouge, Louisiana. In the course of this speech, St. Amant read a series of questions which he had put to J. D. Albin, a member of a Teamsters Union local, and Albin's answers to those questions. The exchange concerned the allegedly nefarious activities of E. G. Partin, the president of the local, and the alleged relationship between Partin and St. Amant's political opponent. One of Albin's answers concerned his efforts to prevent Partin from secreting union records; in this answer Albin referred to Herman A. Thompson, an East Baton Rouge Parish deputy sheriff and respondent here:

"Now, we knew that this safe was gonna be moved that night, but imagine our predicament, knowing of Ed's connections with the Sheriff's office through Herman Thompson, who made recent visits to the Hall to see Ed. We also knew of money that had passed hands between Ed and Herman Thompson . . . from Ed to Herman. We also knew of his connections with State Trooper Lieutenant Joe Green. We knew we couldn't get any help from there and we didn't know how far that he was involved in the Sheriff's office or the State Police office through that, and it was out of the jurisdiction of the City Police."[1]

Thompson promptly brought suit for defamation, claiming that the publication had "impute[d] . . . gross misconduct" and "infer[red] conduct of the most nefarious nature." The case was tried prior to the decision in *New York Times Co. v. Sullivan, supra.* The trial judge ruled in Thompson's favor and awarded $5,000 in damages. Thereafter, in the course of entertaining and denying a motion for a new trial, the Court consid-

1. St. Amant had preceded this question and answer with other answers by Albin asserting that Partin, on learning that a union member had written to the Secretary of Labor charging that Partin had been stealing union funds, had become "pretty riled up" and had decided to "get rid of the safe" containing the union records.

ered the ruling in *New York Times,* finding that rule no barrier to the judgment already entered. The Louisiana Court of Appeal reversed because the record failed to show that St. Amant had acted with actual malice, as required by *New York Times.* 184 So. 2d 314 (1966). The Supreme Court of Louisiana reversed the intermediate appellate court. 250 La. 405, 196 So. 2d 255 (1967). In its view, there was sufficient evidence that St. Amant recklessly disregarded whether the statements about Thompson were true or false. We granted a writ of certiorari. 389 U.S. 1033 (1968).

For purposes of this case we accept the determinations of the Louisiana courts that the material published by St. Amant charged Thompson with criminal conduct, that the charge was false, and that Thompson was a public official[2] and so had the burden of proving that the false statements about Thompson were made with actual malice as defined in *New York Times Co. v. Sullivan* and later cases. We cannot, however, agree with either the Supreme Court of Louisiana or the trial court that Thompson sustained this burden.

Purporting to apply the *New York Times* malice standard, the Louisiana Supreme Court ruled that St. Amant had broadcast false information about Thompson recklessly, though not knowingly. Several reasons were given for this conclusion. St. Amant had no personal knowledge of Thompson's activities; he relied solely on Albin's affidavit although the record was silent as to Albin's reputation for veracity; he failed to verify the information with those in the union office who might have known the facts; he gave no consideration to whether or not the statements defamed Thompson and went ahead heedless of the consequences; and he mistakenly believed he had no responsibility for the broadcast because he was merely quoting Albin's words.

These considerations fall short of proving St. Amant's reckless disregard for the accuracy of his statements about Thompson. "Reckless disregard," it is true, cannot be fully encompassed in one infallible definition. Inevitably its outer limits will be marked out through case-by-case adjudication, as is true with so many legal standards for judging concrete cases, whether the standard is provided by the Constitution, statutes, or case law. Our cases, however, have furnished meaningful guidance for the further definition of a reckless publication. In *New York Times,* supra, the plaintiff did not satisfy his burden because the record failed to show that the publisher was aware of the likelihood that he was circulating false information. In *Garrison v. Louisiana,* 379 U.S. 64 (1964), also decided before the decision of the Louisiana Supreme Court in this case, the opinion emphasized the necessity for a showing that a false publica-

2. The Louisiana Supreme Court concluded, after considering state law, that a deputy sheriff has "substantial responsibility for or control over the conduct of governmental affairs," the test established by Rosenblatt v. Baer, 383 U.S. 75, 85 (1966), "at least where law enforcement and police functions are concerned." 250 La. at 422, 196 So. 2d at 261.

tion was made with a "high degree of awareness of . . . probable falsity." 379 U.S. at 74. MR. JUSTICE HARLAN'S opinion in *Curtis Publishing Co. v. Butts*, 388 U.S. 130, 153 (1967), stated that evidence of either deliberate falsification or reckless publication "despite the publisher's awareness of probable falsity" was essential to recovery by public officials in defamation actions. These cases are clear that reckless conduct is not measured by whether a reasonably prudent man would have published, or would have investigated before publishing. There must be sufficient evidence to permit the conclusion that the defendant in fact entertained serious doubts as to the truth of his publication. Publishing with such doubts shows reckless disregard for truth or falsity and demonstrates actual malice.

It may be said that such a test puts a premium on ignorance, encourages the irresponsible publisher not to inquire, and permits the issue to be determined by the defendant's testimony that he published the statement in good faith and unaware of its probable falsity. Concededly the reckless disregard standard may permit recovery in fewer situations than would a rule that publishers must satisfy the standard of the reasonable man or the prudent publisher. But *New York Times* and succeeding cases have emphasized that the stake of the people in public business and the conduct of public officials is so great that neither the defense of truth nor the standard of ordinary care would protect against self-censorship and thus adequately implement First Amendment policies. Neither lies nor false communications serve the ends of the First Amendment, and no one suggests their desirability or further proliferation. But to insure the ascertainment and publication of the truth about public affairs, it is essential that the First Amendment protect some erroneous publications as well as true ones. We adhere to this view and to the line which our cases have drawn between false communications which are protected and those which are not.

The defendant in a defamation action brought by a public official cannot, however, automatically insure a favorable verdict by testifying that he published with a belief that the statements were true. The finder of fact must determine whether the publication was indeed made in good faith. Professions of good faith will be unlikely to prove persuasive, for example, where a story is fabricated by the defendant, is the product of his imagination, or is based wholly on an unverified anonymous telephone call. Nor will they be likely to prevail when the publisher's allegations are so inherently improbable that only a reckless man would have put them in circulation. Likewise, recklessness may be found where there are obvious reasons to doubt the veracity of the informant or the accuracy of his reports.[3]

3. See, e.g., Curtis Publishing Co. v. Butts, 388 U.S. 130, 169–170 (Warren, C. J., concurring in the result), and 172 (Brennan, J., dissenting) (1967).

By no proper test of reckless disregard was St. Amant's broadcast a reckless publication about a public officer. Nothing referred to by the Louisiana courts indicates an awareness by St. Amant of the probable falsity of Albin's statement about Thompson. Failure to investigate does not in itself establish bad faith. *New York Times Co. v. Sullivan*, supra, at 287–288. St. Amant's mistake about his probable legal liability does not evidence a doubtful mind on his part. That he failed to realize the import of what he broadcast—and was thus "heedless" of the consequences for Thompson—is similarly colorless. Closer to the mark are considerations of Albin's reliability. However, the most the state court could say was that there was no evidence in the record of Albin's reputation for veracity, and this fact merely underlines the failure of Thompson's evidence to demonstrate a low community assessment of Albin's trustworthiness or unsatisfactory experience with him by St. Amant.

Other facts in this record support our view. St. Amant made his broadcast in June 1962. He had known Albin since October 1961, when he first met with members of the dissident Teamsters faction. St. Amant testified that he had verified other aspects of Albin's information and that he had affidavits from others. Moreover Albin swore to his answers, first in writing and later in the presence of newsmen. According to Albin, he was prepared to substantiate his charges. St. Amant knew that Albin was engaged in an internal struggle in the union; Albin seemed to St. Amant to be placing himself in personal danger by publicly airing the details of the dispute.

Because the state court misunderstood and misapplied the actual malice standard which must be observed in a public official's defamation action, the judgment is reversed and the case remanded for further proceedings not inconsistent with this opinion.

Reversed and remanded.

MR. JUSTICE BLACK and MR. JUSTICE DOUGLAS concur in the judgment of the Court for the reasons set out in their concurring opinions in *New York Times Co. v. Sullivan*, 376 U.S. 254, 293 (1964), and *Garrison v. Louisiana*, 379 U.S. 64, 79, 80 (1964).

MR. JUSTICE FORTAS, dissenting.

I do not believe that petitioner satisfied the minimal standards of care specified by *New York Times Co. v. Sullivan*, 376 U.S. 254 (1964). The affidavit that petitioner broadcast contained a seriously libelous statement directed against respondent. Respondent was a public official. He was not petitioner's adversary in the political contest. Petitioner's casual, careless, callous use of the libel cannot be rationalized as resulting from the heat of a campaign. Under *New York Times*, this libel was broadcast by petitioner with "actual malice"—with reckless disregard of whether it was false or not. The principle of Curtis Publishing Co. v. Butts, 388 U.S. 130 (1967), in my opinion, should lead us to affirmance here.

The First Amendment is not so fragile that it requires us to immunize this kind of reckless, destructive invasion of the life, even of public officials, heedless of their interests and sensitivities. The First Amendment is not a shelter for the character assassinator, whether his action is heedless and reckless or deliberate. The First Amendment does not require that we license shotgun attacks on public officials in virtually unlimited open season. The occupation of public officeholder does not forfeit one's membership in the human race. The public official should be subject to severe scrutiny and to free and open criticism. But if he is needlessly, heedlessly, falsely accused of crime, he should have a remedy in law. *New York Times* does not preclude this minimal standard of civilized living.

Petitioner had a duty here to check the reliability of the libelous statement about respondent. If he had made a good-faith check, I would agree that he should be protected even if the statement were false, because the interest of public officials in their reputation must endure this degree of assault. But since he made no check, I agree with the Supreme Court of Louisiana that *New York Times* does not prohibit recovery.

I would affirm.

NOTES

PREFACE

1. This figure is based on citations listed by the Shepherd's service within the LexisNexis database of legal materials.

2. This based on a review of all the biographical books on the justices in the Louisiana State University Middleton (general) and Law libraries.

3. Levine and Wermiel, *The Progeny*, 82–88.

4. The Black papers did not contain any information on the *St. Amant* case, but his involvement was gleaned from memos and other materials in the papers of the other justices.

INTRODUCTION

1. The details of St. Amant's charges against Long in the 1964 campaign come from Long's *New York Times* obituary and transcripts of St. Amant's television address on June 27, 1962, as played and transcribed (twice) during the trial in the subsequent libel case. Trial transcript, Thompson v. St. Amant, La. Dist. Ct. 1964, 15–35, 107–21.

2. Trial transcript, Thompson v. St. Amant, La. Dist. Ct. 1964, 28–29, 116–17.

3. Quoted in Lawhorne, *Defamation and Public Officials*, 263.

1
THE GUMBO OF 1960s LOUISIANA

1. The cleavage is described in Mann, *Legacy to Power*, 72, and in contemporary newspaper reports.

2. The details and circumstances of Huey Long's early life are chronicled in Hair, *The Kingfish and His Realm*, and on the Long Legacy Project's *Huey Long: The Man, His Mission and Legacy* website.

3. Cook and Watson, *Louisiana Labor*, 210.

4. Boulard, *Huey Long Invades New Orleans*, discusses this incident in detail.

5. The split between Earl and Russell in the 1952 election is detailed in Martin, *Dynasty*, 193–95.

6. This incident is discussed in detail in Kurtz and Peoples, *Earl K. Long*, 211; Martin, *Dynasty*, 205–17; and Mann, *Legacy to Power*, 72, 192–93.

7. Long's statements to Thompson and the other deputy were made before a crowd of onlookers. Martin, *Dynasty*, 248.

8. Martin, *Dynasty*, 293. Earl's initial plan was to formally resign before the primary, thus evading the prohibition against succeeding himself as governor. Kurtz and Peoples, *Earl K. Long*, 243–47.

9. "The Returns."

10. Sheridan, *The Fall and Rise of Jimmy Hoffa*, 408.

11. Vaccara and Miller, *Carlos Marcello*, 21.

12. This story is related in various sources, including Davis, *Mafia Kingfish*, 309; Hair, *The Kingfish and His Realm*, 12; and Vaccara and Miller, *Carlos Marcello*, 22.

13. Vaccara and Miller, *Carlos Marcello*, 24.

14. Chandler, "The 'Little Man' Is Bigger Than Ever"; Davis, *Mafia Kingfish*, 31–32.

15. Thompson, *Gambling in America;* and Boulard, *Huey Long Invades New Orleans*, 127–28, 132, 159–60.

16. Marcello's origins and immigration status are analyzed in detail in Kanstroom, "The Long, Complex, and Futile Deportation Saga of Carlos Marcello."

17. Kanstroom, "The Long, Complex, and Futile Deportation Saga of Carlos Marcello," 116; Vaccara and Miller, *Carlos Marcello*, 29–30; Davis, *Mafia Kingfish*, 23, 32.

18. Davis, *Mafia Kingfish*, 43.

19. Davis, *Mafia Kingfish*, 58.

20. The estimated size of Marcello's operations comes from Davis, *Mafia Kingfish*, 127.

21. *Hearings Before the Special Committee to Investigate Organized Crime in Interstate Commerce Pursuant to S. Res. 202*, pt. 8, p. 37.

22. Marcello v. U.S., 196 F.2d 437 (5th Cir. 1952).

23. Quoted in Davis, *Mafia Kingfish*, 60.

24. Kanstroom, "The Long, Complex, and Futile Deportation Saga of Carlos Marcello," 117–25. Marcello's convoluted deportation case is Matter of M____, 5 I. & N. Dec. 261, 270–71 (BIA 1953), *aff'd*, United States ex. rel. Marcello v. Ahrens, 113 F. Supp. 22 (E.D. La. 1953), *aff'd*, 212 F.2d 830 (5th Cir. 1954), *aff'd*, Marcello v. Bonds, 349 U.S. 302 (1955), *reh'g denied*, 350 U.S. 856 (1955).

25. Kanstroom, "The Long, Complex, and Futile Deportation Saga of Carlos Marcello," 128–30. One source claims that Marcello bribed an Italian official to get the revocation. Blakey and Billings, *The Plot to Kill the President*, 242.

26. For details of the CIA-sponsored coup in Guatemala, see Charles D. Brockett, *An Illusion of Omnipotence*. For details on Marcello's fake Guatemalan birth certificate, see Blakey and Billings, *The Plot to Kill the President*, 242.

27. Kanstroom, "The Long, Complex, and Futile Deportation Saga of Carlos Marcello," 133–34; Davis, *Mafia Kingfish*, 108–12, 309, 342, quote at 112 (quoting FBI report, June 16, 1961, Carlos Marcello file, Bureau Serials 126–202). Sources vary on the specifics of Marcello's travels in Central America, including how he returned to the United States.

28. Marcello v. Kennedy, 194 F. Supp. 750 (D.D.C. May 24, 1961), *vacated*, 312 F.2d 874 (D.C. Cir. 1962) (vacating rationale but reaching same result).

29. Kanstroom, "The Long, Complex, and Futile Deportation Saga of Carlos Marcello," 137. See United States ex. rel. Marcello v. District Director, 634 F.2d 964 (5th Cir. 1981), *reh'g and reh'g en banc denied*, 641 F.2d 879 (5th Cir. 1981), *cert. denied*, 452 U.S. 917 (1981).

30. Davis, *Mafia Kingfish*, 116, 118.

31. Davis, *Mafia Kingfish*, 118–19, 122–23, quote at 122.

32. Davis, *Mafia Kingfish*, 188–89, 197–99.

33. Report of the President's Commission on the Assassination of President Kennedy, 19, 21.

34. Davis, *Mafia Kingfish*, 136, 332–33, 367–68.

35. Davis, *Mafia Kingfish*, 331; Mann, *Legacy to Power*, 256; Associated Press, "Garrison Claims Arrests in JFK Probe Far Away." Garrison received a free room and $5,000 in gambling credits at the Sands Hotel in 1967, when it was partially owned by Marcello. Garrison was also tried on charges of taking money from pinball operators in Louisiana, which were controlled by Marcello's organization; he was acquitted despite the seizure of $1,000 in marked bills from Garrison's home. Blakey and Billings, *The Plot to Kill the President*, 50.

36. Moldea, *The Hoffa Wars*, 261; Davis, *Mafia Kingpin*, 358 (quote), 399.

37. Davis, *Mafia Kingpin*, 375–97.

38. Select Committee on Assassinations, *Summary of Findings and Recommendations*, 169, 172.

39. See U.S. v. Roemer, 703 F.2d 805 (5th Cir. 1983), *cert. denied*, 464 U.S. 935 (1983), and U.S. v. Marcello, 731 F.2d 1354 (9th Cir. 1984).

40. U.S. v. Marcello, 876 F.2d 1147 (5th Cir. 1989) (vacating RICO conviction).

41. Quoted in Smith, "Carlos Marcello," 94.

42. Godson, *Menace to Society*, 115.

43. Godson, *Menace to Society*, 176.

44. Chandler, The 'Little Man' Is Bigger Than Ever," 30, 34.

45. Chandler, The 'Little Man' Is Bigger Than Ever," 30, 34; Davis, *Mafia Kingpin*, 100, 112, 309, 342, 343.

46. Cook and Watson, *Louisiana Labor*, 67.

47. Cook and Watson, *Louisiana Labor*, 205–7; Troy and Sheflin, *U.S. Union Sourcebook*, 7–4.

48. Marshall, *Labor in the South*, 303; Troy and Sheflin, *U.S. Union Sourcebook*, 7–4; Mayer, *Union Membership Trends in the United States*, 22; Hirsch, Macpherson, and Vroman, "Estimates of Union Density by State"; Hirsch, Macpherson, and Vroman, *Union Density Estimates by State, 1964–2016*.

49. Partin, *From My Brother's Shadow*, 13–14, 36–38.

50. Trial transcript, Thompson v. St. Amant, La. Dist. Ct. 1964, 29–30, 118; Partin, *From My Brother's Shadow*, 47–48; Hoffa, *Hoffa*, 169; Hoffa, *The Trials of Jimmy Hoffa*, 240. According to Douglas Partin, the lone holdout on the jury in the rape trial later told him that "he just couldn't see a white man going to jail for raping a black woman." Partin, *From My Brother's Shadow*, 48.

51. Partin, *From My Brother's Shadow*, 48–50.

52. Partin, *From My Brother's Shadow*, 55, 58–59, 62.

53. Evans, *And Justice for All*, 38.

54. Neff, *Vendetta*, 252–53.

55. Velle, *Desperate Bargain*, 106; Mollenhoff, *Tentacles of Power*, 374–75.

56. Friedman and Schwarz, *Power and Greed*, 27.

57. Moldea, *The Hoffa Wars*, 3–84; Friedman and Schwartz, *Power and Greed*, 65.

58. Blakey and Billings, *The Plot to Kill the President*, 193; "Reveals Hoffa Signaled How to Cast Votes."

59. James and James, *Hoffa and the Teamsters*,190–91.

60. James and James, *Hoffa and the Teamsters*, 191.

61. Quoted in Zeller, *Devil's Pact*, 46. See also James and James, *Hoffa and the Teamsters*, 273; Moldea, *The Hoffa Wars*, 114–18; Davis, *Mafia Kingfish*, 343, 509.

62. Kennedy, *The Enemy Within*, 161.

63. Partin's brother claims that Ed Partin fabricated the story of Hoffa's plans as a ploy to get out of jail for the kidnapping charges. Partin, *From My Brother's Shadow*, 110–12.

64. Mollenhoff, *Tentacles of Power*, 371–72, 378–79; Partin, *From My Brother's Shadow*, 129; Neff, *Vendetta*, 253–55, 257–60; Hoffa, *The Trials of Jimmy Hoffa*, 243.

65. Hoffa, *The Trials of Jimmy Hoffa*, 168, 243.

66. "Probe Finds No Evidence of Firebomb at Partin Home," 17A.

67. See Hoffa v. United States, 385 U.S. 293 (1966). Hoffa had argued that Partin's testimony had violated his Fourth, Fifth and Sixth Amendment rights.

68. Smith, "The Fix," 22; Davis, *Mafia Kingfish*, 334–35, 344–45; Velle, *Desperate Bargain*, 19, 126; Partin, *From My Brother's Shadow*, 125; Friedman and Schwarz, *Power and Greed*, 189.

69. De Toledano, "In Washington," 4; Partin, *From My Brother's Shadow*, 130–32.

70. Smith, "The Fix," 22; Sheridan, *The Fall and Rise of Jimmy Hoffa*, 415, 497; Davis, *Mafia Kingfish*, 373.

71. Sheridan, *The Fall and Rise of Jimmy Hoffa*, 423; Davis, *Mafia Kingfish*, 328, 329, 366, 373–74; Moldea, *The Hoffa Wars*, 181.

72. Quoted in Moldea, *The Hoffa Wars*, 279–80.

73. Partin, *From My Brother's Shadow*, 162; Sheridan, *The Fall and Rise of Jimmy Hoffa*, 424.

74. Sheridan, *The Fall and Rise of Jimmy Hoffa*, 427–28, 505.

75. Barrow et al., *History Detectives*. President Nixon was recorded on White House tapes discussing the commutation for Hoffa with White House special counsel Charles W. "Chuck" Colson and acknowledged that Teamsters president Frank Fitzsimmons offered the union's support for Nixon's reelection in return for the commutation but also wanted Hoffa barred from seeking to regain the union presidency. "Richard Nixon and Charles W. 'Chuck' Colson on 8 December 1971," conversations 016-053 and 016-060.

76. Evans, *And Justice for All*, 220, 221, 223. See Hoffa v. Saxbe, 378 F. Supp. 1221 (D.D.C. 1974).

2
THE ROAD TO *SULLIVAN*

1. Levy, *Emergence of a Free Press*, 16. Levy's analysis was—and remains—a controversial conclusion; see Cohen and Gleason, *Social Research in Communication and Law*, 59. Roche, "American Liberty," 137; Chapin, *Criminal Justice in Colonial America*, 102–11; Rossiter, *Seedtime of the Republic*, 44; Cook, *Literary Influences in Colonial Newspapers*, 3.

2. Blackstone, *Commentaries on the Laws of England*, 3:125–26, 4:150.

3. Chapin, *Criminal Justice in Colonial America*, 134. Chapin collected 1,969 pre-1660 cases from six colonial superior courts in Connecticut, Maryland, Massachusetts, and Virginia and five county courts in Maryland, Massachusetts, and Virginia.

4. Rosenberg, *Protecting the Best Men*, 22–25.

5. Rosenberg, *Protecting the Best Men*, 25–27.

6. Cook, *Literary Influences in Colonial Newspapers*, 3.

7. Cook, *Literary Influences in Colonial Newspapers*, 140.

8. Levy, *Emergence of a Free Press*, 44, 63–64.

9. This was not the first time Franklin had trouble with the authorities about printed material. In 1722, his brother James was imprisoned for a month for printing that the Massachusetts colonial legislature was weak on piracy. Benjamin, who received a reprimand as his brother's apprentice, continued printing the *New England Courant* in his brother's absence, including criticism of the colonial government's restrictions on the press.

10. Franklin, *An Apology for Printers*, 5–6.

11. Levy, *Emergence of a Free Press*, 120–21.

12. Schlesinger, "The Colonial Newspapers and the Stamp Act," 80.

13. Rosenberg, *Protecting the Best Men*, 54–57.

14. Levy, *Emergence of a Free Press*, 272.

15. Quoted in Rosenberg, *Protecting the Best Men*, 65.

16. Rosenberg, *Protecting the Best Men*, 68.

17. Cook, *Literary Influences in Colonial Newspapers*, 81; Rossiter, *Seedtime of the Republic*, 141; Brant, *The Bill of Rights*, 184; Levy, *Emergence of a Free Press*, 119.

18. Brant, *The Bill of Rights*, 37.

19. Yates [Brutus], Antifederalist No. 84 (1787); Hamilton [Publius], *Federalist* No. 84 (1788). Ironically, Hamilton later called for libel prosecutions of his political opponents.

20. Levy, *Emergence of a Free Press*, 270.

21. The salary provision was eventually ratified as the Twenty-Seventh Amendment in 1992. The fourteen states were the thirteen original colonies plus Vermont, which joined the union in March 1791.

22. Levy, *Emergence of a Free Press*, x.

23. Washington, *Washington's Farewell Address to the People of the United States*.

24. Levy, *Emergence of a Free Press*, 280; Smith, *Printers and Press Freedom*, 59.

25. Recent scholarship has discovered more cases than the traditionally recognized twenty-five. Bird, *Press and Speech under Assault*, 335–90.

26. New York Times v. Sullivan, 376 U.S. at 276.

27. Levy, *Emergence of a Free Press*, 282–83, 285.

28. The states that adopted constitutional provisions allowing limited use of the truth defense were Connecticut, Indiana, Illinois, Maine, Mississippi, and Missouri. The two states without such provisions were Alabama and Massachusetts. Levy, *Emergence of a Free Press*, 302n43.

29. Rosenberg, *Protecting the Best Men*, 121.

30. Rosenberg, *Protecting the Best Men*, 122, 124–28, 133, 303n53; Lawhorne, *Defamation and Public Officials*, 87–110.

31. McMahon, "The Louisiana Code of Civil Procedure," 1. The 1805 code remained the basic criminal law in Louisiana until 1942.

32. La. Const. of 1812, art. 6, § 21.

33. 1808 La. Acts No. 29.

34. 1808 La. Acts No. 29.

35. Although the court labeled the claim as "slander," Louisiana's civil law system does not distinguish between libel (written defamation) and slander (oral defamation).

36. Spotorno v. Fourichon, 4 So. at 71 (La. 1888); Kirk and Rosenthal, "Defamation . . . (Part One)," 281.

37. La. Const. of 1921, art. 1, § 3.

38. See La. Const. of 1974, art. 1, § 7.

39. Guice v. Harvey, 14 La. at 202 (1839); Cox, "Defamation," 98.

40. Cox, "Defamation," 96.

41. Louisiana Revised Statutes § 45:1352 (2016). This correlates with federal law, which prohibits broadcast stations from altering advertisements purchased by legally qualified candidates for public office. See 47 United States Code § 315(a) (2016).

42. Cox, "Defamation," 90 (footnotes omitted).

43. Cox, "Defamation," 91.

44. Kirk and Rosenthal, "Defamation . . . (Part Two)," 418–22, 423.

45. Cox, "Defamation," 91; Kirk and Rosenthal, "Defamation . . . (Part Two)," 422–23; Barnhill v. Times-Picayune Publishing Co., 131 So. at 22 (La. 1930).

46. Cox, "Defamation," 92.

47. Kirk and Rosenthal, "Defamation . . . (Part One)," 282.

48. Kirk and Rosenthal, "Defamation . . . (Part One)," 282; Kirk and Rosenthal, "Defamation . . . (Part Two)," 418–22; Cox, "Defamation," 93–94.

49. Communications scholar W. Joseph Campbell disputes this characterization, arguing that "myth, the blight of serious history, has overrun yellow journalism, distorting popular and scholarly understanding of the genre." Campbell, *Yellow Journalism*, 2.

50. The head of the CPI strongly denied that the agency's work was propaganda. See Creel, *How We Advertised America*, 4: "We did not call it propaganda, for that word, in German hands, had come to be associated with deceit and corruption. Our effort was educational and informative throughout, for we had such confidence in our case as to feel that no other argument was needed than the simple, straightforward presentation of facts."

51. *Gitlow v. New York*, 268 U.S. at 666. Only three years before deciding *Gitlow* the court explicitly rejected the argument that the First Amendment applied to the states by virtue of the Fourteenth Amendment. See Prudential Ins. Co. of America v. Cheek, 259 U.S. at 543: "neither the Fourteenth Amendment nor any other provision of the Constitution of the United States imposes upon the states any restrictions about 'freedom of speech' or the 'liberty of silence.'"

52. Commission on Freedom of the Press, *A Free and Responsible Press*, 11.

53. Commission on Freedom of the Press, *A Free and Responsible Press*, 86; Chafee, *Government and Mass Communication* vol. 1, 103.

54. While court cases are generally shortly referred to by the name of the first litigant in the caption of the case, *New York Times v. Sullivan* is most often referred to as "Sullivan."

55. Dun & Bradstreet, Inc. v. Greenmoss Builders, Inc., 472 U.S. at 767–68 (White, J., concurring).

56. Rosenberg, *Protecting the Best Men*, 236–37.

57. Urofsky, "*New York Times Co. v. Sullivan* as a Civil Rights Case," 167–68.

58. Thomas, "State Finds Formidable Legal Club to Swing at Out-of-State Press," A1; Lewis, *Make No Law*, 34.

59. Lewis, *Make No Law*, 42.

60. Urofsky, "*New York Times Co. v. Sullivan* as a Civil Rights Case," 170.

61. Urofsky, "*New York Times Co. v. Sullivan* as a Civil Rights Case," 158 (footnote omitted).

62. Urofsky, "*New York Times Co. v. Sullivan* as a Civil Rights Case," 181.

63. New York Times v. Sullivan, 376 U.S. at 294 (Black, J., concurring).

64. Kalven, "The New York Times Case," 192.

65. Rosenberg, *Protecting the Best Men*, 247.

66. New York Times v. Sullivan, 376 U.S. at 270.

67. New York Times v. Sullivan, 376 U.S. at 279–80.

68. Rosenberg, *Protecting the Best Men*, 249, 263.

69. See, *e.g.*, Murnaghan, "From Figment to Fiction to Philosophy," 7.

70. Pauling v. News Syndicate, Inc., 335 F.2d 671 (2d Cir. 1964).

71. Cox, "Defamation," 108.

72. Lewis, *Make No Law*, 234–35.

73. Quoted in Kalven, "The New York Times Case," 194, 221n125; quoted in Lewis, *Make No Law*, 163; quoted in Hall and Urofsky, *New York Times v. Sullivan*, 182.

3

PHILOSOPHIES OF COMMUNICATION AND DEFAMATION

1. Siebert, *Freedom of the Press in England, 1476–1776*, 9.

2. Blackstone, *Commentaries on the Laws of England*, 4:151–52.

3. Blackstone, *Commentaries on the Laws of England*, 4:150–51.

4. The origins of this phrase are unclear. Although it is attributed to William Murray—the first Earl of Mansfield, who was chief justice of the King's Bench from 1756 to 1765—it does not appear in any of his judicial rulings.

5. Bates v. City of Little Rock, 361 U.S. at 528 (Black, J., concurring); Konigsberg v. State Bar of California, 366 U.S. at 60–61 (Black, J., dissenting).

6. Cox v. Louisiana, 379 U.S. at 555.

7. Brandenburg v. Ohio, 395 U.S. at 457 (Douglas, J., concurring).

8. Dennis v. U.S., 341 U.S. at 581 (Douglas, J., dissenting); New York Times Co. v. U.S., 403 U.S. at 720 (Douglas, J., concurring).

9. Milton, *Areopagitica;* Altschull, *From Milton to McLuhan*, 169; Mill, "Law of Libel and Liberty of the Press," 34; Mill, *On Liberty*, 53–54.

10. Abrams v. U.S., 250 U.S. at 630 (Holmes, J., dissenting); Gertz v. Robert Welch, Inc., 418 U.S. at 339–40.

11. Ingber, "The Marketplace of Ideas," 3.

12. Smolla, *Free Speech in an Open Society*, 6; Cohen and Gleason, *Social Research in Communication and Law*, 58.

13. Ingber, "The Marketplace of Ideas," 50.

14. Chafee, *Free Speech in the United States*, 3.

15. Chaplinsky v. New Hampshire, 315 U.S. at 571–72; Brandenburg v. Ohio, 395 U.S. at 471.

16. Hall and Urofsky, *New York Times v. Sullivan*, 185; Scardino, "Liberty and Defamation," 3.

17. Scardino, "Liberty and Defamation," 3.

18. Meiklejohn, *Free Speech and Its Relation to Self-Government*, 91.

19. Meiklejohn, *Free Speech and Its Relation to Self-Government*, 94.

20. Meiklejohn, "The First Amendment Is an Absolute," 259.

21. Whitney v. California, 274 U.S. at 377 (Brandeis, J., concurring).

22. Hutchins, "Ideas, Institutions and American Liberty," 25.

23. Commission on Freedom of the Press, *A Free and Responsible Press*, 11, 86.

24. Peterson, "The Social Responsibility Theory of the Press," 74.

25. Peterson, "The Social Responsibility Theory of the Press," 97, 99.

26. Emerson, *Systems of Freedom of Expression*, 6–7, 17–18, 717, 922.

27. Procunier v. Martinez, 416 U.S. at 427; Heyman, *Free Speech and Human Dignity*, 2; Smolla, *Free Speech in an Open Society*, 9 (emphasis in original).

28. Heyman, *Free Speech and Human Dignity*, 11, 37, 39.

29. Heyman, *Free Speech and Human Dignity*, 2.

30. New York Times v. Sullivan at 268.

31. New York Times v. Sullivan at 271–72, 298.

32. New York Times v. Sullivan at 293 (Black, J., concurring).

33. New York Times v. Sullivan at 269 (quoting Stromberg v. California, 283 U.S. at 369).

4
"THE STORY OF POLITICS IN LOUISIANA TODAY"

1. Boulard, *Huey Long Invades New Orleans*, 149; "All Soldiers in State Rush to New Orleans," 8.

2. Phil A. St. Amant in discussion with the author, May 2016.

3. Phil A. St. Amant in discussion with the author, May 2016.

4. "Baton Rougean Plans," 6A; "Phil St. Amant to Seek Senate Post," 8A. In its endorsement of Long in 1964, the *New Orleans Times-Picayune* noted that "in many vital fields, Sen. Long has opposed the Kennedy administration." "Russell B. Long Deserves Re-election to the United States Senate," 12.

5. Phil A. St. Amant, *The Decline and Resurrection of the American Republic*, 5.

6. On July 7 and 8, 1961, a multiracial coalition demanded to use the traditionally whites-only Rainbow Beach on the shores of Lake Michigan, leading to violence. See John Keilman, "Rainbow Beach Wade-Ins' Broke Down Racial Barrier."

7. Phil A. St. Amant in discussion with the author, May 2016.

8. Quoted in "TV Speech Is St. Amant Race Launcher," 10A.

9. Quoted in "TV Speech Is St. Amant Race Launcher," 10A.

10. "In Memory of A. G. Klein, Jr." [advertisement], 2A.

11. Trial transcript, Thompson v. St. Amant, La. Dist. Ct. 1964, 10 (cross-examination of Phil A. St. Amant).

12. Trial transcript, Thompson v. St. Amant, La. Dist. Ct. 1964, 15, 106.

13. Trial transcript, Thompson v. St. Amant, La. Dist. Ct. 1964, 16–17.

14. Trial transcript, Thompson v. St. Amant, La. Dist. Ct. 1964, 28–29, 116–17.

15. Sheridan, *The Fall and Rise of Jimmy Hoffa,* 408, 415, 424, 425.

16. Trial transcript, Thompson v. St. Amant, La. Dist. Ct. 1964, 23–24, 112.

17. Trial transcript, Thompson v. St. Amant, La. Dist. Ct. 1964, 22–23, 111–12.

18. Phil A. St. Amant in discussion with the author, May 2016.

19. Trial transcript, Thompson v. St. Amant, La. Dist. Ct. 1964, 10, 125.

20. "Senate Hopeful Claims Credit for Indictment," 1A, 12A; "Phil. St. Amant Levels Charges of Corruption," 4A.

21. Trial transcript, Thompson v. St. Amant, La. Dist. Ct. 1964, 65.

22. Trial transcript, Thompson v. St. Amant, La. Dist. Ct. 1964, 66.

23. Trial transcript, Thompson v. St. Amant, La. Dist. Ct. 1964, 126.

5
THOMPSON GOES TO COURT

1. Petition for Damages, Thompson v. St. Amant, La. Dist. Ct. 1962, 4.

2. *Deputy Files Slander Suits for $450,000.* The complaints in these other lawsuits are not available in the court's archives.

3. Answer, Thompson v. St. Amant, La. Dist. Ct. 1962, 2, 4.

4. Answer, Thompson v. St. Amant, La. Dist. Ct. 1962, 2.

5. Answer, Thompson v. St. Amant, La. Dist. Ct. 1962, 3, 4.

6. Trial transcript, Thompson v. St. Amant, La. Dist. Ct. 1964, 125.

7. Answers to Interrogatories, Thompson v. St. Amant, La. Dist. Ct. 1962, 2.

8. Interrogatories, Thompson v. St. Amant, La. Dist. Ct. 1962, 3; Answers to Interrogatories, Thompson v. St. Amant, La. Dist. Ct. 1962, 2.

9. Trial transcript, Thompson v. St. Amant, La. Dist. Ct. 1964, 41–42.

10. Trial transcript, Thompson v. St. Amant, La. Dist. Ct. 1964, 45.

11. Trial transcript, Thompson v. St. Amant, La. Dist. Ct. 1964, 38, 40.

12. Trial transcript, Thompson v. St. Amant, La. Dist. Ct. 1964, 40.

13. Trial transcript, Thompson v. St. Amant, La. Dist. Ct. 1964, 40–41.

14. Trial transcript, Thompson v. St. Amant, La. Dist. Ct. 1964, 47.

15. Trial transcript, Thompson v. St. Amant, La. Dist. Ct. 1964, 50–51, 54, 55, 63; "Baseball Clinic Elects McGraw."

16. Trial transcript, Thompson v. St. Amant, La. Dist. Ct. 1964, 69, 65.

17. Trial transcript, Thompson v. St. Amant, La. Dist. Ct. 1964, 67.

18. Trial transcript, Thompson v. St. Amant, La. Dist. Ct. 1964, 92, 93, 95–96, 97.

19. Phil A. St. Amant in discussion with the author, May 2016.

20. Trial transcript, Thompson v. St. Amant, La. Dist. Ct. 1964, 125.

21. Five thousand dollars in 1964 is the equivalent of about $39,900 in 2017. Calculated using the U.S. Department of Labor Statistics CPI Inflation Calculator, http://data.bls.gov/cgi-bin/cpicalc.pl.

22. *Madison v. Bolton* was later overruled for cases involving private figures in matters of private concern, because of the *Sullivan* ruling and subsequent decisions. See Schaefer v. Lynch, 406 So. 2d 188 (La. 1981): "The holding of Madison v. Bolton that a public officer can recover damages for truthful statements containing false and defamatory implications, is overruled."

23. Reasons for Judgment [Verdict], Thompson v. St. Amant, La. Dist. Ct. 1964, 3; U.S. App'x, 144. "U.S. App'x" refers to the reproduction of the verdict in the appendix submitted by parties to U.S. Supreme Court. In the court record available at the Louisiana Nineteenth District Court in Baton Rouge, the Reasons for Judgment [Verdict] document is not available beyond page 5, but the entire document was reproduced in an appendix submitted by the parties submitted to the U.S. Supreme Court.

24. Reasons for Judgment [Verdict], Thompson v. St. Amant, La. Dist. Ct. 1964, 4; U.S. App'x, 146.

25. Reasons for Judgment [Verdict], Thompson v. St. Amant, La. Dist. Ct. 1964, 4; U.S. App'x, 146–47.

26. Reasons for Judgment [Verdict], Thompson v. St. Amant, La. Dist. Ct. 1964, 4; U.S. App'x, 147. Quote from Shakespeare, *Julius Caesar*, act 3, scene 2.

27. Reasons for Judgment [Verdict], Thompson v. St. Amant, La. Dist. Ct. 1964, U.S. App'x, 147, 151.

28. Reasons for Judgment [Verdict], Thompson v. St. Amant, La. Dist. Ct. 1964, U.S. App'x, 149–50.

29. Reasons for Judgment [Verdict], Thompson v. St. Amant, La. Dist. Ct. 1964, U.S. App'x, 151.

30. Phil A. St. Amant in discussion with the author, May 2016.

6
RESULTS SHIFT IN LOUISIANA'S APPEALS COURTS

1. Kalven, "The New York Times Case," 221n125.

2. Adams, "Judge Rules $5,000 Due for Slander," 10A.

3. Reasons for Judgment [Verdict], Thompson v. St. Amant, La. Dist. Ct. 1964, 2; U.S. App'x, 150.

4. Reasons for Judgment [Verdict], Thompson v. St. Amant, La. Dist. Ct. 1965, U.S. App'x, 148.

5. [Defendant's] Motion for a New Trial, Thompson v. St. Amant, La. Dist. Ct. 1964.

6. See Reasons for Judgment [on Motion for Retrial], Thompson v. St. Amant, La. Dist. Ct. 1965, 1–2. The cases cited by Judge Blanche were *Gray v. De Bretton*, 188 So. 722 (La. 1939), *reh'g denied* (La. May 1, 1939) and *State v. Mayeux*, 81 So. 2d 426 (La. 1955).

7. Reasons for Judgment [on Motion for Retrial], Thompson v. St. Amant, La. Dist. Ct. 1965, 3.

8. Reasons for Judgment [on Motion for Retrial], Thompson v. St. Amant, La. Dist. Ct. 1965, 3.

9. Reasons for Judgment [on Motion for Retrial], Thompson v. St. Amant, La. Dist. Ct. 1965, 3.

10. Judgment [Denial of Motion for New Trial]. Thompson's brief to the Louisiana Court of

Appeal erroneously stated that "a new trial *was* granted" (emphasis added) on the question of whether he was a public official. But Judge Blanche's order on the motion, while accompanied by a statement of "Reasons for Judgment" considering the question, declared, "It is ordered, adjudged and decreed that the motion for a new trial filed on behalf of the defendant be denied." Judgment [Denial of Motion for New Trial], 1.

11. Phil A. St. Amant in discussion with the author, May 2016.

12. [Defendant-Appellant's] Original Brief on Appeal, Thompson v. St. Amant, La. Ct. App. 1965, 2. 7, 10.

13. [Defendant-Appellant's] Original Brief on Appeal, Thompson v. St. Amant, La. Ct. App. 1965, 5.

14. [Defendant-Appellant's] Original Brief on Appeal, Thompson v. St. Amant, La. Ct. App. 1965, 6.

15. Phil A. St. Amant in discussion with the author, May 2016.

16. Thompson v. St. Amant, 184 So. 2d at 315–16.

17. Thompson v. St. Amant, 184 So. 2d at 317 (citations omitted).

18. Thompson v. St. Amant, 184 So. 2d at 319–20.

19. Thompson v. St. Amant, 184 So. 2d at 321–22 (quoting *New York Times v. Sullivan*, 376 U.S. at 283n23).

20. Thompson v. St. Amant, 184 So. 2d at 322.

21. Thompson v. St. Amant, 184 So. 2d at 322–23 (citation and quotation omitted).

22. Thompson v. St. Amant, 184 So. 2d at 323.

23. Thompson v. St. Amant, 184 So. 2d at 323.

24. Applications for Certiorari or Review, Thompson v. St. Amant, La. Sup. Ct. 1966, 2 (emphasis in original).

25. Rosenblatt v. Baer, 383 U.S. at 84 (footnote omitted). Following this reasoning and the precepts in *Sullivan* that the First Amendment is meant to ensure robust discussion about public issues and of those in a position to influence these issues, in *Rosenblatt* the court held that the recreation area supervisor was a public official. Because the trial in *Rosenblatt* had occurred before the decision in *Sullivan,* the Supreme Court remanded for a new trial.

26. Applications for Certiorari or Review, Thompson v. St. Amant, La. Sup. Ct. 1966, 6–7.

27. Applications for Certiorari or Review, Thompson v. St. Amant, La. Sup. Ct. 1966, 8–12.

28. Relator's [Thompson's] Brief, Thompson v. St. Amant, La. Sup. Ct. 1966, 11.

29. Relator's [Thompson's] Brief, Thompson v. St. Amant, La. Sup. Ct. 1966, 29, 30, 43–64 (Appendix 1). The article, William O. Bertlesman, "Libel and Public Men," observes that some courts had extended the *Sullivan* requirements to cover not only public officials but also "others in public life as well."

30. Relator's [Thompson's] Brief, Thompson v. St. Amant, La. Sup. Ct. 1966, 33.

31. Original Brief on Behalf of Defendant-Respondent [St. Amant], Thompson v. St. Amant, La. Sup. Ct. 1966, 1–2, 4, 7.

32. Original Brief on Behalf of Defendant-Respondent [St. Amant], Thompson v. St. Amant, La. Sup. Ct. 1966, 1–2, 4, 7.

33. Thompson v. St. Amant, 196 So. 2d at 257, 258.

34. Thompson v. St. Amant, 196 So. 2d at 258.

35. Thompson v. St. Amant, 196 So. 2d at 258.

36. Thompson v. St. Amant, 196 So. 2d at 259.

37. Thompson v. St. Amant, 196 So. 2d at 261; Kirk and Rosenthal, "Defamation . . . (Part One)," 419.

38. Thompson v. St. Amant, 196 So. 2d at 261 (quoting Rosenblatt v. Baer, 383 U.S. at 85 and citing Bertlesman, "Libel and Public Men," the article that had been attached to Thompson's brief, and Gilligan v. King, 264 N.Y.S.2d 309 [N.Y. Sup. Ct. 1965]).

39. Thompson v. St. Amant, 196 So. 2d at 261.

40. Thompson v. St. Amant, 196 So. 2d at 263–65 (McCaleb, J., dissenting).

41. Thompson v. St. Amant, 196 So. 2d at 264 (McCaleb, J., dissenting).

42. Thompson v. St. Amant, 196 So. 2d at 265 (McCaleb, J., dissenting).

43. Time, Inc. v. Hill, 385 U.S. 374 (1967).

44. Time, Inc. v. Hill, 385 U.S. at 411 (Fortas, J., dissenting).

45. Time, Inc. v. Hill, 385 U.S. at 412 (Fortas, J., dissenting).

46. Time, Inc. v. Hill, 385 U.S. at 411 (Fortas, J., dissenting).

7
THE U.S. SUPREME COURT SETS A STANDARD

1. See Garrison v. Louisiana, 379 U.S. 64 (1964); Rosenblatt v. Baer, 383 U.S. 75 (1966); Sheppard v. Maxwell, 384 U.S. 333 (1966).

2. See Time, Inc. v. Hill, 385 U.S. 374 (1967); Curtis Publishing Co. v. Butts, 388 U.S. 130 (1967); Associated Press v. Walker, 388 U.S. 130 (1967) (remanding companion case to *Curtis*). The *Walker* case originated in the Louisiana courts.

3. Scharff made a motion, which was granted June 26, for an extension to file the petition beyond the usual ninety-day limit. See Petition for Writ of Certiorari, St. Amant v. Thompson, U.S. Sup. Ct. 1967, 2.

4. Petition for Writ of Certiorari, St. Amant v. Thompson, U.S. Sup. Ct. 1967, 6.

5. Petition for Writ of Certiorari, St. Amant v. Thompson, U.S. Sup. Ct. 1967, 5–6.

6. Petition for Writ of Certiorari, St. Amant v. Thompson, U.S. Sup. Ct. 1967, 4.

7. Petition for Writ of Certiorari, St. Amant v. Thompson, U.S. Sup. Ct. 1967, 6, 8.

8. Petition for Writ of Certiorari, St. Amant v. Thompson, U.S. Sup. Ct. 1967, 9–11.

9. Harlan Bench Memo [on certiorari], St. Amant v. Thompson, U.S. Sup. Ct. 1967, 1–2.

10. Warren Bench Memo [on certiorari], St. Amant v. Thompson, U.S. Sup. Ct. 1967, 4–5.

11. Warren Bench Memo [on certiorari], St. Amant v. Thompson, U.S. Sup. Ct. 1967, 5.

12. Milkovich v. Lorain Journal Co., 497 U.S. at 9.

13. This word is consistently abbreviated "petr" in the bench memos.

14. Warren Bench Memo [on certiorari], St. Amant v. Thompson, U.S. Sup. Ct. 1967, 6.

15. Warren Bench Memo [on certiorari], St. Amant v. Thompson, U.S. Sup. Ct. 1967, 6–7.

16. Warren Bench Memo [on certiorari], St. Amant v. Thompson, U.S. Sup. Ct. 1967, 7.

17. Fortas Bench Memo [on certiorari], St. Amant v. Thompson, U.S. Sup. Ct. 1967, 1.

18. Abbreviated "La SC."

19. Fortas Bench Memo [on certiorari], St. Amant v. Thompson, U.S. Sup. Ct. 1967, 3.

20. Justice Fortas had recused himself from the *Beckley Newspapers* case because his former law firm represented one of the parties. Fortas Bench Memo [on certiorari], St. Amant v. Thompson, U.S. Sup. Ct. 1967, 3; Beckley Newspapers Corp. v. Hanks, 389 U.S. at 85..

21. Fortas Bench Memo [on certiorari], St. Amant v. Thompson, U.S. Sup. Ct. 1967, 4.

22. Fortas Bench Memo [on certiorari], St. Amant v. Thompson, U.S. Sup. Ct. 1967, 1. It is unclear what Fortas meant by "ask to be noted." Throughout the term, the court's clerk maintains a "granted and noted list" of dispositions of cases in the current term in which the court has granted certiorari. Thus Fortas's note that he would "grant [and] ask to be noted" may indicate his desire that the court grant certiorari in the case and then decide the case on its merits. This interpretation would explain his crossing out of the statement "I'd reverse summarily."

23. Robbins, "Hiding behind the Cloak of Invisibility," 1200–1202.

24. Warren Bench Memo [on certiorari], St. Amant v. Thompson, U.S. Sup. Ct. 1967, 1.

25. Brennan, "State Court Decisions and the Supreme Court," 403.

26. On the Douglas vote sheet, the handwritten note "Respond" next to Justice Harlan's name is crossed out, and "Grant" is written next to it. As for Justice Harlan's attitudes, compare Sacher v. United States, 356 U.S. at 578 (Harlan, J., concurring) (justifying a short per curiam opinion reversing the result below on the grounds that "[the] issue can only be determined by scrutiny of the record, and a full-dress argument could hardly shed further light on the matter") *with* Senko v. LaCrosse Dredging Corp., 352 U.S. at 379n8 (Harlan, J., dissenting) (criticizing an earlier decision as "entered solely on the basis of the petition for certiorari, without the benefit of an opposing brief or oral argument, [so that it] can scarcely be regarded as a precedent of much significance").

27. While no order to this effect was found in either the justices' papers or the court docket available at the Library of Congress, the supplemental memo prepared after receipt of Thompson's response does state that "the response requested by the conference has been received." Supplemental Bench Memo [on certiorari], St. Amant v. Thompson, U.S. Sup. Ct. 1967, 1. Sources differ on the threshold for summary disposition. The latest edition of a Supreme Court practice manual at the time of the *St. Amant* certiorari petition stated that "such summary action occurs when the Court, or a majority thereof, is convinced that the decision below is so clearly erroneous as to make oral argument a waste of time." Stern and Gressman, *Supreme Court Practice,* § 5.12, 186. But an unidentified justice was quoted as saying of summary disposition at the certiorari stage that it was a "convention . . . that it takes six to do that, rather than five." Perry, *Deciding to Decide,* 100. A later edition of the practice manual claims, however, that "this 'rule of six' no longer prevents (if it ever did) five Justices from deciding a case summarily over four dissents that certiorari should be denied. At most it may prevent five Justices from deciding a case summarily if the Court is unanimous that certiorari should be granted but four believe that the case should be fully briefed and argued." Shapiro et al., *Supreme Court Practice,* § 5.12, 343–44 (footnotes omitted).

28. Kirshbaum, "Accelerating Pace of Supreme Court's Summary Reversals of Habeas Relief," 1; Sacks, "The Supreme Court, 1953 Term—Foreword," 103. See also Brown, "The Supreme

Court, 1957 Term—Foreword: Process of Law," 77 ("Even from a point of view which takes into account only the convenience and efficiency of the Court, the practice of summary reversal on certiorari papers seems questionable"); and Hart, "Foreword," 95 (questioning "the degree of intellectual respect which is due [summary] determinations").

29. Sacks, "The Supreme Court, 1953 Term—Foreword," 99.

30. See Response to Application for Writ of Certiorari to the Supreme Court of the State of Louisiana, St. Amant v. Thompson, U.S. Sup. Ct. 1967, 2–3.

31. See Supplemental Bench Memo [on certiorari], St. Amant v. Thompson, U.S. Sup. Ct. 1967, 2.

32. This tally is based on Justice Douglas's vote sheet. Levine and Wermiel, *The Progeny*, reports that Brennan's vote sheet matches Douglas's. Warren's vote sheet shows five votes in favor of granting certiorari, one (Stewart) against, and no votes recorded for justices Fortas, Marshall, and White.

33. St. Amant v. Thompson, 389 U.S. 1033 (Jan, 15, 1968) (granting certiorari).

34. Original Brief on Behalf of Plaintiff-Respondent [Thompson], St. Amant v. Thompson, U.S. Sup Ct. 1967, 1–3.

35. Adams, "Judge Rules $5,000 Due for Slander," 10A.

36. Original Brief on Behalf of Plaintiff-Respondent [Thompson], St. Amant v. Thompson, U.S. Sup Ct. 1967, 5 (quoting Associated Press v. Walker, 388 U.S. at 164). Such individuals are now usually referred to in the defamation context as "public figures."

37. Original Brief on Behalf of Plaintiff-Respondent [Thompson], St. Amant v. Thompson, U.S. Sup Ct. 1967, 5.

38. See Time, Inc. v. Hill, 385 U.S. at 391: "Were this a libel action, the distinction which has been suggested between the relative opportunities of the public official and the private individual to rebut defamatory charges might be germane." This argument was rejected in Rosenbloom v. Metromedia, Inc., 403 U.S. at 45–46 (1971), in which the plurality opinion rejected this argument, as well as any distinction between public and private figures in the defamation context. But it was accepted in Gertz v. Robert Welch, Inc., 418 U.S. at 343, which accepted the argument regarding access to the media as grounds for pulling back from universal application of Sullivan "actual malice" to all defamation plaintiffs, reserving it only for public figures and for private figures involved in matters of public concern.

39. Original Brief on Behalf of Plaintiff-Respondent [Thompson], St. Amant v. Thompson, U.S. Sup Ct. 1967, 5, 6.

40. Original Brief on Behalf of Plaintiff-Respondent [Thompson], St. Amant v. Thompson, U.S. Sup Ct. 1967, 7–9.

41. Original Brief on Behalf of Plaintiff-Respondent [Thompson], St. Amant v. Thompson, U.S. Sup Ct. 1967, 9.

42. Abbreviated "resp."

43. Bench Memo [on merits], St. Amant v. Thompson, U.S. Sup Ct. 1968, 4.

44. Bench Memo [on merits], St. Amant v. Thompson, U.S. Sup Ct. 1968, 10, 11.

45. Bench Memo [on merits], St. Amant v. Thompson, U.S. Sup Ct. 1968, 11.

46. Oral Argument [recording], St. Amant v. Thompson, U.S. Sup Ct. 1968, 00:00:26.

47. Oral Argument [recording], St. Amant v. Thompson, U.S. Sup Ct. 1968, 00:05:54.

48. Oral Argument [recording], St. Amant v. Thompson, U.S. Sup Ct. 1968,00:06:24.

49. Oral Argument [recording], St. Amant v. Thompson, U.S. Sup Ct. 1968, 00:09:36–00:09:56.

50. Oral Argument [recording], St. Amant v. Thompson, U.S. Sup Ct. 1968, 00:11:05–00.11.07.

51. Oral Argument [recording], St. Amant v. Thompson, U.S. Sup Ct. 1968, 00:13:24, 00:13:30, 00:13:55.

52. Oral Argument [recording], St. Amant v. Thompson, U.S. Sup Ct. 1968, 00:15:40, 00:16:03.

53. Oral Argument [recording], St. Amant v. Thompson, U.S. Sup Ct. 1968, 00:17:03, 00:21:10.

54. Oral Argument [recording], St. Amant v. Thompson, U.S. Sup Ct. 1968, 00:22:22. This was Justice Marshall's first oral argument in a defamation case as a member of the court. Levine and Wermiel, *The Progeny,* 84.

55. Oral Argument [recording], St. Amant v. Thompson, U.S. Sup Ct. 1968, 00:28:37.

56. Oral Argument [recording], St. Amant v. Thompson, U.S. Sup Ct. 1968, 00:29:59.

57. Oral Argument [recording], St. Amant v. Thompson, U.S. Sup Ct. 1968, 00:30:34.

58. Oral Argument [recording], St. Amant v. Thompson, U.S. Sup Ct. 1968, 00:31:53, 00:31:59.

59. Quoted in Levine and Wermiel, *The Progeny,* 85. Regarding Stewart's comments, the notes on Earl Warren's vote sheet actually state that Stewart stated that "it is up to deft [defendant] to prove reckless disregard." But this is inconsistent with the law of *Sullivan,* which puts this burden on the plaintiff. See New York Times v. Sullivan, 376 U.S. 254, 279–80 (1964): "The constitutional guarantees require, we think, a federal rule that prohibits a public official from recovering damages for a defamatory falsehood relating to his official conduct *unless he proves* that the statement was made with 'actual malice'" (emphasis added). So either Warren made an error in recording Stewart's comment or Stewart was referring to the defendant (respondent) in the case at the Supreme Court level: Thompson. Levine and Wermiel report that Douglas's notes state that Stewart "asserted that a public official 'must show that there was malice' and the Louisiana Supreme Court had 'put burden of proof on [the] wrong party.'" Levine and Wermiel, *The Progeny,* 85.

60. This reading is consistent with Warren's prior use of "record" to indicate votes for summary reversal at the certiorari stage. This position was a change from White's position at the certiorari stage, when he advocated full briefing on the merits rather than a summary reversal.

61. Under "4 April 1968—Argument" in the notes, "[Reverse]" is written, then crossed out, with "[Affirm*]" written next to it. Lower on the page is an asterisk with the incomplete phrase "on my dissent in," which may effectively be a "footnote" to the word "affirm" above. If so, Fortas may have contemplated basing his vote to affirm on his dissent in another case. *Time, Inc. v. Hill,* 385 U.S. 374 (1967), was the only other libel or privacy case that was decided during Fortas's tenure on the court prior to *St. Amant.* Since Fortas dissented in that case, 385 U.S. at 411 (Fortas, J., dissenting), it seems likely that he planned to vote to affirm in the *St. Amant* case on grounds similar to his dissent in *Time, Inc. v. Hill.*

62. Abe Fortas, 517—*St. Amant v. Thompson* [personal notes], St. Amant v. Thompson, U.S. Sup Ct. 1968.

63. On Marshall's copy of the circulated draft of White's opinion, someone anonymously wrote, "I agree," followed by what appear to be the initials "PMJ." It is unclear who this is, since there was no clerk at the court at the time with these initials. Underneath, with another color ink but the same handwriting, is the notation "except for 1 sentence of p. 4 about which I agree with Nick." The identity of "Nick" is unclear, since there does not appear to have been a clerk with the first name Nick or Nicholas at the court at the time. One of Chief Justice Warren's clerks for the October 1967 term was named J. Larry Nichols, and "Nick" may be a reference to him. There is another notation elsewhere on the page that reads, "I join this one," which is initialed "TM" and appears to have been written by Justice Marshall himself. On the fourth page of the draft opinion is an annotation in the margin to change one sentence, along with a rationale for the change; the annotation was signed with the initials "JNMh" or "JNML." The identity of this annotator is also unclear, since there was no clerk with those initials at the court at the time. It is possible that the annotation reflects a comment by Justice Harlan, with his initials used, especially since the relevant sentence discussed the implications of Justice Harlan's plurality opinion in Curtis Publishing Co. v. Butts, 388 U.S. 130 (1967). But it is unclear why Harlan's sentiment would be reflected on Justice Marshall's copy of the draft opinion and not Harlan's own copy, which has no edits or comments at all.

64. Memo from Hugo Black to Byron White (Apr. 19, 1968), St. Amant v. Thompson, U.S. Sup Ct. 1968. See New York Times v. Sullivan, 376 U.S. at 293 (Black, J., concurring); Garrison v. Louisiana, 379 U.S. at 79 (Douglas, J., concurring); and Garrison v. Louisiana, 379 U.S. at 80 (Black, J., concurring).

65. Circulated draft opinion (Justice Fortas's copy, circulated Apr. 19, 1968), St. Amant v. Thompson, U.S. Sup Ct. 1968, 1, 4.

66. St. Amant v. Thompson, 390 U.S. at 728.

67. St. Amant v. Thompson, 390 U.S. at 729.

68. St. Amant v. Thompson, 390 U.S. at 729.

69. St. Amant v. Thompson, 390 U.S. at 729, 730–31 (citing New York Times v. Sullivan, 376 U.S. 254 (1964); Garrison v. Louisiana, 379 U.S. at 74 (1964); and Curtis Publishing Co. v. Butts, 388 U.S. at 153.

70. St. Amant v. Thompson, 390 U.S. at 731.

71. Hopkins, *Actual Malice*, 121.

72. Hopkins, *Actual Malice*, 121. See also St. Amant v. Thompson, 390 U.S. at 733.

73. St. Amant v. Thompson, 390 U.S. at 731–32.

74. Hopkins, *Actual Malice*, 135; see Harte-Hanks Communications, Inc. v. Connaughton, 491 U.S. at 666n7 (1989) (approving of trial judge's instruction that "actual malice may not be inferred alone from evidence of personal spite, ill-will or intention to injure on the part of the writer").

75. St. Amant v. Thompson, 390 U.S. at 731–32.

76. St. Amant v. Thompson, 390 U.S. at 730, 732.

77. St. Amant v. Thompson, 390 U.S. at 732–33.

78. St. Amant v. Thompson, 390 U.S. at 733.

79. St. Amant v. Thompson, 390 U.S. at 733 (Black, J., and Douglas, J., concurring) (citations omitted).

80. St. Amant v. Thompson, 390 U.S. at 734 (Fortas, J., dissenting).

81. St. Amant v. Thompson, 390 U.S. at 735 (Fortas, J., dissenting).

82. St. Amant v. Thompson, 390 U.S. at 734 (Fortas, J., dissenting).

83. St. Amant v. Thompson, 390 U.S. at 734–35 (Fortas, J., dissenting).

84. St. Amant v. Thompson, 390 U.S. at 734 (Fortas, J., dissenting).

85. Time, Inc. v. Hill, 385 U.S. at 411–12, 420 (Fortas, J., dissenting). In NAACP v. Button, 371 U. S. 415 (1963), the court declared that Virginia statutes that barred suggesting that potential civil rights litigants contact particular attorneys to pursue their cases violated the First and Fourteenth amendments.

8
THE AFTERMATH

1. U.S. Representative Lawrence G. Williams to Chief Justice Earl Warren, May 9, 1968; Newman, *Hugo Black*, 552. Before his election to Congress Williams had spent thirty years as an executive with the Curtis Publishing Co., which published various magazines including the *Saturday Evening Post*. The *Post* suspended publication in 1969, and one factor in the *Post*'s demise was damages it had to pay as the result of a libel case brought by University of Georgia football coach Wally Butts, which the U.S. Supreme Court affirmed in Curtis Publishing Co. v. Butts, 388 U.S. 130 (1967).

2. Select Committee on Assassinations, *Report of the Select Committee on Assassinations of the U.S. House of Representatives, Part 2*. Despite the committee's conclusion, believers in conspiracies involving the Kennedy and King assassinations continue to suspect Thompson. See, *e.g.*, Pepper, *Orders to Kill*, 370 (describing Thompson as "a close friend of Edward Grady Partin").

3. "Solons Renamed; Chasez, Hall Win"; "Phil St. Amant Comments on Recent Senator's Race"; "10 Firms File Charters Here."

4. "Phil St. Amant Comments on Recent Senator's Race."

5. Snowden v. Pearl River Broadcasting Corp., 251 So. 2d 411 (La. App. 1968).

6. Snowden v. Pearl River Broadcasting Corp., 251 So. 2d at 413 (Blanche, J., concurring).

7. Snowden v. Pearl River Broadcasting Corp., 251 So. 2d at 413 (Blanche, J., concurring).

8. Lawhorne, *Defamation and Public Officials*, 255.

9. Lawhorne, *Defamation and Public Officials*, 261.

10. Levine and Wermiel observe that "literally hundreds of reported cases, published books and articles refer to '*New York Times Co. v. Sullivan* and its progeny' or some variation of the phrase." Levine and Wermiel, *The Progeny*, xviii.

11. Lewis, *Make No Law*, 234–35.

12. Garrison v. Louisiana, 379 U.S. at 67 (1964) (reversing State v. Garrison, 154 So. 2d 400 [La. 1963], *reh'g denied* [La. June 28, 1963]). After the initial argument on April 22, 1964, the court could not muster a clear majority in the case, since Justice Brennan's draft majority opinion

would have held all criminal libel prosecutions for statements involving public officials unconstitutional. See Levine and Wermiel, *The Progeny*, 35–39. The case was reargued on October 19, 1964, and finally decided on November 23, 1964.

13. Curtis Publishing Co. v. Butts, 388 U.S. 130 (1967) (football coach); Associated Press v. Walker, 388 U.S. 130 (1967) (companion case to Curtis) (retired military official); Monitor Patriot Co. v. Roy, 401 U.S. 265 (1971) (candidate).

14. Rosenblatt v. Baer, 383 U.S. at 86.

15. Begeley Newspapers Corp. v. Hanks, 389 U.S. at 85.

16. Van Alstyne, "Corliss Lamont and the Postmaster General," 114–15; Gaffney, "A First Amendment Analysis of the Annenberg Libel Reform Proposal," 606.

17. Levine and Wermiel, *The Progeny*, 82.

18. St. Amant v. Thompson, 390 U.S. at 731.

19. Lawhorne, *Defamation and Public Officials*, 263; Lawhorne, *The Supreme Court and Libel*, 62; Smolla, *Law of Defamation*, § 3:40, 3–55.

20. Lawhorne, *The Supreme Court and Libel*, 62.

21. 419 U.S. at 252–53: "The District Judge was clearly correct in believing that the evidence introduced at trial was sufficient to support a jury finding that the respondents . . . published knowing or reckless falsehoods about the [plaintiffs]."

22. 441 U.S. at 160.

23. 466 U.S. at 498; 491 U.S. at 690–93.

24. Pedrick, "Freedom of the Press and the Law of Libel," 597; Hopkins, *Actual Malice*, 135, 145; see also Carpenter, "Note: Constitutional Law—Defamation under the First Amendment," 394.

25. Gaffney, "A First Amendment Analysis of the Annenberg Libel Reform Proposal," 601–2.

26. Rosenblatt v. Baer, 383 U.S. at 84–85.

27. Adams, "Comment," 1155–56.

28. Sack, *Sack on Defamation*, § 5:21, 5-10–5-11; Sanford, *Libel and Privacy*, § 7.2, 7–31.

29. Curtis Publishing Co. v. Butts, 388 U.S. at 155.

30. Gertz v. Robert Welch, Inc., 418 U.S. at 347.

31. Gertz v. Robert Welch, Inc., 418 U.S. at 347.

32. See Philadelphia Newspapers v. Hepps, 475 U.S. at 777 (1986) (plaintiffs suing the media in cases involving matters of public concern must show falsity), and Dun & Bradstreet, Inc. v. Greenmoss Builders, Inc., 472 U.S. at 763 (plurality).

33. In some states, the private figure / public concern standards described here apply only when the defendant is a media entity. In these states, the private figure / private concern standards apply when the case is filed against a nonmedia entity.

34. Pickering v. Board of Educ., 391 U.S. at 573–75.

35. Time, Inc. v. Pape, 401 U.S. at 291–92.

36. Monitor Patriot Co. v. Roy, 401 U.S. at 276 (quoting St. Amant v. Thompson, 390 U.S. at 730–31).

37. Ocala Star-Banner Co. v. Damron, 401 U.S. at 300–301.

38. Rosenbloom v. Metromedia, 403 U.S. at 30n1.

39. Dun & Bradstreet, Inc. v. Grove, 404 U.S. at 901n3 (Douglas, J., dissenting from denial of certiorari).

40. 424 U.S. at 472 (Brennan, J., dissenting).

41. Lawrence v. Bauer Publishing & Printing, 459 U.S. at 1004 (Rehnquist, J., dissenting from denial of certiorari).

42. Coughlin v. Westinghouse Broadcasting & Cable, Inc., 603 F. Supp. at 388 (quoting St. Amant v. Thompson, 390 U.S. at 731).

43. Coughlin v. Westinghouse Broadcasting & Cable, Inc., 476 U.S. at 1187 (Burger, C. J., dissenting).

44. Harte-Hanks Communications, Inc. v. Connaughton, 491 U.S. at 692 (citation omitted).

45. Masson v. New Yorker Magazine, 501 U.S. at 510.

46. The primary search was conducted on August 19, 2017, using LexisNexis Academic Shepard's service to find cases decided by state and federal trial and appellate courts (including state supreme courts but excluding decisions by the U.S. Supreme Court) from 1968 (the year that *St. Amant* was decided) until the end of 2016 that cite or mention the *St. Amant* decision. It was supplemented by an additional search for 2017 cases on January 5, 2018.

47. Kaplar and Maines, *The Government Factor,* 50; Labunski, *Libel and the First Amendment,* 1.

48. Sanford, *Libel and Privacy,* § 1.3, 1–7.

49. Note that in cases with multiple opinions, *St. Amant* may have been cited more than once.

50. Labunski, *Libel and the First Amendment,* 89.

51. Wylie v. Arnold Transportation Services, 494 F. Supp. 2d at 730.

52. Sack, *Sack on Defamation,* § 1:3.1, 1–26.

9
THE LEGACY OF *ST. AMANT V. THOMPSON*

1. Reasons for Judgment [Verdict], Thompson v. St. Amant, La. Dist. Ct. 1964, 5; U.S. App'x, 146.

2. Partin, *From My Brother's Shadow,* 205.

3. Levine and Wermiel, *The Progeny,* 33.

4. Hall and Urofsky, *New York Times v. Sullivan,* 182.

BIBLIOGRAPHY

ARTICLES: LEGAL AND SCHOLARLY

Adams, Kate M. "Comment: (Re)defining Public Officials and Public Figures: A Washington State Primer." *Seattle University Law Review* 23, no. 4 (2000): 1155–88.

Adams, Kristin David. "Blaming the Mirror: The Restatements and the Common Law." *Indiana Law Review* 40, no. 1 (2007): 205–70.

Anderson, David A. "Is Libel Law Worth Reforming?" *University of Pennsylvania Law Review* 140, no. 2 (1992): 487–554.

———. "The Origins of the Press Clause." *UCLA Law Review* 30, no. 3 (1983): 455–541.

Anderson, William. "The Bill of Rights, the Fourteenth Amendment, and the Federal System." In *Aspects of Liberty: Essays Presented to Robert E. Cushman*, edited by Milton R. Konvitz and Clinton Rossiter., 287–308, Ithaca, NY: Cornell University Press, 1958.

Astbury, Raymond. "The Renewal of the Licensing Act in 1693 and Its Lapse in 1695." *Library* 296 (1978): 5–33.

Barron, Jerome. "Access to the Press—A New First Amendment Right." *Harvard Law Review* 80, no. 8 (1967): 1641–78.

Berch, Michael A. "We've Only Just Begun: The Impact of Remand Orders from Higher to Lower Courts on American Jurisprudence." *Arizona State Law Journal* 36, no. 2 (2004): 493–512.

Bernstein, Richard B. "The Sleeper Wakes: The History and Legacy of the Twenty-Seventh Amendment." *Fordham Law Review* 61, no. 3 (1992): 497–558.

Bertlesman, William O. "Libel and Public Men." *American Bar Association Journal* 52, no. 7 (1966): 657–62.

Billings, Warren M. "In Search of Fundamental Law: Constitutionalism in Louisiana." In *In Search of Fundamental Law: Louisiana's Constitutions, 1812–1974*, edited by Warren M. Billings and Edward F. Hass, 189–202. Lafayette, LA: Center for Louisiana Studies, University of Southwestern Louisiana, 1993.

Blair, David C., and Maron, M. E. "An Evaluation of Retrieval Effectiveness for a Full-Text Document Retrieval System." *Communications of the Association for Computing Machinery* 28, no. 3 (1985): 289–99.

Brennan, William J., Jr. "State Court Decisions and the Supreme Court." *Pennsylvania Bar Association Quarterly* 31, no. 4 (1990): 393–407.

———. "The Supreme Court and the Meiklejohn Interpretation of the First Amendment." *Harvard Law Review* 79, no. 1(1965): 1–20.

Brockett, Charles D. "An Illusion of Omnipotence: U.S. Policy toward Guatemala, 1954–1960." *Latin American Politics and Society* 44, no. 1 (2002): 91–126.

Brown, Ernest J. "The Supreme Court, 1957 Term—Foreword: Process of Law." *Harvard Law Review* 72, no 1 (1958): 77–198.

Carpenter, James R., Jr. "Note, Constitutional Law—Defamation under the First Amendment: The Actual Malice Test and 'Public Figures.'" *North Carolina Law Review* 46, no. 2 (1968): 392–98.

Cavicchi, Jon R. "Lexis v. Westlaw for Research: Better, Different, or Same and the QWERTY Effect?" *Idea* 47, no. 3 (2007): 363–406.

Chafee, Zechariah, Jr. "Essential Conditions for the Maintenance of a Healthy Public Opinion." In *Freedom of the Press From Hamilton to the Warren Court,* edited by Harold L. Nelson, 25–34. Indianapolis: Bobbs-Merrill, 1967.

Coates, John C., IV. "Corporate Speech and the First Amendment: History, Data, and Implications." *Constitutional Comment* 30, no. 2 (2015): 223–75.

Cox, John T., Jr. "Defamation: A Compendium." *Louisiana Law Review* 28, no. 1 (1967): 82–109.

Coyle, Erin K. "E. L. Godkin's Criticism of the Penny Press Antecedents to a Legal Right to Privacy." *American Journalism* 31, no. 2 (2014): 262–82.

Cross, Pearson. "The Law and Legal System of Louisiana." In *First Amendment Law in Louisiana,* edited by William R. Davie and T. Michael Maher, 8–25. Lafayette, LA: University of Louisiana at Lafayette Press, 2015.

Dabney, Daniel P. "The Curse of Thamus: An Analysis of Full-Text Legal Document Retrieval." *Law Library Journal* 78, no. 1 (1986): 5–40.

Denbeaux, Mark P. "The First Word of the First Amendment." *Northwestern University Law Review* 80, no. 5 (1986): 1156–1221.

Dudley, Earl C. "A Two-For Clerkship: Stanley F. Reed and Earl Warren." In *Of Courtiers and Kings: More Stories of Supreme Court Law Clerks and Their Justices,* edited by Todd C. Peppers and Clare Cushman, 231–52. Charlottesville: University of Virginia Press, 2015.

Eldridge, Larry. "Before Zenger: Truth and Seditious Speech in Colonial America, 1607–1700." *American Journal of Legal History* 39, no. 3 (1995): 337–58.

Fargo, Anthony. "Social Science Research in Judges' First Amendment Decisions." In *Communication and Law: Multidisciplinary Approaches to Research,* edited by Amy Reynolds and Brooke Barnett., 23–38. Mahwah, NJ: Lawrence Erlbaum Associates, 2006.

Feldstein, Mark. "A Muckraking Model: Investigative Reporting Cycles in American History." *Press/Politics* 11, no. 2 (2006): 105–20.

Fernandez, Mark F. "The Rules of the Courts of the Territory of Orleans." *Louisiana History* 38, no. 1 (1997): 63–86.

Fontenot, H. Ward. "The Louisiana Judicial System and the Fusion of Cultures." *Louisiana Law Review* 63, no. 4 (2003): 1151–60.

Gaffney, Paul. "A First Amendment Analysis of the Annenberg Libel Reform Proposal." *University of Chicago Legal Forum* 1990, no. 1 (1990): 601–23.

Gibson, Michael T. "The Supreme Court and Freedom of Expression from 1791 to 1917." *Fordham Law Review* 55, no. 3 (1986): 263–333.

Glancy, Dorothy J. "The Invention of the Right to Privacy." *Arizona Law Review* 21, no. 1 (1979): 1–199.

Graves, E. B. "Circumspecte Agatis." *English History Review* 43, no. 1 (1928): 1–20.

Green, Barbara. "Cracking the Code: Interpreting and Enforcing the Appellate Court's Decision and Mandate." *Stetson Law Review* 32, no. 2 (2003): 393–414.

Hart, Henry M., Jr. "Foreword: The Time Chart of the Justices." *Harvard Law Review* 73, no. 1 (1959): 84–125.

Harum, Albert E. "Federal Occupation of Political Defamation." *American Bar Association Journal* 49, no. 11 (1963): 1096–1100.

———. "Remolding of Common Law Defamation." *American Bar Association Journal* 49, no. 2 (1963): 149–54.

Helmholz, Richard H. "Canonical Defamation in Medieval England." *American Journal of Legal History* 15, no. 4 (1971): 255–68.

Hemel, Daniel Jacob. "Executive Action and the First Amendment's First Word." *Pepperdine Law Review* 40, no. 3 (2013): 601–24.

Henkin, Louis. "The Supreme Court, 1967 Term." *Harvard Law Review* 82, no. 1 (1968): 63–317.

Hirsch, Barry T., David A. Macpherson, and Wayne G. Vroman. "Estimates of Union Density by State." *Monthly Labor Review* 124, no. 7 (2001): 51–55. Available at http://unionstats.gsu.edu/MLR_7-01_StateUnionDensity.pdf.

———. "Union Density Estimates by State, 1964–2016." Database. http://unionstats.gsu.edu/MonthlyLaborReviewArticle.htm.

Hood, John T., Jr. "The History and Development of the Louisiana Civil Code." *Louisiana Law Review* 19, no. 1 (1958): 18–33.

Hulme, Harold. "The Winning of Freedom of Speech by the House of Commons." *American History Review* 61, no. 4 (1956): 825–53.

Hutchins, Robert M. "Ideas, Institutions and American Liberty." In *Aspects of Liberty: Essays Presented to Robert E. Cushman*, edited by Milton R. Konvitz and Clinton Rossiter, 3–14. Ithaca, NY: Cornell University Press, 1958.

Ingber, Stanley. "The Marketplace of Ideas: A Legitimizing Myth." *Duke Law Journal* 1984, no. 1 (1984): 1–91.

Kalven, Harry, Jr. "The New York Times Case: A Note on 'The Central Meaning of the First Amendment.'" *Supreme Court Review* 1964 (1964): 191–221.

Kanstroom, Daniel. "The Long, Complex, and Futile Deportation Saga of Carlos Marcello." In *Immigration Stories*, edited by David A. Martin and Peter H. Schuck, 113–46. New York: Foundation, 2004.

Kaufman, Henry. "Trends on Damage Awards, Insurance Premiums and the Cost of Media Libel Litigation." In *The Cost of Libel: Economic and Policy Implications*, edited by Everette E. Dennis and Eli M. Noam, 1–20. New York: Columbia University Press, 1989.

Kirk, Martha E., and Morris D. Rosenthal. "Defamation—Conditional Privilege in Louisiana (Part One)," *Louisiana Law Review* 6, no. 2 (1945): 281–85.

———. "Defamation—Conditional Privilege in Louisiana (Part Two)." *Louisiana Law Review* 6, no. 3 (1945): 417–24.

Kirshbaum, Jonathan M. "Accelerating Pace of Supreme Court's Summary Reversals of Habeas Relief Suggests Impatience with Circuit Courts' Failure to Defer to State Tribunals." *Bloomberg BNA Criminal Law Reporter* 13 (June 27, 2012): 429,

Landes, William M., and Posner, Richard A. "The Best for Last: The Timing of U.S. Supreme Court Decisions." *Duke Law Journal* 64, no. 6 (2015): 992–1022.

Layrisson, Louis Edward, III. "Note: Kennedy v. Sheriff of East Baton Rouge: A Hollow Victory for Louisiana Defamation Plaintiffs?" *Louisiana Law Review* 68, no. 1 (2007): 300–329.

Leiman, Joan Maisel, "The Rule of Four." *Columbia Law Review* 57, no. 7 (1957): 975–92.

Levy, Leonard W. "On the Origins of the Free Press Clause." *UCLA Law Review* 32, no. 2 (1984): 177–218.

Lewis, John B., and Bruce L. Ottley. "*New York Times v. Sullivan* at 50: Despite Criticism, the Actual Malice Standard Still Provides 'Breathing Space' for Communications in the Public Interest." *DePaul Law Review* 64, no. 1 (2014): 2–64.

Ludlum, Robert P. "The Antislavery 'Gag Rule': History and Argument." *Journal of Negro History* 26, no. 2 (1941): 203–43.

Maitland, F. W. "Slander in the Middle Ages." *Green Bag* 2, no. 4 (1890): 4–7.

Matthews, Albert. "The Snake Devices, 1754–1776, and of the Constitutional Courant of 21 September, 1765." *Transactions of the Colonial Society of Massachusetts* 9 (1907): 409–53.

McMahon, Henry G. "The Louisiana Code of Civil Procedure." *Louisiana Law Review* 21, no. 1 (1960): 1–52.

Meiklejohn, Alexander, "The First Amendment Is an Absolute." *Supreme Court Review* 1961 (1961): 245–66.

Mercieca, Jennifer Rose. "The Culture of Honor: How Slaveholders Responded to the Abolitionist Mail Crisis of 1835." *Rhetoric and Public Affairs* 10, no. 1 (2007): 51–76.

Merrill, John C. "The Four Theories of the Press Four and a Half Decades Later: A Retrospective." *Journalism Studies* 3, no. 1 (2002), 133–36.

Millon, David. "Circumspecte Agatis Revisited." *Law and History Review* 2, no. 1 (Spring 1984): 105–27.

Murnaghan, Francis D. "From Figment to Fiction to Philosophy—The Requirement of Proof of Damages in Libel Actions." *Catholic University Law Review* 22, no. 1 (1972): 1–38.

Note (R.W.C.). "The Developing Privilege of Neutral Reportage." *Virginia Law Review* 69, no. 5 (1983): 853–74.

Note. "The Pre–*Thorley v. Kerry* Case Law of the Libel-Slander Distinction." *University of Chicago Law Review* 22, no. 1 (1955): 132–50.

O'Neil, Robert M. "Television, Tort Law, and Federalism." *California Law Review* 53, no. 2 (1965): 421–85.

Page, Kathryn. "A First Born Child of Liberty: The Constitution of 1864." In *In Search of Fundamental Law: Louisiana's Constitutions, 1812–1974*, edited by Warren M. Billings and Edward F. Hass, 52–68. Lafayette, LA: Center for Louisiana Studies, University of Southwestern Louisiana, 1993.

Papandrea, Mary-Rose. "The Story of *New York Times Co. v. Sullivan*." In *First Amendment Stories*, edited by Richard W. Garnett and Andrew Koppelman, 229–63. New York, NY: Foundation Press/Thomas Reuters, 2012.

Pedrick, Willard H. "Freedom of the Press and the Law of Libel: The Modern Revised Translation." *Cornell Law Review* 49, no. 4 (1964): 581–608.

Peirce, Clyde. "The Panama Libel Cases." *Indiana Magazine of History* 33, no. 2 (1937): 171–86.

Peterson, Theodore. "The Social Responsibility Theory of the Press." In *Four Theories of the Press: The Authoritarian, Libertarian, Social Responsibility, and Soviet Communist Concepts of What the Press Should Be and Do*, edited by Fred S. Siebert, Theodore Peterson, and Wilbur Schramm, 73–103. Urbana: University of Illinois Press, 1956.

Powe, L. A., Jr. "Evolution to Absolutism: Justice Douglas and the First Amendment." *Columbia Law Review* 74, no. 3 (1974): 371–411.

Powell, Alden L. "A History of Louisiana Constitutions." In Louisiana State Law Inst., *Project of a Constitution for the State of Louisiana with Notes and Studies*, vol. 1, pt. 1, 392–508. Baton Rouge: Thos. J. Moran, 1954.

Remmers, Donald H. "Recent Legislative Trends in Defamation by Radio." *Harvard Law Review* 64, no. 5 (1951): 727–58.

Robbins, Ira P. "Hiding behind the Cloak of Invisibility: The Supreme Court and Per Curiam Opinions." *Tulane Law Review* 86, no. 6 (2012): 1197–1242.

Roche, John P. "American Liberty: An Examination of the 'Tradition' of Freedom." In *Aspects of Liberty: Essays Presented to Robert E. Cushman*, edited by Milton R. Konvitz and Clinton Rossiter, 129–62. Ithaca, NY: Cornell University Press, 1958.

Roosevelt, Kermit, III. "Choice of Law in Federal Courts: From Erie and Klaxo to Cafa and Shady Grove." *Northwestern Law Review* 106, no. 1 (2012): 1–53.

Sacks, Albert M. "The Supreme Court, 1953 Term—Foreword." *Harvard Law Review* 68, no. 1 (1954): 96–103.

Saef, Scott E. "Neutral Reportage: The Case for a Statutory Privilege." *Northwestern University Law Review* 86, no. 417 (1992).

Scanlon, Thomas. "A Theory of Freedom of Expression." *Philosophy and Public Affairs* 1, no. 2 (1972): 204–26.

Scardino, Daniel. "Liberty and Defamation." *Communications Lawyer* 19, no. 3 (2002): 1–5.

Schlesinger, Arthur M. "The Colonial Newspapers and the Stamp Act." *New England Quarterly* 8, no. 1 (1935): 63–83.

Schmidt, Christopher W. "*New York Times v. Sullivan* and the Legal Attack on the Civil Rights Movement." *Alabama Law Review* 66, no. 2 (2014): 293–335.

Schopler, E. H. "Libel and Slander: Who Is a Public Official or Otherwise within the Federal Constitutional Rule Requiring Public Officials to Show Actual Malice." In *American Law Reports*, 3:19, § 5[d]. Rochester, NY: Lawyers Co-operative, 1964, supp. 2005.

Siebert, Fred S. "The Authoritarian Theory of the Press." In *Four Theories of the Press: The Authoritarian, Libertarian, Social Responsibility, and Soviet Communist Concepts of What the Press Should Be and Do*, edited by Fred S. Siebert, Theodore Peterson, and Wilbur Schramm, 9–37. Urbana: University of Illinois Press, 1956.

———. "The Libertarian Theory of the Press," In *Four Theories of the Press: The Authoritarian, Libertarian, Social Responsibility, and Soviet Communist Concepts of What the Press Should Be and Do*, edited by Fred S. Siebert, Theodore Peterson and Wilbur Schramm, 39–71. Urbana: University of Illinois Press, 1956.

Smith, J. Denson. "How Louisiana Prepared and Adopted a Criminal Code." *Journal of Criminal Law and Criminology* 41, no. 2 (1951): 125–35.

Solimine, Michael E., and Rafael Gely. "The Supreme Court and the DIG: An Empirical and Institutional Analysis." *Wisconsin Law Review* 2005, no. 6 (2005): 1421–80.

Stevens, John D., Robert L. Bailey, Judith F. Krueger, and John Mollwitz. "Criminal Libel as Seditious Libel." *Journalism Quarterly* 43, no. 1 (1966): 110–13.

Tucker, John H., Jr. "Source Books of Louisiana Law, Part I: Civil Code." *Tulane Law Review* 6, no. 2 (1932): 280–300.

———. "Source Books of Louisiana Law, Part III: Spanish Laws," *Tulane Law Review* 8, no. 3 (1934): 396–416.

———. "Source Books of Louisiana Law, Part IV: Constitutions, Statutes, Reports and Digests." *Tulane Law Review* 9, no. 2 (1935): 244–67.

Urofsky, Melvin I. "*New York Times Co. v. Sullivan* as a Civil Rights Case." *Communications Law and Policy* 19, no. 2 (2014): 157–83.

Van Alstyne, William. "Corliss Lamont and the Postmaster General: A Synecdoche for the First Amendment in the Era of the Warren Court (1953–1969)." In *Earl Warren and the Warren Court: The Legacy in American and Foreign Law*, edited by Harry N. Scheiber, 113–36. Lanham, MD: Rowman and Littlefield, 2007.

Veeder, Van Vechten. "The History and Theory of the Law of Defamation I." *Columbia Law Review* 3, no. 8 (1903): 546–73.

———. "The History and Theory of the Law of Defamation II." *Columbia Law Review* 4, no. 1 (1904): 35–56.

Warren, Samuel, and Brandeis, Louis. "The Right to Privacy." *Harvard Law Review* 4, no. 5 (1890): 193–220.

Yiannopoulos, A. N. "The Civil Codes of Louisiana." *Civil Law Commentary* 1, no. 1 (2008): 1–23.

ARTICLES: NEWSPAPER AND MAGAZINE

Adams, Art. "Johnson Withdraws; New Filings Made as Qualifying Ends." *Baton Rouge Morning Advocate*, Aug. 20, 1971.

Adams, Gibbs. "Judge Rules $5,000 Due for Slander." *Baton Rouge Morning Advocate*, May 6, 1964, 1A, 10A.

"Alabamians Assail Ad Backing Dr. King." *New York Times*, Apr. 8, 1960.

"All Soldiers in State Rush to New Orleans." *Chicago Daily Tribune*, Sept. 8, 1934, 1.

Anders, Smiley. "Special People Dept." *Baton Rouge Advocate*, Feb. 3, 2016.

Associated Press. "Cursing, Fighting Long Taken to Mental Hospital." *Dallas Morning News*, June 19, 1959.

———. "Garrison Claims Arrests in JFK Probe Far Away." *Baton Rouge Advocate*, Feb. 21, 1967, 1.

———. "Obituary: Edward Partin, 66; Union Aide Became Anti-Hoffa Witness." *New York Times*, Mar. 13, 1990.

———. "Sen. Long, St. Amant Quicken Tempo of Campaigns." *New Orleans Times-Picayune*, July 20, 1962, 1.

———. "St. Amant Hits Long Who Cites Own Record." *Baton Rouge State-Times*, July 20, 1962, 8A.

Bartels, Paul. "St. Amant Attacks Busing, Simoneaux." *Baton Rouge Morning Advocate*, Dec. 2, 1971, 1.

"Baseball Clinic Elects McGraw." *Baton Rouge Morning Advocate*, Mar. 12, 1971, 5C.

"Baton Rougean Plans to Run for Senator." *Baton Rouge State-Times*, Sept. 19, 1961, 1A, 6A.

"Blasts Union Activity" (photo and caption). *Baton Rouge Morning Advocate*, June 28, 1962, 12A.

Bliss, George. "Meany Calls Hoffa Key to Union's Status." *Chicago Daily Tribune*, Dec. 5, 1957.

Boyd, Richard. "Marcello Wins Look at Jeff Files." *New Orleans Times-Picayune / States Item*, Sept. 17, 1980, I-18.

Brill, Stephen. "Inside the Jury Room at the Washington Post Libel Trial." *American Lawyer*, November 1982.

Burrough, Bryan. "Killing Him Softly." *New York Times*, June 20, 2004.

Chandler, David. "The 'Little Man' Is Bigger Than Ever." *Life*, Apr. 10, 1970.

"Chasez, Hall Win." *New Orleans Times-Picayune*, July 29, 1962, 1.

"Court Report," *Baton Rouge State-Times*, July 6, 1962, 4A.

Cullen, Ed. "The Center of the Universe," *Baton Rouge Advocate*, Mar. 22, 2009, D1.

De Toledano, Ralph. "In Washington: The Partin Case: Justice Bound and Gagged," *Reading (PA) Eagle*, Mar. 4, 1970, 4.

Dean, John W. "The Telling Tale of the Twenty-Seventh Amendment." *Findlaw*, Sept. 27, 2002, http://writ.news.findlaw.com/dean/20020927.html.

"Deputy Denies Charges Made by Candidate." *Baton Rouge State-Times*, June 29, 1962, 8A.

"Deputy Files Slander Suits for $450,000." *Baton Rouge State-Times*, July 4, 1962, 33A.

"'Fantasy' Is Theme of Dance." *Baton Rouge Morning Advocate*, May 22, 1960, 1D.

"Federal Jury Indicts Partin for Embezzling." *Baton Rouge Morning Advocate*, June 27, 1962, 1A.

"Former Senator Russell B. Long Dies at 84." *New York Times*, May 10, 2003.

"The Free Press." *New York Herald*, June 1, 1869, 5. Reproduced in Frederic Hudson, *Journalism in the United States from 1690 to 1872*, 742–47. New York: Harper & Brothers, 1873.

"Funeral Set for Man Killed in Accident." *Baton Rouge Morning Advocate*, June 9, 1962, 6A.

Godkin, E. L. "Libel and Its Legal Remedy." *Atlantic Monthly* 46, no. 278 (1880): 729–38.

"Harris Falls to DeBileux." *Baton Rouge Sunday Advocate*, Jan. 12, 1964, 1.

"Herman Thompson to Run for Sheriff." *Baton Rouge Morning Advocate*, July 15, 1975, 7A.

Hughes, Frank. "A Free Press (Hitler Style) Sought for U.S.: Totalitarians Tell How It Can Be Done." *Chicago Daily Tribune*, Mar. 27, 1947.

"In Memory of A. G. Klein, Jr." (advertisement). *Baton Rouge Morning Advocate*, Dec. 14, 1962, 2A.

"Joseph Daniel 'J. D.' Albin." Obituary. *Baton Rouge Advocate*, Mar. 3, 2006.

Keilman, John. "Rainbow Beach 'Wade-Ins' Broke Down Racial Barrier." *Chicago Tribune*, July 10, 2011.

Krouse, Peter. "Testimony of Key Witness in Jimmy Hoffa Case Unsealed." *Cleveland Plain Dealer*, Apr. 19, 2009.

"LBJ Slogans on St. Amant Car Causes a Shot in the Dark." *Baton Rouge Morning Advocate*, Sept. 8, 1964, 1A.

"Lamplighters Entertain at Party." *Baton Rouge State-Times*, Apr. 24, 1961, 14A.

"Law Enforcement Officers Leaving City-Parish Gov't." *Baton Rouge Morning Advocate*, June 1, 1972, 2A.

Leubsdorf, Carl P. "Deep Dixie May Be Headed for Three-Party System." *Baton Rouge Advocate*, Jan. 7, 1962, 6B.

———. "It's Plain Enough a Long Has Hit Louisiana Campaign Trail." *Baton Rouge Morning Advocate*, July 15, 1962, 16A.

Lewis, Anthony. "Black Doubts Suits for Libel Are Legal." *New York Times*, June 11, 1962, 1.

"Lieut. Colonel Phil A. St. Amant, Ret. . . . Will Present . . ." (advertisement). *New Orleans Times-Picayune*, Nov. 29, 1961, 30.

"Lt. Col. St. Amant Retires from Army." *Baton Rouge State-Times*, Sept. 10, 1959, 13.

Loftus, Joseph A. "F.B.I. Seizes Hoffa in a Plot to Bribe Senate Staff Aide." *New York Times*, Mar. 14, 1957, 1.

———. "Hoffa Acquitted of Bribery Plot; Seeks Beck Post." *New York Times*, July 20, 1957.

"Man Crushed to Death under Tandem Trailer." *Baton Rouge Morning Advocate*, June 8, 1962, 1.

McHale, Ed. "'Brilab' Convictions Overturned." Associated Press, June 23, 1989.

"Mobilization Necessary Says Retired Officer." *Baton Rouge State-Times*, July 12, 1961, 31.

Moses, Gerald. "Libel Award to Office Reinstated." *Baton Rouge Morning Advocate*, Feb. 21, 1967, 1.

"New Filings Made as Qualifying Ends." *Baton Rouge Morning Advocate*, Aug. 20, 1971, 1.

"One Candidate Asks to Leave Sheriff's Race." *Baton Rouge Morning Advocate*, Sept. 11, 1975, 15A.

"Open Letter" (advertisement). *Baton Rouge State-Times*, Dec. 20, 1961, 24.

Partin, Edward G. "Scheme to Kill Bob Kennedy . . . and Kennedy's Kids." *Life*, May 15, 1964, 45.

"Phil A. St. Amant" (advertisement). *Baton Rouge Morning Advocate*, Apr. 26, 1962, 38.

"Phil A. St. Amant, II Has Party on Third Birthday." *Baton Rouge Morning Advocate*, Oct. 8, 1944, 14.

"Phil St. Amant Comments on Recent Senator's Race." *Baton Rouge Morning Advocate*, Aug. 14, 1962, 32.

"Phil. St. Amant Levels Charges of Corruption." *Baton Rouge State-Times*, June 28, 1962, 4A.

"Phil St. Amant to Seek Senate Post Next Year." *Baton Rouge Morning Advocate*, Sept. 19, 1961, 1A, 8A.

"Pitcher Still Probing St. Amant-Clemmons Spat." *Baton Rouge Morning Advocate*, Sept. 10, 1964, 4C.
"Political Exposé" (advertisement). *Baton Rouge Morning Advocate*, July 27, 1962, 25.
"Probe Finds No Evidence of Firebomb at Partin Home." *Baton Rouge Morning Advocate*, July 9, 1983, 17A.
"Radio Special Event" (advertisement). *Baton Rouge Morning Advocate*, Sept. 25, 1961, 19.
"Radio Special Event" (advertisement). *Baton Rouge State-Times*, July 11, 1961, 22.
"Recusal Is Offered in Clay Shaw Suit." *New Orleans Times-Picayune*, Nov. 26, 1974, 16.
"Reseating Session of Solons is Urged." *Baton Rouge Morning Advocate*, Dec. 18, 1970, 11.
"The Returns." Editorial. *Baton Rouge Morning Advocate*, Dec. 10, 1959, 8.
"Reveals Hoffa Signaled How to Cast Votes." *Chicago Daily Tribune*, Dec. 5, 1957, pt. 2, p. 3.
"Robert L. 'Buck' Kleinpeter." Obituary. *Baton Rouge Advocate*, May 18, 2013.
"Russell B. Long Deserves Re-election to the United States Senate." Editorial. *New Orleans Times-Picayune*, July 11, 1962, 12.
"Safe Stolen Here in March Found in River." *Baton Rouge Morning Advocate*, June 10, 1961, 1.
"St. Amant May Give Talk on Shooting Incident Here." *Baton Rouge Morning Advocate*, Sept. 11, 1964, 11A.
"St. Amant Planning Television Speech." *Baton Rouge Morning Advocate*, June 17, 1962, 4.
St. Amant, Phil A. "Letters from the People." Letter to the editor. *Baton Rouge State-Times*, July 17, 1961, 28.
"Solons Renamed; Chasez, Hall Win." *New Orleans Times-Picayune*, July 29, 1962, 1.
Seghers, Frances. "Candidates for EBR Sheriff Address Kiwanis Club." *Baton Rouge Morning Advocate*, Aug. 29, 1975, 1B.
"Senate Accepts Sedition Bill." *New York Times*, May 4, 1918.
"Senate Hopeful Claims Credit for Indictment." *Baton Rouge Morning Advocate*, June 28, 1962, 1A, 12A.
"Sentence Delayed for Six Teamsters in Beating Case." *Baton Rouge Morning Advocate*, Jan. 30, 1963, 47A.
"Sheriff Promotes Lt. Thompson." *Baton Rouge Morning Advocate*, May 24, 1956, 11B.
Smith, Sandy. "Carlos Marcello: King Thug of Louisiana," *Life*, September 8, 1967, 94.
———. "The Fix." *Life*, Sept. 1, 1967, 22.
Tedesco, Larie. "Anti-Italian Mood Led to 1891 Lynchings." *New Orleans Times-Picayune*, Mar. 14, 1991, B1.
"10 Firms File Charters Here." *Baton Rouge State-Times*, Aug. 18, 1962, 7.
Thibodeaux, Ron. "Partin Left Legacy of Power, Controversy." *Baton Rouge Morning Advocate*, June 28, 1980, 16A.

Thomas, Rex. "State Finds Formidable Legal Club to Swing at Out-of-State Press." *Montgomery (AL) Advertiser,* Sept. 25, 1960.

"3 Promotions Listed by Local Sheriff's Office." *Baton Rouge Morning Advocate,* Feb. 17, 1956, 22.

"TV Speech Is St. Amant Race Launcher." *Baton Rouge Morning Advocate,* Mar. 30, 1962, 10A.

"U.S. Senatorial Candidate Given Free TV Time." *Baton Rouge Morning Advocate,* June 11, 1962, 13.

United Press International. "Alabamians Assail Ad Backing Dr. King." *New York Times,* April 8, 1960.

White, Gordon S. "Wally Butts, Ex-Georgia Coach, Dies: Won Large Libel Suit." *New York Times,* Dec. 18, 1973.

"With the Colors." *Baton Rouge State-Times,* Sept. 20, 1943, 1B.

"Woman Files Suit for $9000 against Sheriff, Deputy." *Baton Rouge Morning Advocate,* Sept. 2, 1949, 1.

BOOKS, MONOGRAPHS, AND SIMILAR MATERIALS

Adler, Renata. *Reckless Disregard: Westmoreland v. CBS et al., Sharon v. Time.* New York: Knopf, 1986.

Alexander, James [attrib.]. *A Brief Narrative of the Case and Tryal of John Peter Zenger, Printer of the New-York Weekly Journal.* Boston: Thomas Fleet, 1738.

Altschull, J. Herbert. *From Milton to McLuhan: The Ideas behind American Journalism.* New York: Longman, 1990.

Berkin, Carol. *The Bill of Rights: The Fight to Secure America's Liberties.* New York: Simon and Schuster, 2015.

Bilder, Mary Sarah. *Madison's Hand: Revising the Constitutional Convention.* Cambridge, MA: Harvard University Press, 2015.

Billings, Warren M., and Edward F. Hass, eds. *In Search of Fundamental Law: Louisiana's Constitutions, 1812–1974.* Lafayette, LA: Center for Louisiana Studies, University of Southwestern Louisiana, 1993.

Bird, Wendell. *Press and Speech under Assault: The Early Supreme Court Justices, the Sedition Acts of 1798, and the Campaign Against Dissent.* New York: Oxford University Press, 2016.

Blackstone, William. *Commentaries on the Laws of England.* 1769, 4 vols.; Chicago: University of Chicago Press, 1979.

Blakey, G. Robert, and Richard N. Billings. *The Plot to Kill the President.* New York: Times Books, 1981.

Blumberg, Phillip L. *Repressive Jurisprudence in the Early American Republic: The First Amendment and the Legacy of English Law.* New York: Cambridge University Press, 2010.

Boulard, Garry. *Huey Long Invades New Orleans: The Siege of a City, 1934–36.* Gretna, LA: Pelican, 1998.

Brant, Charles. *"I Heard You Paint Houses": Frank "the Irishman" Sheeran and Closing the Case on Jimmy Hoffa.* Hanover, NH: Steerforth, 2016.

Brant, Irving. *The Bill of Rights: Its Origin and Meaning.* Indianapolis: Bobbs-Merrill, 1965.

Calhoun, Milburn, ed. *Louisiana Almanac.* New Orleans: Pelican, 2012.

Campbell, W. Joseph. *Yellow Journalism: Puncturing the Myths, Defining the Legacies.* Westport, CT: Praeger, 2001.

Chafee, Zechariah, Jr.. *Free Speech in the United States.* Cambridge, MA: Harvard University Press, 1941.

———. *Government and Mass Communication.* 2 vols. Chicago: University of Chicago Press, 1947.

Chapin, Bradley. *Criminal Justice in Colonial America, 1606–1660.* Athens: University of Georgia Press, 1983.

Cohen, Jeremy, and Timothy Gleason. *Social Research in Communication and Law.* Newbury Park, CA: Sage, 1990.

Commission on Freedom of the Press. *A Free and Responsible Press: A General Report on Mass Communication, Newspapers, Radio, Motion Pictures, Magazines, and Books.* Chicago: University of Chicago Press, 1947.

Cook, Bernard A., and James R. Watson. *Louisiana Labor: From Slavery to "Right-to-Work."* Lanham, MD: University Press of America, 1985.

Cook, Elizabeth Christine. *Literary Influences in Colonial Newspapers.* 1912; reprint, Port Washington, NY: Kennikat, 1966.

Coyle, Erin K. *The Press and Rights to Privacy: First Amendment Freedoms vs. Invasion of Privacy Claims.* El Paso: LFB Scholarly, 2012.

Crawford, William E. *Louisiana Civil Law Treatise: Tort Law.* 2d ed. Eagan, MN: West, 2009; supp. 2015.

Creel, George. *How We Advertised America: The First Telling of the Amazing Story of the Committee on Public Information That Carried the Gospel of Americanism to Every Corner of the Globe.* New York: Harper and Brothers, 1920.

Dart, Benjamin W. *Constitutions of the State of Louisiana and Selected Federal Laws.* Indianapolis: Bobbs-Merrill, 1932.

Davis, John H. *Mafia Kingfish: Carlos Marcello and the Assassination of John F. Kennedy.* New York: McGraw-Hill, 1989.

De Tocqueville, Alexis. *Democracy in America.* Edited by Richard Heffner. 1835; reprint, New York: New American Library, 1956.

Dickson, Del. *The Supreme Court in Conference (1940–1985): The Private Discussions behind Nearly 300 Supreme Court Decisions.* Oxford: Oxford University Press, 2001.

Dray, Philip. *There Is Power in a Union: The Epic Story of Labor in America.* New York: Doubleday, 2010.

Eakin, Sue, Manie Culbertson, and Marta Long. *Louisiana: The Land and Its People.* 5th ed. Gretna, LA: Pelican, 2007.

Ellsberg, Daniel. *Secrets: A Memoir of Vietnam and the Pentagon Papers.* New York: Viking, 2003.

Emerson, Thomas I. *The System of Freedom of Expression.* New York: Random House, 1969.

Epstein, Lee, Jeffrey Allan Segal, Harold J. Spaeth, and Thomas G Walker. *The Supreme Court Compendium: Data, Decisions and Developments.* 6th ed. Washington, DC: Congressional Quarterly, 2015.

Evans, Laird. *And Justice for All . . . Even Teamsters.* Morrisville, NC: Lulu, 2016.

Evans, William David. *Collection of Statutes Connected with the General Administration of the Law.* London: W. H. Bond, 1836.

Forde, Kathy Roberts. *Literary Journalism on Trial: Masson v. New Yorker and the First Amendment.* Amherst: University of Massachusetts Press, 2008.

Franklin, Benjamin. *An Apology for Printers.* Edited by Randolph Goodman. 1731; reprint, New York: Book Craftsmen Associates, 1955.

Friedman, Allen, and Ted Schwarz. *Power and Greed: Inside the Teamsters Empire of Corruption.* New York: Franklin Watts, 1989.

Friendly, Fred W. *Minnesota Rag: Corruption, Yellow Journalism, and the Case That Saved Freedom of the Press.* New York: Vintage Books, 1982.

Garvey, Joan B., and Mary Lou Widmer. *Louisiana: The First 300 Years.* New Orleans: Garmer, 2001.

Godson, Roy. *Menace to Society: Political-Criminal Collaboration around the World.* New Brunswick, NJ: Transaction, 2003.

Goodale, James A. *Fighting for the Press: The Inside Story of the Pentagon Papers and Other Battles.* New York: CUNY Journalism Press, 2013.

Greiner, Meinrad. *Louisiana Digest, 1804–1841.* New Orleans: B. Levy, 1841.

Hair, William Ivy. *The Kingfish and His Realm: The Life and Times of Huey P. Long.* Baton Rouge: Louisiana State University Press, 1991.

Hall, Kermit L., and Melvin I. Urofsky. *New York Times v. Sullivan: Civil Rights, Libel Law, and the Free Press.* Lawrence: University Press of Kansas, 2011.

Hansen, Arthur. *Libel and Related Torts.* New York: American Newspaper Publishers Association Foundation, 1969.

Hargrave, W. Lee. *The Louisiana State Constitution: A Reference Guide.* New York: Greenwood, 1991.

Heyman, Steven J. *Free Speech and Human Dignity.* New Haven, CT: Yale University Press, 2008.

Hoffa, James R. (as told to Donald I. Rogers). *The Trials of Jimmy Hoffa: An Autobiography.* Chicago: Henry Regnery, 1970.

———. *Hoffa: The Real Story.* New York: Stein and Day, 1975.

Hopkins, W. Wat. *Actual Malice: Twenty-Five Years after Times v. Sullivan.* New York: Praeger, 1989.

Hryb, Willie. *Vanished: The Life and Disappearance of Jimmy Hoffa.* Rock Hill, SC: Strategic Media Books, 2013.

Hughes, Frank. *Prejudice of the Press: A Restatement of the Principle of Freedom of the Press with Specific Reference to the Hutchins-Luce Commission.* New York: Devin-Adair, 1950.

International Brotherhood of Teamsters. *100th Anniversary: A Strong Legacy, a Powerful Future.* [Philadelphia?]: DeLancey, 2003.

James, Ralph, and Estelle Dinerstein James. *Hoffa and the Teamsters: A Study of Union Power.* Princeton, NJ: D. Van Nostrand, 1965.

Jenks, Edward. *Law and Politics in the Middle Ages.* New York: H. Holt, 1898.

Kalven, Harry, Jr. *A Worthy Tradition: Freedom of Speech in America.* Edited by Jamie Kalven. New York: Harper and Row, 1988.

Kaplar, Richard T., and Patrick D. Maines. *The Government Factor: Undermining Journalistic Ethics in the Information Age.* Washington, DC: Cato Institute, 1995.

Kennedy, Robert. *The Enemy Within: The McClellan Committee's Crusade against Jimmy Hoffa and Corrupt Labor Unions.* New York: Harper, 1960.

Kerr, Lewis. *An Exposition of the Criminal Laws of the Territory of Orleans, 1806.* New Orleans: John Mowry, 1986.

Knight, Carol Lynn. *The American Colonial Press and the Townshend Crisis, 1766–1770: A Study in Political Imagery.* Lewiston, ME: E. Mellen, 1990.

Kurtz, Michael L., and Morgan Peoples. *Earl K. Long: The Saga of Uncle Earl and Louisiana Politics.* Baton Rouge: Louisiana State University Press, 1992.

Labunski, Richard E. *Libel and the First Amendment: Legal History and Practice In Print and Broadcasting.* New Brunswick, NJ: Transaction Books, 1987.

Lawhorne, Clifton O. *Defamation and Public Officials: The Evolving Law of Libel.* Carbondale: Southern Illinois University Press, 1971.

———. *The Supreme Court and Libel.* Carbondale: Southern Illinois University Press, 1981.

Levine, Lee, and Stephen Wermiel. *The Progeny: Justice William J. Brennan's Fight to Preserve the Legacy of New York Times v. Sullivan.* Chicago: American Bar Association, 2011.

Levy, Leonard W. *Emergence of a Free Press.* New York: Oxford University Press, 1985.

Lewis, Anthony. *Make No Law: The Sullivan Case and the First Amendment.* New York: Random House, 1991.

Lislet, L. Moreau. *A General Digest of the Acts of the Legislature of Louisiana.* New Orleans: B. Levy, 1828.

Long Legacy Project. Huey Long: The Man, His Mission and Legacy, http://www.hueylong.com/index.php.

Maier, Pauline. *Ratification: The People Debate the Constitution, 1787–1788.* New York: Simon and Schuster, 2010.

Malcolm, Janet. *The Journalist and the Murderer.* New York: Knopf, 1990.

Mann, Robert. *Legacy to Power: Senator Russell Long of Louisiana.* New York: Paragon House, 1992.

Marshall, F. Ray. *Labor in the South.* Cambridge, MA: Harvard University Press, 1967.

Martin, Michael S. *Russell Long: A Life in Politics.* Jackson: University Press of Mississippi, 2014.

Martin, Thomas. *Dynasty: The Longs of Louisiana.* New York: G. P. Putnam's Sons, 1960.

Mayer, G. *Union Membership Trends in the United States.* Washington, DC: Congressional Research Service, 2004.

Meiklejohn, Alexander. *Free Speech and Its Relation to Self-Government.* New York: Harper, 1948.

Mill, John Stuart. *On Liberty.* 2d ed. London: John W. Parker and Son, 1859.

Miller, William Lee. *Arguing about Slavery: John Quincy Adams and the Great Battle in the United States Congress.* New York: Knopf, 1995.

Milton, John. *Areopagitica: A Speech for the Liberty of Unlicensed Printing to the Parliament of England.* 1664. https://www.dartmouth.edu/~milton/reading_room/areopagitica/text.html.

Moldea, Dan E. *The Hoffa Wars: The Rise and Fall of Jimmy Hoffa.* New York: Shapolsky, 1993.

Mollenhoff, Clark R. *Tentacles of Power: The Story of Jimmy Hoffa.* Cleveland: World Publishing, 1965.

Morgan, Edmund S., and Helen M. Morgan. *The Stamp Act Crisis: Prologue to Revolution.* 2d ed. Chapel Hill: University of North Carolina Press, 1962.

Neff, James. *Vendetta: Bobby Kennedy versus Jimmy Hoffa.* New York: Little, Brown, 2015.

Nelson, Harold L., ed. *Freedom of the Press from Hamilton to the Warren Court.* Indianapolis: Bobbs-Merrill, 1967.

Newman, Roger K. *Hugo Black: A Biography.* New York: Pantheon Books, 1997.

Nugent, Henry Paul. *An Account of the Proceedings Had in the Superior Court of the Territory of Orleans, against Thierry & Nugent for Libels and Contempt of Court.* Philadelphia, 1810.

Partin, Douglas W. *From My Brother's Shadow: Teamster Doug Partin Tells His Side of the Story.* Greenwell Springs, LA: Oak of Acadiana, 2013.

Pepper, William. *Orders to Kill: The Truth behind the Murder of Martin Luther King.* New York: Skyhorse, 2015.

Perry, H. W., Jr. *Deciding to Decide: Agenda Setting in the United States Supreme Court.* Cambridge, MA: Harvard University Press, 1991.

Pollock, Frederick, and Frederic W. Maitland. *The History of English Law before the Time of Edward.* Cambridge: Cambridge University Press, 1895.

Pugh, Robert G., Jr. *The Influence of the Nationalization of the U.S. Bill of Rights on Constitution-Making in the States: The Case of Louisiana.* Baton Rouge: Louisiana State University, 1976.

Restatement of Torts. Philadelphia: American Law Institute, 1938.

Richards, Robert D. *Uninhibited, Robust, and Wide Open: Mr. Justice Brennan's Legacy to the First Amendment.* Boone, NC: Parkway, 1994.

Robinson, M. M. *Digest of the Penal Law of the State of Louisiana.* New Orleans: A. S. Gould, 1841.

Rosenberg, Norman L. *Protecting the Best Men: An Interpretive History of the Law of Libel.* Chapel Hill: University of North Carolina Press, 1986.

Rossiter, Clinton. *Seedtime of the Republic: The Origin of the American Tradition of Political Liberty.* New York: Harcourt, Brace, 1953.

Roth, M. Patricia. *The Juror and the General.* New York: Morrow, 1986.

Rothenberg, Eliot C. *The Taming of the Press: Cohen v. Cowles Media Company.* Westport, CT: Praeger, 1999.

Rudenstine, David. *The Day the Presses Stopped: A History of the Pentagon Papers Case.* Berkeley: University of California Press, 1996.

Rutherford, Livingston. *John Peter Zenger: His Press, His Trial, and a Bibliography of Zenger Imprints.* New York: Holt, 1904.

Sack, Robert D. *Sack on Defamation: Libel, Slander, and Related Problems.* New York: Practising Law Institute, 2016.

Salmon, David W. *The Jimmy Hoffa I Knew.* Provo, UT: D. W. Salmon, 1995.

Sanford, Bruce W. *Libel and Privacy.* Englewood Cliffs, NJ: Prentice Hall Law and Business, 2005.

Scalia, Antonin, and Bryan A. Garner. *Making Your Case: The Art of Persuading Judges.* St. Paul, MN: Thomson/West, 2008.

Schliesser, Eric. "On the Right to Work in Adam Smith and the Origin of the Harm Principle." *Digressions & Impressions* (blog). Nov. 10, 2015. http://digressionsnimpressions.typepad.com/digressionsimpressions/2015/11/strengthanddexterity.html.

Schwartz, Bernard, *The Unpublished Decisions of the Warren Court.* New York: Oxford University Press, 1985.

Schwartz, Bernard, and Stephan Lesher. *Inside the Warren Court.* Garden City, NY: Doubleday, 1983.

Shapiro, Stephen M., Kenneth Geller, Timothy S. Bishop, Edward A. Hartnett, and Dan Himmelfarb. *Supreme Court Practice.* Arlington, VA: Bloomberg BNA, 2013.

Sheridan, Walter. *The Fall and Rise of Jimmy Hoffa.* New York: Saturday Review Press, 1972.

Siebert, Frederick S. *Freedom of the Press in England, 1476–1776: The Rise and Decline of Government Controls.* Urbana: University of Illinois Press, 1952.

Smith, Adam. *An Inquiry into the Nature and Causes of the Wealth of Nations.* Edited by Katheryn Sutherland. New York: Oxford University Press, 2008.

Smith, Jeffery Alan. *Printers and Press Freedom: The Ideology of Early American Journalism.* New York: Oxford University Press, 1988.

Smolla, Rodney A. *Free Speech in an Open Society.* New York: Knopf, 1992.

———. *Law of Defamation.* St. Paul, MN: West Group, 2011.

Special Committee to Investigate Organized Crime in Interstate Commerce. *Hearings Before the Special Committee to Investigate Organized Crime in Interstate Commerce Pursuant to S. Res. 202, Part 8: Louisiana.* Transcript of January 25 and 26 and February 7, 1951, hearings. 82nd Congress, 1st Session.

St. Amant, Phil A. *The Decline and Resurrection of the American Republic.* Baton Rouge [?]: n.d. [1962?]. Box 713, folder 36, Russell B. Long Papers, Louisiana and Lower Mississippi Valley Collections, Special Collections, Hill Memorial Library, Louisiana State University.

Stern, Robert L., and Eugene Gressman. *Supreme Court Practice.* Washington, DC: BNA, 1962.

Thompson, William N. *Gambling in America: An Encyclopedia of History, Issues and Society.* Santa Barbara, CA: ABC-CLIO, 2015.

Troy, Leo. *Trade Union Membership, 1897–1962.* Cambridge, MA: National Bureau of Economic Research, 1965.

Troy, Leo, and Neil Sheflin. U.S. *Union Sourcebook: Membership, Finances, Structure, Directory.* West Orange, NJ: Industrial Relations Data and Information Services, 1985.

Ungar, Sanford J. *The Papers & The Papers: An Account of the Legal and Political Battle over the Pentagon Papers.* New York: Notable Trials Library, 1989.

Vaccara, Stefano, and Robert Miller. *Carlos Marcello: The Man behind the JFK Assassination.* New York: Enigma Books, 2013.

Veit, Helen E., Kenneth R. Bowling, and Charlene B. Bickford, eds. *Creating the Bill of Rights: The Documentary Record from the First Federal Congress.* Baltimore: Johns Hopkins University Press, 1991.

Velle, Lester. *Desperate Bargain: Why Jimmy Hoffa Had to Die.* New York: Reader's Digest, 1977.

Ward, Artemis, and David L. Weiden. *Sorcerers' Apprentices: 100 Years of Law Clerks at the United States Supreme Court.* New York: New York University Press, 2006.

Washington, George. "Washington's Farewell Address 1796." The Avalon Project: Documents in Law, History & Diplomacy. Lillian Goldman Law Library, Yale Law School, 1796. http://avalon.law.yale.edu/18th_century/washing.asp.

Weslager, C. A. *The Stamp Act Congress.* Newark: University of Delaware Press, 1976.

Woodward, Bob, and Scott Armstrong. *The Brethren: Inside the Supreme Court.* New York: Simon and Schuster, 1979.

Zeller, F. C. Duke. *Devil's Pact: Inside the World of the Teamsters Union.* New York: Carol Publishing Group, 1996.

Zenger, John Peter. *The Trial of John Peter Zenger of New York, Printer.* London: J. Wilford, 1738.

CASES

Abrams v. U.S., 250 U.S. 616 (1919).

Ardoin v. Hartford, 360 So. 2d 1331 (La. 1978), reh'g denied (La. July 26, 1978)

Associated Press v. Walker, 389 U.S. 28 (1967), reh'g denied, 389 U.S. 997 (1967).

Austin v. Mich. State Chamber of Commerce, 494 U.S. 652 (1990).

Barnhill v. Times-Picayune Publishing Co., 131 So. 21 (La. 1930).

Barron v. Baltimore, 32 U.S. (7 Pet.) 243 (1833).

Barry v. Time, Inc., 584 F. Supp. 1110 (N.D. Cal. 1984).

Bates v. City of Little Rock, 361 U.S. 516 (1960).

Batson v. Time, Inc., 298 So. 2d 100 (La. Ct. App.), writ denied, 299 So. 2d 803 (La. 1974).

Begeley Newspapers Corp. v. Hanks, 389 U.S. 81 (1967).

Blanke v. Time, Inc., 308 F. Supp. 378 (E.D. La. 1970).

Bose v. Consumers Union, 466 U.S. 485 (1984), reh'g denied, 467 U.S. 1267 (1984).

Boynton v. Virginia, 364 U.S. 454 (1960).

Brandenburg v. Ohio, 395 U.S. 444 (1969).

Brown v. Board of Education ("Brown I"), 347 U.S. 483 (1954).

Brown v. Board of Education of Topeka ("Brown II"), 349 U.S. 294 (1955).

Bussie v. Larson, 501 F. Supp. 1107 (M.D. La. 1980).

Cantrell v. Forest City Publishing Co., 419 U.S. 245 (1974).

Carlin v. Stewart, 2 La. 73 (1830).

Chaplinsky v. New Hampshire, 315 U.S. 568 (1942).

Commissioner v. Gordon, 391 U.S. 83 (No. 67-760) (1968).

Cooper v. Aaron, 358 U.S. 1 (1958).

Cottin v. Cottin, 5 Mart. (o.s.) 93 (La. 1817).

Coughlin v. Westinghouse Broadcasting & Cable, Inc., 603 F. Supp. 377 (E.D. Pa. 1985), 780 F.2d 340 (3d Cir. 1985), cert. denied, 476 U.S. 1187 (1986).
Cox v. Louisiana, 379 U.S. 536 (1965).
Curtis Publishing Co. v. Butts, 388 U.S. 130 (1967).
D'Echaux v. D'Echaux, 62 So. 597 (La. 1913).
Davies v. Gardiner, Popham 36, 79 Eng. Rep. 1155 (C.P. 1593).
De Jonge v. Oregon, 299 U.S. 353 (1937).
De Libellis Famosis, 5 Co. Rep. 125a, 77 Eng. Rep. 250 (K.B. 1606).
Debs v. United States, 249 U.S. 211 (1919).
Dennis v. U.S., 341 U.S. 494 (1951).
Dickey v. CBS, Inc., 583 F.2d 1221 (3d Cir. 1978).
Dun & Bradstreet, Inc. v. Greenmoss Builders, Inc., 472 U.S. 749 (1985).
Edwards v. National Audubon Soc., 556 F.2d 113, 120 (2d Cir. 1977).
Erie R.R. v. Tompkins, 304 U.S. 64 (1938).
Farmers Educational & Co-operative Union v. WDAY, Inc., 360 U.S. 525, 534 (1959).
Fellman v. Dreyfous, 17 So. 422 (La. 1895).
Fitzgerald v. Tucker, 737 So. 2d 706 (La. 1999).
Fowler v. Griffith, 6 Mart. (n.s.) 89 (La. 1827).
Frohwerk v. United States, 249 U.S. 204 (1919).
Garrison v. Louisiana: see State v. Garrison, infra.
General Truckdrivers, Chauffeurs, etc. v. NLRB, 389 F.2d 757 (5th Cir. 1968).
Gertz v. Robert Welch, Inc., 418 U.S. 323 (1974).
Gilligan v. King, 264 N.Y.S.2d 309 (N.Y. Sup. Ct. 1965).
Gitlow v. New York, 268 U.S. 652 (1925).
Graves v. Blanchet, 2 Salk. 696, 91 Eng. Rep. 589 (K.B. 1704).
Gray v. De Bretton, 188 So. 722 (La. 1939), reh'g denied (La. May 1, 1939).
Greenbelt Cooperative Publishing Association v. Bresler, 398 U.S. 6 (1970).
Grove v. Dun & Bradstreet, Inc., 438 F.2d 433 (3d Cir. 1971).
Guice v. Harvey, 14 La. 198 (1839).
Hanner v. DeMarcus, cert. granted, 389 U.S. 926 (1967), cert. dismissed, 390 U.S. 736 (1968).
Harrison v. United States, 392 U.S. 219 (1968).
Hart v. Playboy Enters., 1979 U.S. Dist. LEXIS 995, 5 Media L. Rep. 1811 (D. Kansas 1979).
Harte-Hanks Communications, Inc. v. Connaughton, 491 U.S. 657 (1989).
Herbert v. Lando, 441 U.S. 153 (1979).
Herndon v. Lowry, 301 U.S. 242 (1937).
Himango v. Prime Time Broadcasting, Inc., 680 P.2d 432 (Wn. App. 1984).
Hoffa v. United States, 385 U.S. 293 (1966).

Hutchinson v. Proxmire, 443 U.S. 111 (1979).
Jacron Sales Co. v. Sindorf, 350 A.2d 688 (Md. 1976).
Jagers v. Royal Indemnity Co., 276 So. 2d 309 (La. 1973).
Johnson v. Massachusetts, cert. granted, 389 U.S. 816 (1967), cert. dismissed, 390 U.S. 511 (1968).
Johnson v. St. Paul Mercury Ins. Co., 236 So. 2d 216 (La. 1970), reh'g denied (La. May 4, 1970).
Kidder v. Anderson, 354 So. 2d 1306 (La. 1978), reh'g denied (La. Mar. 2, 1978), cert. denied, 439 U.S. 829 (1978).
Kiesau v. Bantz, 686 N.W. 2d 164 (Iowa 2004).
Konigsberg v. State Bar of California, 366 U.S. 36 (1961).
Korematsu v. United States, 323 U.S. 214 (1944).
Lamont v. Postmaster General, 381 U.S. 301 (1965).
Lawrence v. Bauer Publishing & Printing, 459 U.S. 999 (1982).
Le Marc's Mgmt. Corp. v. Valentin, 709 A.2d 1222, 1225 (Md. 1998).
Lorain Journal Co. v. Milkovich, cert. denied, 474 U.S. 953 (1985) (denying certiorari in Milkovich v. News-Herald, 473 N.E.2d 1191 [Ohio 1984]).
Louisiana State Bar Ass'n v. Van Buskirk, 191 So. 2d 497 (La. 1966).
Madison v. Bolton, 102 So. 2d 433 (La. 1958), reh'g denied (La. May 26, 1958).
Mashburn v. Collin, 355 So. 2d 879 (La. 1977).
Massachusetts v. Painten, cert. granted, 386 U.S. 931 (1967), cert. dismissed, 389 U.S. 560 (1968).
Masson v. New Yorker Magazine, Inc., 501 U.S. 496 (1991).
Matassa v. Bel, 164 So. 2d 332, 335 (La. 1964), reh'g denied (La. June 8, 1964).
McCusker v. Valley News, 428 A.2d 493 (N.H. 1981), cert. denied, 454 U.S. 1017 (1981).
McHale v. Lake Charles American Press, 390 So. 2d 556 (La. Ct. App. 3d Cir. 1980), reh'g denied (La. Ct. App., 3d Cir. Dec. 1, 1980), cert. denied, 452 U.S. 941 (1981).
McLaurin v. Oklahoma State Regents for Higher Education, 339 U.S. 637 (1950).
Milkovich v. Lorain Journal Co., 497 U.S. 1 (1990).
Milkovich v. Lorain Journal Co., cert. denied, 449 U.S. 966 (1980) (denying certiorari in Milkovich v. Lorain Journal Co., 416 N.E.2d 662 (Ohio App. 1979), rev. denied [Ohio Mar. 20, 1980]).
Miller v. California, cert. granted, 389 U.S. 968 (1967), cert. dismissed, 392 U.S. 616 (1968).
Miller v. Holstein, 16 La. 389 (1840), aff'd after reargument, 16 La. 395 (1840).
Monitor Patriot Co. v. Roy, 401 U.S. 265 (1971).
NAACP v. Alabama, 357 U.S. 449 (1958).
NAACP v. Button, 371 U.S. 415 (1963).
Near v. Minnesota, 283 U.S. 697 (1931).

New York Times Co. v. U.S., 403 U.S. 713.

New York Times v. Sullivan: see Sullivan v. New York Times, infra.

Ocala Star-Banner Co. v. Damron, 401 U.S. 295 (1971).

Patterson v. Colorado ex. rel. The Attorney General of the State of Colorado, 205 U.S. 454 (1906).

Pauling v. News Syndicate, Inc., 335 F.2d 659 (2d Cir. 1964).

Peck v. Tribune Co., 214 U.S. 185 (1909).

People v. Croswell, 3 Johns. Cas. 337 (N.Y. 1803).

Philadelphia Newspapers v. Hepps, 475 U.S. 767 (1986).

Pickering v. Board of Education, 391 U.S. 563 (1968).

Procunier v. Martinez, 416 U.S. 396 (1974).

Prudential Ins. Co. of America v. Cheek, 259 U.S. 530 (1922).

R. v. Zenger, 17 St. Tr. 678 (N.Y. 1735).

Reynolds v. Swain, 13 La. 193 (1839).

Robertson v. Baldwin, 165 U.S. 275 (1897).

Romero v. Abbeville Broadcasting Serv., 420 So. 2d 1247 (La. Ct. App., 3rd Cir. 1982).

Rosenblatt v. Baer, 383 U.S. 75 (1968).

Rosenbloom v. Metromedia, Inc., 403 U.S. 29 (1971).

Sacher v. United States, 356 U.S. 576 (1958).

Sassone v. Elder, 626 So. 2d 345 (La. 1993).

Schaefer v. Lynch, 406 So. 2d 185 (La. 1981).

Schenck v. United States, 249 U.S. 47 (1919).

Senko v. LaCrosse Dredging Corp., 352 U.S. 370 (1957).

Skinner v. Oklahoma, 16 U.S. 535 (1942).

Smith v. Clemmons, 48 So. 2d 813 (La. Ct. App. 1950).

Snowden v. Pearl River Broadcasting Corp., 251 So. 2d 405 (La. Ct. App., 1st Cir. 1971), reh'g denied (La. Ct. App., 1st Cir. Sept. 2, 1971), writ refused, 253 So. 2d 217 (La. 1971).

Snyder v. Ware, 314 F. Supp. 335 (W.D. La. 1970), aff'd without opinion, 397 U.S. 589 (1970) (per curiam).

Spotorno v. Fourichon, 4 So. 71 (La. 1888).

St. Amant v. Thompson: see Thompson v. St. Amant, infra.

Stackpole v. Hennen, 6 Mart. (o.s.) 481 (La. 1828).

State v. American Sugar Refinery Co., 68 So. 742 (1915).

State v. Defley, 395 So. 2d 759 (La. 1981).

State v. Garrison, 154 So. 2d 400 (La. 1963), reh'g denied (La. June 28, 1963), rev'd sub. nom. Garrison v. Louisiana, 379 U.S. 64 (1964).

State v. Mayeux, 81 So. 2d 426 (La. 1955).

State v. Time, Inc., 249 So. 2d 328 (La. Ct. App.), writ denied, 259 La. 761, 252 So. 2d 456 (1971).

Stromberg v. California, 283 U.S. 359 (1931).

Sullivan v. New York Times, 144 So. 2d 25 (Ala. 1962), rev'd sub. nom. New York Times v. Sullivan, 376 U.S. 254 (1964).

Sweatt v. Painter, 339 U.S. 629 (1950).

Teamsters, Local 5 (Ryder Truck Lines, Inc.), 161 N.L.R.B. 493 (1966).

Territory v. Nugent, 1 Mart. (o.s.) 103 (La. Terr. 1810).

Territory v. Nugent, 1 Mart. (o.s.) 108 (La. Terr. 1810).

Territory v. Nugent, 1 Mart. (o.s.) 169 (La. Terr. 1810).

Territory v. Thierry, 1 Mart. (o.s.) 101 (La. Terr. 1810).

Thomas v. Collins, 323 U.S. 516 (1945).

Thompson v. Airwaves, Inc., No. 88781 (La. Dist. Ct., 19th Dist. filed June 3, 1962), dismissed (order Mar. 5, 1970) (ordering retroactive dismissal as of Dec. 31, 1967).

Thompson v. Albin, No. 88780 (La. Dist. Ct., 19th Dist. filed June 3, 1962).

Thompson v. St. Amant, No. 48184 (verdict May 5, 1964), reh'g denied, No. 48184 (La. order Jan. 22, 1965), reversed, 184 So. 2d 314 (La. App., 1st Cir.1966), writ granted, 186 So. 2d 627 (No. 48184) (La. order June 9, 1966) (issuing writ of review and ordering transmittal of record from Court of Appeal), reversed, 196 So. 2d 255 (La. 1967), reh'g denied (La. Mar. 27, 1967), cert. granted sub. nom. St. Amant v. Thompson, 389 U.S. 1033 (Jan. 15, 1968), reversed, 390 U.S. 727 (1968).

Thorley v. Lord Kerry, 4 Taunt. 355, 128 Eng. Rep. 367 (Ex. Ch. 1812).

Time, Inc. v. Firestone, 424 U.S. 448 (1976).

Time, Inc. v. Pape, 401 U.S. 279 (1971).

Time, Inc. v. Hill, 385 U.S. 374 (1967).

Trentecosta v. Beck, 677 So. 2d 1013 (La. Ct. App., 4th Cir. May 1, 1996), reh'g refused (La. App., 4th Cir. Aug. 29, 1996), cert. granted, 692 So. 2d 362 (La. 1996), rev'd in part and remanded in part, 703 So. 2d 552 (La. 1997), on remand, 714 So. 2d 721 (La. Ct. App. 4th Cir. Feb. 25, 1998), reh'g denied, 714 So. 2d 721 (La. Ct. App., 4th Cir. 1998), writ denied, 726 So. 2d 28 (La. 1998), appeal after remand, 786 So. 2d 885 (La. App., 4th Cir. 2001) (affirming trial court judgment).

Umans v. United States, cert. granted, 386 U.S. 940 (1967), cert. dismissed, 389 U.S. 80 (1967).

United States v. Carolene Products, 304 U.S. 144 (1938).

United States v. Partin (I), 493 F.2d 750 (5th Cir. 1974) (reversing and remanding).

United States v. Partin (II), 552 F.2d 621 (5th Cir. Ga. 1977), reh'g denied (5th Cir. June 5, 1977), cert. denied, 434 U.S. 903 (1977).

United States v. Press Publishing Co., 219 U.S. 1 (1911).

Wainwright v. New Orleans, cert. granted, 385 U.S. 1001 (1967), cert. dismissed, 392 U.S. 598 (1968).

Walker v. Associated Press, cert. denied, 194 So. 2d 97 (La. 1967) (denying certiorari as to defendant Associated Press), cert. granted, 194 So. 2d 99 (La. 1967) (granting certiorari as to defendant Times-Picayune Publishing Corp.), reversed, 389 U.S. 28 (1967) (reversing as to Associated Press), reh'g denied, 389 U.S. 997 (1967), 206 So. 2d 489 (La. 1968) (ruling as to Times-Picayune Publishing Corp.), reh'g denied (La. Feb. 19, 1968), on remand, 209 So. 2d 806 (La. Ct. App. 2d Cir. 1968), reh'g denied (La. Ct. App., 2d Cir. May 9, 1968), cert. denied, 211 So. 2d 331 (La. June 21, 1968).

Wattigny v. Lambert, 453 So. 2d 1272 (La. Ct. App., 3d Cir. 1984).

Whitney v. California, 274 U.S. 357 (1927).

Whitney v. Florida, cert. granted, 386 U.S. 970 (1967), cert. dismissed, 389 U.S. 138 (1967).

Wolston v. Reader's Digest Ass'n, 443 U.S. 157 (1979).

Wylie v. Arnold Transportation Services, 494 F. Supp. 2d 717 (S.D. Ohio 2006).

Young v. Meyer, 527 So. 2d 391 (La. Ct. App., 4th Cir. 1988).

LEGAL BRIEFS

(SEE BELOW FOR LEGAL BRIEFS FROM ST. AMANT V. THOMPSON)

Brief for Respondent L. B. Sullivan, Abernathy v. Sullivan, 376 U.S. 254 (1964). In *West's Encyclopedia of American Law*, edited by Jeffrey Lehman and Shirelle Phelps, 2d ed., 11:465. Eagan, MN: West, 2005.

Brief of Petitioner Ralph David Abernathy et al., New York Times v. Sullivan, 376 U.S. 254 (1964).

LETTERS AND MEMORANDA

Hugo Black to Bryon White. Memorandum. Apr. 19, 1968. Earl Warren Papers, Manuscript Division, Library of Congress, Washington, DC (box 556, folder 7).

William Brennan to Byron White. Memorandum. Apr. 19, 1968. William J. Brennan Papers, Manuscript Division, Library of Congress, Washington, DC (box I:173, folder 11).

John Harlan II to Byron White. Memorandum. Apr. 23, 1968. John Marshall Harlan II Papers, Princeton University, Princeton, NJ (box 315, "No. 517, St. Amant v. Thompson" folder).

James Madison to Thomas Jefferson. Letter. Oct. 17, 1788. James Madison Papers, Library of Congress, Washington, DC (series 1, General Correspondence, 1723–1859, microfilm reel 3, available at http://hdl.loc.gov/loc.mss/mjm.03_0714_0719).

James Madison to Thomas Jefferson. Letter. May 27, 1789. James Madison Papers, Library of Congress, Washington, DC (series 1, General Correspondence, 1723–1859, microfilm reel 3, available at http://hdl.loc.gov/loc.mss/mjm.03_1135_1137).

Thurgood Marshall to Byron White. Memorandum. Apr. 23, 1968. Byron White Papers, Manuscript Division, Library of Congress, Washington, DC (box I:126, folder 18).

Stephen Penderson to Governor Claiborne. Letter. Aug. 16, 1809. In *The Territorial Papers of the United States: The Territory of Orleans, 1803–1812*, edited by Clarence Edwin Carter, 9:849. Washington, DC: Government Printing Office, 1940.

Henry Putzel Jr. to Byron White. Memorandum. May 3, 1968. Byron White Papers, Manuscript Division, Library of Congress, Washington, DC (box I:126, folder 18).

Potter Stewart to Byron White. Memorandum. Apr. 19, 1968. Earl Warren papers, Manuscript Division, Library of Congress, Washington, DC (box 556, folder 7).

Earl Warren to Byron White. Memorandum. April 26, 1968, Earl Warren Papers, Manuscript Division, Library of Congress, Washington, DC (box 556, folder 7).

Byron White to Henry Putzel Jr. Memorandum. May 3, 1968. Byron White Papers, Manuscript Division, Library of Congress, Washington, DC (box I:126, folder 18).

Lawrence G. Williams to Earl Warren. Letter. May 9, 1968. William J. Brennan Papers, Manuscript Division, Library of Congress, Washington, DC (box I:173, folder 11).

ST. AMANT V. THOMPSON MATERIALS (CHRONOLOGICAL)

Louisiana District Court

Petition for Damages [Complaint], Thompson v. St. Amant, No. 88779 (La. Dist. Ct. filed July 3, 1962).

Answer, Thompson v. St. Amant, No. 88779 (La. Dist. Ct. filed July 10, 1962).

Answers to Interrogatories, Thompson v. St. Amant, No. 88779 (La. Dist. Ct. filed Dec. 26, 1962).

Interrogatories, Thompson v. St. Amant, No. 88779 (La. Dist. Ct. interrogatories filed [n.d.] 1962).

Trial Transcript, Thompson v. St. Amant, No. 88779 (La. Dist. Ct. trial May 5, 1964).

Reasons for Judgment [Verdict], Thompson v. St. Amant, No. 88779 (La. Dist. Ct. ruling May 5, 1964).

[Defendant's] Motion for a New Trial, Thompson v. St. Amant, No. 88779 (La. Dist. Ct. motion filed May 18, 1964).

Reasons for Judgment [on Motion for Retrial], Thompson v. St. Amant, No. 88779 (La. Dist. Ct. Jan. 22, 1965).

Judgment [Denial of Motion for New Trial], Thompson v. St. Amant, No. 88779 (La. Dist. Ct. Jan. 27, 1965).

Notice of Appeal, Thompson v. St. Amant, No. 8877 (La. Dist. Ct. Feb. 1, 1965).

Louisiana Court of Appeal

[Defendant-Appellant's] Original Brief on Appeal, Thompson v. St. Amant, No. 6571 (La. Ct. App., 1st Dist. filed Feb. 2, 1965).

[Plaintiff-Appellee's] Answer to Appeal, Thompson v. St. Amant, No. 6571 (La. Ct. App. 1st Dist. filed Oct. 25, 1965).

Original Brief on Behalf of Plaintiff-Appellee, Thompson v. St. Amant, No. 6571 (La. Ct. App. 1st Dist. filed Oct. 25, 1965).

Louisiana Supreme Court

Applications for Certiorari or Review, Thompson v. St. Amant, No. 48184 (La. n.d. [May 3, 1966]).

Original Brief on Behalf of Defendant-Respondent [St. Amant], Thompson v. St. Amant, No. 48184 (La. filed Nov. 4, 1966), 1–2.

[Plaintiff-Appellee's] Application for Rehearing, Thompson v. St. Amant, No. 6571 (La. App. 1st Dist. filed Mar. 11, 1966).

Notice (denying petition for rehearing), Thompson v. St. Amant, No. 6571 (La. Ct. App. 1st Dist. Apr. 4, 1966).

Certiorari, or Writ of Review, Thompson v. St. Amant, No. 48184 (La. order June 9, 1966).

Motion and Order to be Admitted as Counsel of Record, Thompson v. St. Amant, No. 48184 (La. entered Oct. 10, 1966).

Relator's [Thompson's] Brief, Thompson v. St. Amant, No. 48184 (La. brief submitted Oct. 24, 1966).

Application for Rehearing, Thompson v. St. Amant, No. 48184 (La. Mar. 6, 1967).

U.S. Supreme Court

Petition for Writ of Certiorari, St. Amant v. Thompson, 390 U.S. 727 (1968) (No. 67-517) (filed Aug. 19, 1967).

Harlan Bench Memorandum [on certiorari], 20 Oct. 1967, St. Amant v. Thompson, 390 U.S. 727 (1968) (No. 67-517). John Marshall Harlan II Papers, Seeley G. Mudd Manuscript Library, Princeton University, Princeton, NJ (box 315, folder 517).

Warren Bench Memorandum [on certiorari], 23 Oct. 1967, St. Amant v. Thompson, 390 U.S. 727 (1968) (No. 67-517). Earl Warren Papers, Manuscript Division, Library of Congress, Washington, DC (box 312, folder 8).

Fortas Bench Memorandum [on certiorari], 25 Oct. 1967, St. Amant v. Thompson, 390 U.S. 727 (1968) (No. 67-517). Abe Fortas Papers, Sterling Memorial Library, Yale University, New Haven, CT (box 64, folder 1288).

Douglas Vote Sheet, 3 Nov. 1967, St. Amant v. Thompson, 390 U.S. 727 (1968) (No. 67-517). William O. Douglas Papers, Manuscript Division, Library of Congress, Washington, DC (box 292).

Warren Vote Sheet, 3 Nov. 1967, St. Amant v. Thompson, 390 U.S. 727 (1968) (No. 67-517). Earl Warren Papers, Manuscript Division, Library of Congress, Washington, DC (box 312, folder 8).

Response to Application for Writ of Certiorari to the Supreme Court of the State of Louisiana, St. Amant v. Thompson, 390 U.S. 727 (1968) (No. 67-517) (Dec. 8, 1967).

Original Brief of Defendant-Relator [St. Amant], St. Amant v. Thompson, 390 U.S. 727 (1968) (No. 67-517) (filed Feb. 29, 1968).

Original Brief on Behalf of Plaintiff-Respondent [Thompson], St. Amant v. Thompson, 390 U.S. 727 (1968) (No. 67-517) (filed Mar. 30, 1968).

Briefs [summaries of arguments] and Appearances of Counsel, St. Amant v. Thompson, 20 L.Ed.2d 1491 (argued Apr. 4, 1968).

Oral Argument [recording], St. Amant v. Thompson, 390 U.S. 727 (1968) (No. 67-517) (argued Apr. 4, 1968), available at https://apps.oyez.org/player/#/warren15/oral_argument_audio/15482.

Fortas, Abe, *517—St. Amant v. Thompson* (legal notepad paper with handwritten notes), n.d. [1968?]. Abe Fortas Papers, Sterling Memorial Library, Yale University, New Haven, CT (box 64, folder 1288).

Circulated draft opinion (Justice Marshall's copy), Apr. 19, 1968, St. Amant v. Thompson, 390 U.S. 727 (1968) (No. 67-517). Thurgood Marshall Papers, Manuscript Division, Library of Congress, Washington, DC (box 47, folder 4).

Mandate [in St. Amant v. Thompson, 390 U.S. 727 (1968) (No. 67-517)], Thompson v. St. Amant, No. 48184 (La. received May 28, 1968).

STATUTES, REGULATIONS, AND LEGISLATIVE MATERIALS

Louisiana (as Orleans territory and as state)

Act of March 26, 1804, 2 La. Stat. 283 (1804).

An Act to revise the laws of the State of Louisiana of a general or public nature and to consolidate them into a system of laws to be known as the Louisiana Revised Statutes of 1950; to enact the necessary legislation in connection therewith; to provide for the continuous revision of the laws; and to repeal certain enumerated statutes, 1950 La. Acts No. 2.

Crimes Act of May 4, 1805, 1805 La. Acts p. 416.
A Digest of the Civil Laws Now in Force in the Territory of Orleans (1808/repub. 1968).
[Enabling Act, Louisiana Civil Code], 1808 La. Acts No. 29.
Great Repealing Act, 1828 La. Acts No. 83.
Louisiana Acts No. 468 (1950).
Louisiana Civil Code (1825), published in Louisiana Legal Archives, vol. 1. New Orleans: Moran, 1937.
Louisiana Civil Code (1870), republished in Louisiana Legal Archives, vol. 3. New Orleans: Moran, 1937.
Louisiana Civil Code (1988).
Louisiana Civil Code (1992).
Louisiana Civil Code (1999).
Louisiana Civil Code of Practice (1835)
Louisiana Code of Civil Procedure (1960).
Louisiana Constitution of 1812.
Louisiana Constitution of 1845.
Louisiana Constitution of 1852.
Louisiana Constitution of 1864.
Louisiana Constitution of 1868.
Louisiana Constitution of 1879.
Louisiana Constitution of 1898.
Louisiana Constitution of 1913.
Louisiana Constitution of 1921.
Louisiana Constitution of 1931.
Louisiana Constitution of 1974.
Louisiana Revised Statutes, various sections.
Resolution to express the sincere and heartfelt condolences of the Senate of the Legislature of Louisiana upon the death of Robert L. "Buck" Kleinpeter, S. Res. No. 177 (La. Senate 2013).
Return of Proclamations, Pardons and Appointments, June 30, 1808. In *The Territorial Papers of the United States: The Territory of Orleans, 1803–1812*, edited by Clarence Edwin Carter, 9:796. Washington, DC: Government Printing Office, 1940.

United States (federal)

An Act Relative to the Election of a President and Vice President of the United States, 1 Stat. 239 (1792).
Alien Registration Act, c. 439, 54 Stat. 670 (1940).

1 Annals of Congress 443–59 (June 8, 1789).
6 Annals of Congress 945–76 (Jan. 25, 1801).
Cuban Assets Control Regulations, 31 CFR §505.101 et seq.
Espionage Act, Public Law 65-24, 40 Stat. 217 (1917).
Joint Congressional Committee on Inaugural Ceremonies. *The 57th Presidential Inaugural Ceremonies, Monday, January 21, 2013: Guide for Producers and Correspondents to the Inaugural Ceremonies and Capitol Hill Events.* Washington, DC: U.S. Congress, 2013.
Interstate Income Act of 1959, Pubic Law No. 86–274, 73 Stat. 557 (1959).
Sedition Act of 1798, Sess. 2, ch. 74, 1 Stat. 596 (1798).
Sedition Act of 1918, Public Law 65–150, 40 Stat. 553 (1918).
Select Committee on Assassinations. *Report of the Select Committee on Assassinations of the U.S. House of Representatives*, pt. 2 (H. Rpt. 95-1828, pr. 2) Washington, DC: Government Printing Office, 1979.
U.S. House of Representatives. *Statistics of the Congressional Election of Nov. 6, 1962.* Washington, DC: Government Printing Office, 1963.
28 USC § 2101 (1968).
47 USC § 315 (2016).
U.S. Sup. Ct. Rules (2016).
U.S. Sup. Ct. Rules (1968).

England/Great Britain (chronological)

Statute of Westminster, 3 Edward I, c. 34 (1275) (Eng.).
Statute of Westminster, 13 Edw. I, c. 1 (stat. 4) (1285) (Eng.).
Star-Chamber Act, 17 Car. I, c. 10 (1640) (Eng.).
An Ordinance for the Regulating of Printing (14 June 1643). In *Acts and Ordinances of the Interregnum, 1642–1660*, edited by C. H. Firth and R. S. Rait. London: H. M. Stationery Office, Wyman and Sons, 1911.
Licensing of the Press Act, 14 Charles II, c. 33 (1662) (Eng.).
An Act for reviving, continuing, and explaining several Laws therein mentioned, which are expired and near expiring, 4 & 5 William & Mary, c. 24 (1693).
Duties in American Colonies Act 1765, 5 George III, c. 12 (Eng.).
Libel Act (Fox's Libel Act), 1792, 32 Geo. III c. 60 (Eng.).
Treason Act, 36 Geo. III, c.7 (1795) (Eng.)
Seditious Meetings Act 1795, 36 Geo. III, c.8 (Eng.).
Lord Campbell's Act, 1843, 6 & 7 Vict. c. 96 (Eng.).
An Act for Abolishing the Jurisdiction of the Ecclesiastical Courts of England and Wales in Suits for Defamation, 18 & 19 Vic., c. 41 (1855).
Coroners and Justice Act, Eliz. II, c. 25 (2009) (Eng.).

Other Jurisdictions

Kentucky Constitution of 1799, Art. 10, § 7.
28 N.Y. Laws chap. 90 (1805).
Pennsylvania Constitution of 1776, Decl. Rts. § XII.
Pennsylvania Constitution of 1790, Art. IX, § 11.

MISCELLANEOUS

Barrow, Bruce, Lisa Kalikow, Billy Shebar, and Annie Wong, directors. (2014). "History Detectives: Who Killed Jimmy Hoffa?" In *History Detectives*, produced by Bruce Barrow. Oregon Public Broadcasting. Video and transcript available at http://www.pbs.org/opb/historydetectives/investigation/who-killed-jimmy-hoffa/.

Bent, Samuel Arthur, ed. *Familiar Short Sayings of Great Men*. 6th ed.. Boston: Ticknor, 1887.

Bryce, James. "Edwin Lawrence Godkin." In James Bryce, *Studies in Contemporary Biography*, 363–81. New York: Macmillan, 1903.

Cato. "Discourse on Libels, No. 100." In *Cato's Letters, or Essays on Liberty Civil and Religious, and Other Important Subjects*, edited by Thomas Gordon, 4th ed., 1:252. London: W. Wilkins, 1737.

———. "Of Freedom of Speech: That the Same Is Inseparable from Publick Liberty, No. 15." In *Cato's Letters, or Essays on Liberty Civil and Religious, and Other Important Subjects*, edited by Thomas Gordon, 4th ed., 1:96–103, London: W. Wilkins, 1737.

———. "Reflecting upon Libelling." In *Cato's Letters, or Essays on Liberty Civil and Religious, and Other Important Subjects*, edited by Thomas Gordon, 4th ed., 1:246–47. London: W. Wilkins, 1737.

———. "Second Discourse on Libels." In *Cato's Letters, or Essays on Liberty Civil and Religious, and Other Important Subjects*, edited by Thomas Gordon, 4th ed., 3:302–3. London: W. Wilkins, 1737.

Declaration of the Rights of Man and of the Citizen (1789). English translation available at http://www.conseil-constitutionnel.fr/conseil-constitutionnel/root/bank_mm/anglais/cst2.pdf.

Devon Energy Corp. "Board of Directors." http://www.devonenergy.com/about-us/board-of-directors.

"Earl Kemp Long Leaving for State Hospital" (photograph). 1959. Historic Photograph Collection, State Library of Louisiana.

"Foreword." In *Louisiana Legal Archives*, 1:v. New Orleans: Moran, 1937.

"Fred A. Blanche, Jr." In *Louisiana Supreme Court, Louisiana Supreme Court Justices, 1813–Present*. http://www.lasc.org/Bicentennial/justices/Blanche_Fred.aspx.

Greelegs, Edward. *Citizens Look at Congress: Russell B. Long, Democratic Senator from Louisiana*. Ralph Nader Congress Project. Washington, DC: Grossman, 1972.

Hamilton, Alexander [Publius]. *Federalist* No. 84. 1788.

International Brotherhood of Teamsters. *Constitution and Bylaws*. http://old1.teamster.org/about/constitution/toc.htm.

Johnson, Erica Robin. "Louisiana Identity on Trial: The Superior Court Case of Pierre Benonime Dormenon, 1790–1812. Master's thesis, University of Texas, Austin, 2007. https://uta-ir.tdl.org/uta-ir/handle/10106/622.

Kant, Immanuel. "On the Common Saying: This May Be True in Theory but Does Not Apply in Practice." In *Basic Writings of Kant*, edited by Allen W. Wood. New York: Modern Library, 2001.

"Larry Simon" (faculty listing). USC College of Law. http://weblaw.usc.edu/faculty/contactInfo.cfm?detailID=308.

"Long, Russell Billiu." In *Biographical Directory of the U.S. Congress*. Washington, DC: U.S. Congress. http://bioguide.congress.gov/scripts/biodisplay.pl?index=L000428.

"Louis R. Cohen, Senior Counsel." WilmerHale.com. https://www.wilmerhale.com/louis_cohen.

Media Law Resource Center. "2016 Report on Trials and Damages." *MLRC Bulletin*, no. 1 (2016).

Mill, John Stuart. "Law of Libel and Liberty of the Press." In *The Collected Works of John Stuart Mill: Essays on Equality, Law, and Education*, edited by John M. Robson, 21:1–34. Toronto: University of Toronto Press, 1984.

National Archives. *Tally of Electoral Votes for the 1800 Presidential Election, February 11, 1801*. http://www.archives.gov/legislative/features/1800-election/1800-election.html.

"Peter L. Zimroth, Retired Partner." ArnoldPorter.com. http://www.arnoldporter.com/en/people/z/zimroth-peter-1.

"Richard Nixon and Charles W. 'Chuck' Colson on 8 December 1971." Conversation 016-053, *Presidential Recordings Digital Edition* [Nixon Telephone Tapes 1971], edited by Ken Hughes. Charlottesville: University of Virginia Press, 2014–. Retrieved from http://prde.upress.virginia.edu/conversations/4006699.

"Richard Nixon and Charles W. 'Chuck' Colson on 8 December 1971." Conversation 016-060, *Presidential Recordings Digital Edition* [Nixon Telephone Tapes 1971], edited by Ken Hughes. Charlottesville: University of Virginia Press, 2014–. Retrieved from http://prde.upress.virginia.edu/conversations/4006700.

Scalia, Antonin. "Interview with Associate Justice Antonin Scalia." By Bryan Garner. LawProse.com, available at http://www.lawprose.org/bryan-garner/

garners-interviews/supreme-court-interviews/justice-antonin-scalia-supreme-court-of-the-united-states-part-2/ and https://youtu.be/zbZmKjpLV8w.

Spaeth, Harold J., Lee Epstein, Andrew D. Martin, Jeffrey A. Segal, Theodore J. Ruger, and Sara C. Benesh. *2016 Supreme Court Database* (2015 release 03). http://supremecourtdatabase.org.

St. Amant, Phil A. *A Statement of Principles* (campaign brochure), n.d. [1962?]. Box 713, folder 36, Russell B. Long Papers, Louisiana and Lower Mississippi Valley Collections, Special Collections, Hill Memorial Library, Louisiana State University.

U.S. Dept. of Labor Statistics. *CPI Inflation Calculator.* Available at http://data.bls.gov/cgi-bin/cpicalc.pl.

Virginia Declaration of Rights (1776). http://www.gunstonhall.org/georgemason/human_rights/vdr_final.html.

"Williams, Lawrence Gordon." In *Biographical Directory of the U.S. Congress.* Washington, DC: U.S. Congress. http://bioguide.congress.gov/scripts/biodisplay.pl?index=W000525.

Yates, Robert [Brutus]. *Antifederalist* No. 84. 1787. http://resources.utulsa.edu/law/classes/rice/Constitutional/AntiFederalist/84.htm.

INDEX